C000246880

Continued on next page

Vilma Espín
Asela de los Santos
Yolanda Ferrer

Women in Cuba: The making of a revolution within the revolution

PATHFINDER
NEW YORK LONDON MONTREAL SYDNEY

Edited by Mary-Alice Waters

ISBN 978-1-60488-036-6
Library of Congress Control Number 2011945974
Manufactured in the United States of America

First edition, 2012

COVER DESIGN: Toni Gorton
COVER PHOTO: A militia unit of women department store workers
    and brewery employees, Plaza of the Revolution, Havana,
    Cuba, May Day 1959.

Cover photo copyright © Raúl Corrales
    The family of photographer Raúl Corrales has granted
    permission to use, free of charge in this edition, the cover
    photo and three others.

PHOTO PAGES: Eva Braiman, Carole Caron

Pathfinder
www.pathfinderpress.com
E-mail: pathfinder@pathfinderpress.com

Contents

Top: Vilma Espín with other combatants in Rebel Army's Second Eastern Front, end of 1958. **Middle:** Melba Hernández and Espín (left and right) with Nguyen Thi Dinh, deputy commander during Vietnam War of Southern Liberation Armed Forces, Havana, 1974. **Bottom:** Espín and Fidel Castro at event in Havana marking International Women's Day, March 8, 2005.

Vilma Espín Guillois

VILMA ESPÍN, a leader of the Cuban Revolution for more than fifty years, was born in 1930 in Santiago de Cuba, in Oriente province. Her mother, Margarita, was a housewife. Her father, José, was chief accountant of the Bacardi rum company and executive assistant to its president.

Espín entered the University of Oriente in 1948, a year after it opened. There she took part in her first political activity—the fight to win official recognition and funding from the government in Havana for the new university.

Following the military coup of March 10, 1952, that established the US-backed dictatorship of Fulgencio Batista, she joined the Revolutionary National Movement, whose action coordinator in Oriente was student leader Frank País.

On July 26, 1953, 160 revolutionaries under the leadership of Fidel Castro carried out an armed attack on Batista's military garrisons in Santiago de Cuba and Bayamo. As word spread that dozens of captured combatants had been tortured and killed, Espín and three other young women, one of whom was Asela de los Santos, went to the Moncada military compound to learn the truth. Espín soon joined the newly formed Oriente Revolutionary Action, led by País.

In May 1955 Castro and thirty-one other Moncada combatants who had been captured and imprisoned were freed through a national amnesty campaign. The following month Castro led a regroupment of forces to found the July 26 Revolutionary Movement. Espín became one of its first members.

In 1954 Espín graduated as one of the first chemical engineers educated in Cuba and among the few women in the field. She left Cuba in the summer of 1955 for a year of study in the United States at the Massachusetts Institute of Technology. In June 1956, as she prepared to return to Cuba, she was asked by the July 26 Movement leadership to travel through Mexico to meet with Fidel Castro. July 26 Movement cadres were training there for what a few months later became the *Granma* expedition—the landing of the yacht *Granma* in eastern Cuba, transporting eighty-two combatants under Fidel Castro's command to launch a revolutionary war to overthrow the Batista regime.

Upon her return to Santiago, Espín began to assume major responsibilities in the July 26 Movement, working closely with Frank País. She helped prepare the November 30, 1956, armed action there, intended to draw Batista's military forces away from the area of the *Granma* landing. For a period of time, her family's home became the organizing center for the July 26 Movement's underground leadership in Santiago.

In February 1957, Espín took part in the first national leadership meeting of the July 26 Movement to be held in the Sierra Maestra mountains. In July, shortly before País was gunned down by Batista's police, she became the July 26 Movement's coordinator for Oriente province.

In June 1958, with Batista's cops combing the province to find her, Espín was transferred to the Rebel Army's Frank País Second Eastern Front. Following the July 1958 defeat of the Batista army's "encircle and annihilate" offensive, the Second Front became a vast liberated zone north and east of Santiago that combatants under Raúl Castro defended and in which they began to establish a civilian governmental structure. There Espín shouldered numerous responsibilities, including as an instructor in the school training combatants as teachers.

After the triumph over the dictatorship on January 1, 1959, women who wanted to organize to support the deepening revolutionary transformation turned for leadership to Espín, who was among the best known of the women who were leaders of the underground and Rebel Army combatants. She led the efforts to launch the Federation of Cuban Women and was its president and principal leader from its founding in August 1960 until her death in 2007.

Among her many responsibilities, Espín was director of the National Center on Sex Education, founded in 1989, and the National Commission for Attention to and Prevention of Social Problems, founded in 1986. She was vice president of the Women's International Democratic Federation from 1973 on.

Espín was a member of the Central Committee of the Communist Party from its inception in 1965, a member of the party's Political Bureau from 1980 to 1991, and a member of Cuba's Council of State from 1976 on. As a member of the National Assembly of People's Power from 1976 on, she chaired the Committee on Childhood, Youth, and Equality of Rights for Women. She received the honorary title Heroine of the Republic of Cuba in 2003.

Espín was married to Raúl Castro Ruz, minister of the Revolutionary Armed Forces 1959–2008 and today president of the Council of State and Council of Ministers. They had four children.

Top: Asela de los Santos (left) with Zoila Ibarra, assistant head of Rebel Army's Education Department, Second Eastern Front, late 1958.
Right: De los Santos receives Ana Betancourt award, 1974. From left: Vilma Espín, Fidel Castro, Raúl Castro, de los Santos.
Bottom: De los Santos, November 2011.

Asela de los Santos Tamayo

ASELA DE LOS SANTOS was born in 1929 in Santiago de Cuba. Her father, José de los Santos, was a retired army lieutenant; her mother, Parmenia Tamayo, was a housewife. She entered the University of Oriente in 1949, shortly before student and faculty demonstrations won official recognition for the new institution. Studying there to become a teacher, she met Vilma Espín. The two became lifelong friends and comrades-in-arms.

De los Santos and Espín were among the students who immediately took to the streets to protest Fulgencio Batista's US-backed military coup of March 10, 1952. In 1954 de los Santos graduated from the university and took a job teaching in nearby El Caney. That same year she began to work with Oriente Revolutionary Action, led by Frank País. In 1955 she joined the newly formed July 26 Revolutionary Movement, of which País became the central leader in Santiago and later its national action coordinator.

On November 30, 1956, de los Santos was among the July 26 Movement members who organized and carried out an armed action in Santiago de Cuba, which had been timed to coincide with the anticipated landing of the *Granma*. Soon after, de los Santos left her teaching job to devote herself full time to the July 26 Movement.

In March 1957 she worked alongside Celia Sánchez and Vilma Espín transporting the first fifty-one reinforcements for the Rebel Army from Santiago to Manzanillo, the staging point for the combatants joining the rebel front in the Sierra Maestra mountains. In July she was one of the July 26 Movement cadres who helped assure the success of the massive spontaneous outpouring that shut down the city of Santiago in response to the murder of Frank País.

In 1957–58 de los Santos made nine trips to Miami as a courier, arranging the transport of weapons, ammunition, money, and messages for the revolutionary movement in Cuba. In August 1958, on the proposal of Vilma Espín, de los Santos was transferred to the Rebel Army's Frank País Second Eastern Front and placed in charge of the schools being organized there. Within months the Department of Education de los Santos headed had responsibility for four hundred primary schools as well as educational programs for the combatants, many of whom did not know how to read or write.

After the revolutionary victory of January 1, 1959, de los Santos remained in charge of schools in the area formerly governed by the Second Front. Later that year she accepted responsibility for education in all of Oriente province.

From 1960 to 1966 de los Santos worked alongside Vilma Espín in launching and building the Federation of Cuban Women. She served as organizational secretary of the FMC's National Bureau, then as its general secretary. She is currently a member of the FMC's National Committee and an adviser to its general secretary.

In 1965 de los Santos was a founding member of the Cuban Communist Party and served on its Central Committee from 1975 to 1991.

From 1966 to 1970, she was director of education for the Revolutionary Armed Forces, holding the rank of captain.

She helped establish the Camilo Cienfuegos Military Schools where students, popularly known as Camilos, acquired military skills and training as they earned a high school degree.

In 1970 de los Santos became director of personnel training in the Ministry of Education. She was vice minister of education from 1974 to 1979 and minister from 1979 to 1981.

She is married to Reserve Division General José Ramón Fernández, vice president of the Council of Ministers. Fernández commanded the main column of combatants that in April 1961, at Playa Girón, defeated the US-organized "Bay of Pigs" invasion.

De los Santos was awarded the Order of Playa Girón in 2009 and received the honorary title Hero of Labor in 2011. She is today a researcher in the Revolutionary Armed Forces Office of History.

Top left: Yolanda Ferrer (right) with Vilma Espín at an international gathering, late 1970s. **Top right:** Yolanda Ferrer, general secretary of Federation of Cuban Women, November 2011. **Bottom:** (From left to right) Ricardo Alarcón, president of Cuba's National Assembly; Vilma Espín; Raúl Castro, minister of Revolutionary Armed Forces; and Yolanda Ferrer, International Women's Day, March 8, 2004.

ganized working people to take charge of health care and education, justice, agriculture, construction, communications, taxation, and established their own radio station and other means of providing news and orientation. The toilers within the Second Front began to implement the program outlined in *History Will Absolve Me*.

It became a "virtual republic," as Vilma Espín affirms here. And one with a new class character.

A congress of peasants in arms was organized by the Rebel Army in September 1958, land reform was codified by military decree in the liberated territories, and titles were issued to those who worked the land.

More than four hundred primary schools were opened, organized by the Rebel Army's department of education headed by Asela de los Santos, as peasant families enthusiastically carried out a census of the children, searched for suitable classrooms, found books, and built desks and benches. Nighttime classes for combatants often used the same premises.

Clinics and field hospitals were established, treating combatants, including wounded enemy soldiers, and local residents alike. They provided the first medical care most peasants had ever received.

With the participation of all, roads were repaired and new ones opened.

Taxes on output were collected from the owners of sugar mills, mining operations, and coffee plantations. The workers knew exactly how much had been produced and shipped out.

Disputes were settled and marriages celebrated.

A popular revolution, a proletarian revolution-in-becoming, was organized in the mountains of the east, as the workers and peasants mobilized to begin transforming social relations. It spread across Cuba with the victory of January 1, 1959.

■

"When a deepgoing revolution takes place women, who have been oppressed for millennia, want to take part," Asela de los Santos reminds us here.

The growing participation of women was a seamless part of this revolutionary upheaval. Forged in the heat of popular mobilizations in the opening months of 1959, what became the Federation of Cuban Women grew out of women's determination to participate in the revolution—not the other way around. As Vilma Espín describes, women insisted on organizing themselves, and being organized, into the most pressing tasks of the revolution. In the process they created an organization that would enable them to do just that.

Many years later, a journalist for the Cuban daily *Granma* asked Vilma Espín whether she had anticipated all this when she was fighting in the mountains of eastern Cuba. Had she ever imagined she would be so involved and identified with making—as Fidel Castro called it—a revolution within the revolution? Espín's spontaneous response was:

> Never! It hadn't even remotely occurred to me that a women's organization should exist. I had never even thought about it. I joined the struggle as part of a group that included young women and men. It never occurred to me we'd have to carry out special work with women. . . .
>
> When the idea of creating a women's organization was suggested to me, it came as a surprise. . . . But soon after it was created I realized that yes, it was indispensable. . . . It was an enormous revolutionary force.[2]

2.   Interview with Mirta Rodríguez Calderón, August 1985, in *La mujer en Cuba* [Women in Cuba] (Havana: Editora Política, 1990) pp. 79–81.

Part II of *The Making of a Revolution Within the Revolution* takes us through this "Birth of the Federation of Cuban Women" in interviews with Vilma Espín and Yolanda Ferrer.

What strikes the reader more than anything else in Espín's account is the absence of dogma or schemas, the absence of clotted political jargon. There was only one guide: opening the way for the broadest layers of women to become involved—with organization, effectiveness, and discipline—in ongoing struggles and the construction of a new social order.

In the beginning was the deed. Leaders were those who led.

"Learn in the morning and teach in the afternoon" became a popular revolutionary slogan, reflecting a fact of life. Often that meant doing so under fire—literally—as Washington tried unsuccessfully, over and over, to organize and arm a counterrevolutionary cadre. As on every other front of the advancing revolution, form followed content, and organizational structures were codified as the struggle permitted.

Nothing captures this better than the image of the school for young women from the countryside, training to staff child care centers, being strafed and bombed by US-based planes a few days prior to the US-organized invasion at the Bay of Pigs in April 1961. "Not a single one asked to go home," Espín notes. "Everyone stayed."

"When I talk about how the federation was created," Espín says here,

> I always emphasize that at the time we didn't talk about women's liberation. We didn't talk about women's emancipation, or the struggle for equality. We didn't use those terms then. What we did talk about was participation. Women wanted to participate....
>
> There was real proof, every day, that the revolution

wasn't just hot air, it wasn't empty phrases of the kind
people were used to hearing from politicians in the past.
This was the genuine thing. And women wanted to be part
of it, to *do* something. The more the revolutionary laws
strengthened this conviction, the more women demanded
a chance to contribute—and the more they saw how
necessary their contribution was.

Cuba in the 1950s was one of the more economically developed countries of Latin America, not one of the poorest. Yet
only 13.5 percent of women worked outside the home in 1953,
many of them without pay. By 1981, barely twenty years after the triumph of the revolution, that figure had risen to 44.5
percent, and by 2008 stood at 59 percent.

In 1953, of those women in the workforce "with or without
pay," the largest single category, totaling more than 70,000,
were domestic servants, a large proportion of whom were
black. That was close to 30 percent of all women who had
jobs. Some worked for as little as 20 cents a day or for room
and board alone—which could mean a mat to sleep on and
leftover food from the plates of their employer.

The social dynamic of the early years of the revolution is
dramatically represented by the FMC-organized night schools
for former domestic workers, women left with no way to make
a living as their well-off employers abandoned the country.
Retrained for jobs ranging from taxi drivers and auto mechanics to bank clerks, secretaries, child care workers, and poultry
farmers, they began new lives—with confidence and pride.

The same dynamic was central to one of the most extensive FMC campaigns in the first years of the revolution, the
establishment of the Ana Betancourt School for young peasant women. Between 1961 and 1963, twenty-one thousand,
with their parents' consent, came to Havana for an intensive

six-month course during which they learned to read and write, cut and sew, and acquired the foundations of scientific nutrition and hygiene. Some learned basic office-work skills as well.

One of the charges leveled against the Cuban Revolution by its opponents in other countries, often by women who came out of some of the feminist organizations of the 1960s and 70s, is that the FMC, by teaching women how to make clothes for themselves and their families, reinforced traditional female stereotypes. It bolstered women's oppression rather than advancing women's liberation, they claimed. In the *Granma* interview quoted earlier, Espín was asked if she still thought they had done the right thing.

"Yes, I do," was her immediate answer, "because at that time it was what allowed us to draw women out of their homes. It's what made it possible for young women from the Escambray mountains and the Baracoa region, where the counterrevolution was working intensively on peasant families, to come to the capital, learn what the revolution was really about, and become the first cadres of the revolution in those areas.

"This was important, not only in combating the counterrevolution," Espín said, "but in terms of the development of women as cadres. . . . We started from where women were at to raise them to a new level."

The revolution in women's social, economic, and political status was not a phenomenon *parallel* to the revolutionary advance of Cuba's toilers. It took place *within* that advance.

■

Addressing a leadership meeting of the Federation of Cuban Women in December 1966, Cuban prime minister Fidel Castro called attention to the antiwoman prejudices that prevailed in prerevolutionary Cuba, as throughout class societies the world over. "Prejudices that have existed, not just for decades or centuries," Castro said, "but for millennia." He pointed

> to the belief that all a woman was good for was to scrub dishes, wash, iron, cook, keep house, and bear children—age-old prejudices that placed women in an inferior position in society. In effect women did not have a productive place in society.

Under capitalism, he went on, the big majority of women are "doubly exploited or doubly humiliated."

> A poor woman, whether a worker or belonging to a working-class family, was exploited simply because of her humbler status, because she was a worker. Moreover, within her own class, as a working woman, she was looked down on and underrated. Not only was she underestimated, exploited, and looked down on by the exploiting classes, but even within her own class she was the object of countless prejudices. . . .
> There are two sectors in this country, two components of society that, aside from economic reasons, have had other motives for sympathizing with and feeling enthusiasm for the revolution: the black population of Cuba and the country's women.

The political clarity and decisive leadership given the fight for women's equality by Fidel Castro, the central leader of the Cuban Revolution for more than half a century, is one of the truest measures of the working-class character of that revolution and the caliber of its leadership. It has been so from the earliest days of the fight against the Batista dictatorship. That same clarity and decisiveness has been a guarantee of the revolutionary alliance of workers and farmers in Cuba over those decades.

At every point in the struggle, women were part of the vanguard and its leadership. Women such as Haydée Santamaría and Melba Hernández, who joined the assault on the Moncada military garrison in Santiago de Cuba on July 26, 1953. Women like Celia Sánchez, the principal organizer of the July 26 Movement in Manzanillo, the first woman to join the Rebel Army as a combatant, and a member of its general staff. Women like Vilma Espín, whose story you will read in the pages to follow.

The Cuban Revolution is distinguished from all previous revolutions in the history of the modern working-class movement, among other things, by the number of women who were central to its day-to-day leadership.

Moreover, the speed of women's economic and social advances in the thirty years between 1960 and 1990—advances measured by education, employment, infant and maternal mortality rates, and other gauges—allowed Cuban women to conquer a degree of equality that it took women in the United States and other industrialized capitalist countries more than a century and a half to achieve.

But none of this was inevitable.

"One of the ways our revolution will be judged in coming years," Fidel Castro told the Second Congress of the FMC in 1974, "is how we have resolved the problems facing women in our society and our country."

Without the clear course charted by Fidel as well as other central leaders—including Abel Santamaría, Frank País, and Raúl Castro, all of whom readers come to know better in the pages of this book—the record of Cuba's revolutionary struggle would have been far less exemplary. Espín notes, for example, that Frank País's leadership and "attitude toward women" is what made it possible for women in the July 26 Movement in Santiago de Cuba "to work as complete equals with men."

The political determination of Fidel Castro to challenge the antiwoman prejudices held by some who were among the best cadres of the movement was demonstrated by the fight he waged in 1958 to organize the Mariana Grajales Women's Platoon of the Rebel Army—something Espín points to as "an extraordinary moment in the history of women's participation in the revolution."

"Some of our comrades were still very machista," Fidel told a June 1988 send-off for a battery of the First Women's Antiaircraft Artillery Regiment of Guantánamo leaving for Angola the next day. The women had volunteered for an internationalist mission, defending newly built airstrips in southern Angola from attack by the air force of the South African apartheid regime. Also invited to that gathering were ambassadors of African countries accredited in Cuba. Fidel continued:

> Some of the men asked "How can you give those rifles to those women when we are unarmed?"
>
> That reaction really made me mad. So I told one of them: "I'll tell you why we're going to give those rifles to those women: because they're better soldiers than you." I didn't say another word.
>
> We were living in a class society, a society where women were discriminated against, a society where a revolution had to come about, a revolution in which women would have to demonstrate their capacity and their merits.

"What was our objective?" Fidel asked.

> First, we believed in women's capacity, women's courage, their capacity to fight; and second, we knew that such a

precedent would have enormous importance in the future, when the moment came to raise the question of equality in our society.[3]

The combat record of the Mariana Grajales Women's Platoon proved to be one of the most outstanding in the revolutionary war. And the precedent set was never lost.

Addressing the guests from the diplomatic corps attending the send-off for the women's antiaircraft regiment, Castro joked, "Perhaps our guests could be asking themselves this evening if it's necessary for a battery of women to go to southern Angola ... whether there are no more Cuban men to send over there and we have to resort to sending Cuban women. In truth, that's not the way it is."

The deployment of the women's antiaircraft artillery battery to Angola "is not a military necessity," Fidel told them. "It is a moral necessity, a revolutionary necessity."

What the reader will find in these pages is the consistency of the revolutionary leadership of Cuba on the fight for women's equality over more than half a century. And its continuity reaching all the way back to Karl Marx and Frederick Engels, founders of the modern working-class movement.

■

The three authors of this book, who knew each other and worked together over some five decades, reflect two different generations in the leadership of "a revolution

3.   Speech at June 24, 1988, meeting with members of the First Women's Antiaircraft Artillery Regiment of Guantánamo, in *Mujeres y Revolución* (Havana: Editorial de la Mujer, 2006, 2010), pp. 216–17.

within the revolution."

Espín and de los Santos were lifelong friends and co-combatants from their earliest days as students at the University of Oriente in Santiago de Cuba. Following the March 10, 1952, military coup that brought Batista to power, they were among the first to become involved in the struggle against the increasingly brutal US-backed dictatorship. They worked side by side in Santiago's underground and in the Rebel Army's Second Eastern Front. After the 1959 victory, de los Santos joined Espín from 1960 to 1966 in the leadership of the newly formed Federation of Cuban Women, serving as the organization's first general secretary.

Yolanda Ferrer, general secretary of the Federation of Cuban Women today, tells the story of the tremendous leaps made by women in the first years of the revolution from a different perspective. She was part of a new generation, too young to have been involved in the struggle against the dictatorship, that threw itself into the great social battles that pushed forward the revolution. Barely in their teens, these young women joined the first militia units and helped build the communist youth organization. They formed the core of the historic countrywide campaign that in 1961, in a single year-long mobilization, wiped out illiteracy among the adult population of Cuba—23 percent of whom, the majority women, had never had the opportunity to learn to read or write.

It was the intertwining of these two generations in the tasks of the revolution that assured the energy and discipline of the campaigns that marked the character of the FMC at its birth. In the accounts of the three authors we see—firsthand—the impact of the revolutionary struggles that transformed them along with millions of other Cuban women, as they fought to build a society in which, as Frederick Engels expressed it more than a hundred and twenty-five years ago, exploitation by capital has been abolished and "true equality between men and women can become a reality"—if the struggle continues.

■

The Making of a Revolution Within the Revolution would not have been possible without the extensive collaboration provided by the leadership of the Federation of Cuban Women over a number of years, including the help of its cadres in cities from Havana to Santiago de Cuba and Holguín.

Special thanks is due above all to FMC general secretary Yolanda Ferrer and to Asela de los Santos for the many hours they devoted to reading drafts, correcting errors, and explaining aspects of the history of the Cuban Revolution that would have otherwise remained obscure.

Carolina Aguilar, one of the founding cadres and longtime leaders of the FMC, and Isabel Moya, director of Editorial de la Mujer, the FMC's publishing house, offered their time, suggestions, collaboration, and encouragement at every turn, including the scouring of archives for photos, documents, and long out-of-print sources.

Iraida Aguirrechu, senior editor at Editora Política, the publishing house of the Central Committee of the Communist Party of Cuba, provided unstinting support, help, and editorial expertise, as always.

The Office of Historical Affairs of the Council of State, through its director, Eugenio Suárez, and Elsa Montero, organizer of the photographic archive (and herself a Rebel Army messenger at fourteen and combatant in the Third Front under the command of Juan Almeida), provided invaluable assistance, making available numerous historic photos reproduced in this book and identifying individuals, locations, dates, and circumstances of many others.

Directors of the archives at *Bohemia* and *Granma*, Magaly Miranda Martínez and Alejandro Debén, were generous in the time they made available to aid in the search for many other photos capturing specific moments and events in the history of the revolution.

Last but far from least, we express appreciation to the family of photographer Raúl Corrales for allowing reproduction, free of cost in this edition, not only of three photographs that are reproduced inside the book, but the evocative photo of a workers' militia unit that appears on the cover.

The armed women department store employees in their white-dress workclothes—marching side by side on May 1, 1959, with their compañero brewery workers, each ready to give her or his life to defend their revolution—captures an indelible image of the vanguard of the Cuban working class at that decisive moment in the class struggle. It does so with an insight that few photographers other than Raúl Corrales ever achieved.

Department store salesperson was one of the few jobs deemed appropriate for a woman in Cuba in the 1950s. And there was good reason for them to be armed. Two of the most destructive actions of the counterrevolution were the fire-bombings of two famous department stores in central Havana, El Encanto and La Epoca. A militia member on guard duty that night, a woman like those on the cover of this book, died as she rushed back into the inferno of El Encanto to try to retrieve funds the workers had collected to build a child care center there. In 1960–61 alone, nine Havana department stores were the targets of such attacks.

The Making of a Revolution Within the Revolution is dedicated to the new generations of women and men, in Cuba and worldwide, for whom the accurate history of the Cuban Revolution and how it was made is, and will be, an indispensable armament in the tumultuous class battles whose initial skirmishes are already upon us.

January 2012

HAVANA   MATANZAS

GUANIGUANICO

P I N A R   D E L   R I O

H A V A N A

M A T A N Z A S

PINAR DEL RÍO

ZAPATA SWAMP

SANTA CLARA

CIENFUEGOS

L A S
V I L L A S

ESCAMBRAY

Isle of Pines

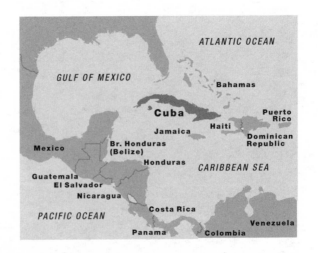

ATLANTIC OCEAN

GULF OF MEXICO

Bahamas

Cuba

Puerto
Rico

Jamaica

Haiti

Dominican
Republic

Mexico

Br. Honduras
(Belize)

Honduras

CARIBBEAN SEA

Guatemala
El Salvador
Nicaragua

PACIFIC OCEAN

Costa Rica

Venezuela

Panama   Colombia

CAMAGÜEY

CAMAGÜEY

ORIENTE

SAGUA BARACOA

SIERRA MAESTRA

SANTIAGO DE CUBA

GUANTÁNAMO
U.S. NAVAL BASE

| 0 | 50 | 100 miles |
| 0 | 80 | 160 kilometers |

Cuba 1959

From Santiago de Cuba to the Rebel Army Second Front

Introduction to Part I

Independence fighters in Cuba, one of Spain's last remaining colonies in the New World, battled thirty years, arms in hand, for national liberation. In 1898, as they were on the verge of winning that historic struggle, the rising imperialist power to the north stepped in to snatch victory from the Cuban people.

Under the terms of the 1898 Treaty of Paris, which ended the first war of the imperialist epoch—a treaty between Washington and Madrid with no Cuban representation—Spain ceded the US government possession of Puerto Rico in the Caribbean and Guam in the Pacific, and sold the Philippines to Washington for twenty million dollars.

Relinquishing all claim of sovereignty over Cuba, Madrid handed the country over to US military occupation, and Cuba became a US protectorate in all but name. The notorious Platt Amendment—named after the US senator who sponsored it—was written into the 1901 Cuban constitution and embodied in a treaty imposed on Cuba to boot. It established the "right" of the US government "to intervene for the preservation of Cuban independence" or to guarantee "maintenance of a government adequate for the protection of life, property, and individual liberty" whenever Washington deemed it necessary. The amendment also provided for establishing what is now the infamous US naval base at Guantánamo Bay, Cuban territory that to this day continues to be occupied against the will of the Cuban people.

For more than half a century, America's ruling families plundered the riches produced by Cuba's peasants, plantation workers, petty commodity producers, and the small but growing urban working class. To protect their profits, the US rulers imposed a succession of brutal and corrupt governments submissive to Washington's dictates. Those regimes doled out fat rewards to buy off Cuban capitalists and landlords, as well as the politicians who acted on their behalf.

By the middle of the twentieth century, US capitalist families held title to 75 percent of Cuba's cultivated land. Eighty percent of the public utilities and 90 percent of all mineral wealth was US owned. All three oil refineries were owned by US or British companies. Meanwhile, more than 700,000 rural laborers remained landless, and some 600,000 totally unemployed.

A 1957 survey conducted by the University Catholic Association in Havana documented conditions of life for the families of nearly a million agricultural workers, some 34 percent of the population. Only four percent said meat was part of their diet; barely two percent consumed eggs. Forty-four percent had never attended a day of school. According to the official government census of 1953, forty-two percent of those living in the countryside were illiterate.

Women in Cuba: The Making of a Revolution Within the Revolution picks up the threads of this history as it begins to unfold after the March 10, 1952, coup, organized by US-backed military strongman Fulgencio Batista, overthrowing the elected government of President Carlos Prío Socarrás. Determined to fight the dictatorship and end the decades of US economic and political domination and rampant government corruption, a new generation of revolutionary leaders emerged. Fidel Castro, Raúl Castro, Frank País, Vilma Espín, all central figures in this book, were among them.

On July 26, 1953, 160 combatants, including two women, under the leadership of Fidel Castro, carried out the first large-scale assault on the military forces of the Batista regime—an attack on the Moncada army garrison in Santiago de Cuba and the Carlos Manuel de Céspedes garrison in Bayamo. The attempt failed. In addition to five combatants killed during the attack, fifty-six taken prisoner were murdered that week by Batista's army, many after brutal torture. As mounting outrage over this butchery brought pressure on the regime, thirty-two other participants in the action were convicted in October 1953 and sentenced to up to fifteen years in prison. These included Fidel Castro, Raúl Castro, and Juan Almeida, as well as Melba Hernández and Haydée Santamaría, the two combatants who were women.

From behind prison walls, the voice of the revolutionary forces continued to grow louder. In an effort propelled by Haydée Santamaría and Melba Hernández, the first two Moncada combatants to be released, Fidel Castro's powerful courtroom defense speech, written on scraps of paper, was smuggled out of the gates and published clandestinely in October 1954. *History Will Absolve Me*, the program of the revolutionary movement, quickly passed from hand to hand across the island.

A broad, organized public campaign for amnesty won release of the prisoners in May 1955. A month later the July 26 Revolutionary Movement was founded, bringing together combatants from the Moncada attack and cadres of other groups committed to revolutionary action to bring down the dictatorship.

Forced into exile by repression, revolutionary forces regrouped in Mexico, where they recruited and collected funds, arming and training themselves for a return to Cuba. In late November 1956, pledging "we shall be free or we shall be martyrs," eighty-two combatants under the command of Fidel Castro set out from Tuxpan, Mexico, aboard the small yacht *Granma*. Their landing in southeast Cuba December 2, 1956, marked the birth of the Rebel Army and the opening of the revolutionary war.

At the same time, as Asela de los Santos and Vilma Espín recount, on November 30 a major action was carried out in Santiago de Cuba, timed to coincide with the anticipated arrival of the *Granma*. With broad support from the local population, more than three hundred sixty cadre of the July 26 Movement, led by Frank País, participated in attacks on the police headquarters, naval police station, and other targets.

The Rebel Army forces, after an initial devastating defeat near the site of the *Granma* landing, established a base in the Sierra Maestra mountain range northwest of Santiago de Cuba. Over the next two years, these combatants became the spearhead of growing mass opposition to the dictatorship. To a greater degree than ever before in history, women shouldered major responsibilities for the work of the revolutionary movement in the cities and countryside, as well as in the Rebel Army fronts that were organized in the mountains.

In the pages that follow, Asela de los Santos and Vilma Espín tell this story firsthand—from the earliest days of the revolutionary underground in Oriente province; to their responsibilities in the Frank País Second Eastern Front of the Rebel Army; to the defeat of the Batista dictatorship, sealed by the nationwide popular insurrection and general strike that swept the country in the opening days of January 1959.

As the Freedom Caravan of the Rebel Army crossed the country, greeted by jubilant throngs of tens of thousands, from Santiago to Havana, the next stage of the revolutionary struggle began.

"The urban underground movement supported and supplied the Rebel Army with revolutionary cadres as well as equipment. It got out the word about what was happening in the mountains, the insurgency in towns and cities, what Fidel was leading."—Asela de los Santos

Participating in March 1958 meeting of National Directorate of July 26 Movement in Sierra Maestra mountains were leaders of both urban underground and Rebel Army. (From left) sitting: Celia Sánchez, Vilma Espín, Fidel Castro; standing: Haydée Santamaría; René Ramos Latour (Daniel), Marcelo Fernández, David Salvador, and Faustino Pérez.

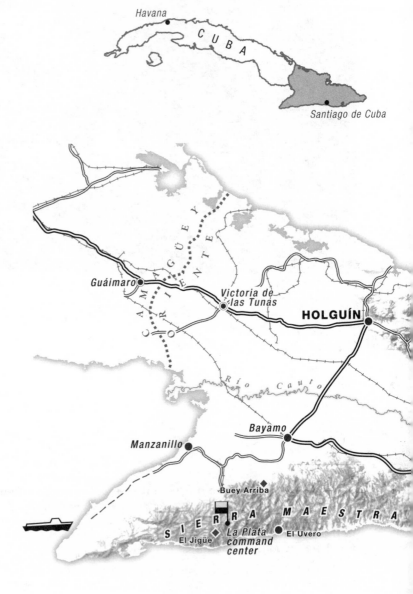

Oriente Province 1958

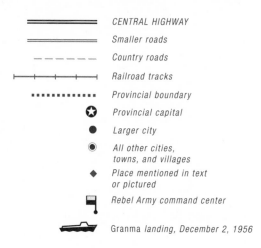

══════════	CENTRAL HIGHWAY
──────────	Smaller roads
- - - - - - -	Country roads
├─┼─┼─┼─┤	Railroad tracks
••••••••••••	Provincial boundary
✪	Provincial capital
●	Larger city
◉	All other cities, towns, and villages
◆	Place mentioned in text or pictured
🚩	Rebel Army command center
🚤	Granma landing, December 2, 1956

Banes

Atlantic Ocean

Mayari
Nicaro
Moa
SIERRA CRISTAL

SAGUA BARACOA MOUNTAINS

Baracoa

Palma Soriano
San Luis
Ermita
Guantánamo
El Cobre
El Escandel
El Caney
Caimanera

SANTIAGO DE CUBA

U.S. NAVAL BASE

Caribbean Sea

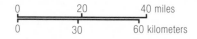

0	20	40 miles
0	30	60 kilometers

It Gave Us a Sense of Worth

INTERVIEW WITH ASELA DE LOS SANTOS

MARY-ALICE WATERS: As a young woman growing up in Santiago de Cuba in the 1950s, you responded to the social and political struggles erupting throughout the country and became one of the earliest members of the July 26 Revolutionary Movement. What were the events that propelled you along this course?

ASELA DE LOS SANTOS: The times I had the good fortune to live through were truly historic. When Batista's military coup took place on March 10, 1952, I was studying at the University of Oriente to become a teacher. In student circles at the time there was deep concern over the country's economic, political, and social situation.

Before January 1959, when the revolution triumphed, the big majority of the Cuban people faced increasingly intolerable conditions. Ours was a society dominated by large landowners. Few peasants had access to land. High unemployment, illiteracy, disease, and neglect of public services were rampant. Politicians were corrupt thieves.

The insurrectional struggle to overthrow the Batista dicta-

Pathfinder Press editors Mary-Alice Waters and Martín Koppel interviewed Asela de los Santos in Havana, February 26, 2008. Two additional interviews took place in March 2009 and March 2010.

torship began July 26, 1953, with the attack on the Moncada army barracks led by Fidel. There followed the slaughter of nearly sixty Moncadistas by Batista's army and police, and then the trial of Fidel and others, their imprisonment, the amnesty campaign, and their release. That, in turn, was followed by their exile to Mexico and the recruitment and intensive training of the eighty-two revolutionary fighters who set out aboard the *Granma* in late November 1956 to begin the armed struggle in the Sierra Maestra mountains.[1]

I joined the July 26 Movement as soon as it was founded in June 1955, after Fidel and the others were released from prison. But I had decided to fight the dictatorship the moment the coup occurred in early 1952.

WATERS: You and Vilma Espín, who was soon to become one of the most capable leaders of the revolutionary struggle, were among the first students at the University of Oriente, weren't you?

DE LOS SANTOS: Yes. The university was just taking its first steps. Vilma, who was studying engineering, enrolled in 1948. I went there in 1949 to study education.

The school had opened its doors in 1947 under the sponsorship of a group of broadly educated professionals who wanted Santiago de Cuba to be the site of a center of higher education serving all of Oriente province. The only other university at the time was in Havana. One of our first battles— students and professors together—was to gain official status, that is, national recognition, for the university. In March 1949 it won full official standing, including funds from Cuba's national budget.

The creation of an educational institution with high aca-

---

1.   For these and other events, individuals, and organizations referred
     to, see chronology and glossary.

demic standards for both students and teachers was a very important step for Santiago de Cuba. The university was true to its motto of "science and consciousness." A number of professors from Spain were hired, people who had supported the republican side in the 1936–39 Spanish Civil War. Some, such as Rendueles and Galbe,[2] had been members of the Communist Party in Spain. All had a high level of professional training, and quite a bit of influence among the student body as well as among the professors who were Cuban.

Most students and professors at the university leaned toward positions on the left. Many students liked the professors best who held new, revolutionary ideas, who supported just causes.

MARTÍN KOPPEL: Who were some of those professors?

DE LOS SANTOS: Some of the Cubans, like José Antonio Portuondo, were members of the Communist Party. Others, like Regino Boti, Pedro Cañas Abril, and Max Figueroa were what I would call progressive-minded.

Not all students at the university became revolutionaries, of course. Some did. Others, while they didn't like the regime, just went home to wait and see what would happen.

WATERS: Tell us about your activities following the coup.

DE LOS SANTOS: I saw the March 1952 coup as an act of brutality and opposed it from the outset. When it took place the university shut its doors as an act of protest. A group of us stayed there, however, to see what would happen and then figure out what we would do. Vilma was already becoming the central figure among us. She was courageous, calm, and unpretentious. Her patriotism had a deep impact on us.

I'll tell you a personal experience. The group occupying the university after the coup decided to pass out some printed

2.   See glossary, Julio López Rendueles, José Luis Galbe.

leaflets in the city to denounce the dictatorship. Vilma chose the text, including a few lines from a poem by José María Heredia, a great Cuban poet of the nineteenth century, addressing the role of a people confronting tyranny:

> If people do not dare
> to break their chains with their own hands,
> they may find it easy to remove a tyrant
> but will never be free.

We paid the price for this act. We were arrested and taken to the garrison for questioning. But others at the university mobilized, and we were freed within a few hours.

This was in the first days of the dictatorship, when they were still trying to present Batista as an honest person, someone who had come to solve all of Cuba's problems. That's how they started out.

At the Moncada army garrison, where they had taken us, the officers gave us some advice. "We used to be young, too," they told us. "Twenty years ago, at the time of the Machado dictatorship, we also did things. But now we have a man who will take care of everything. His name is Batista."

We argued with them.

Finally they decided we were incorrigible and let us go.

Moncada attack

Within a few months of the coup, the University of Oriente returned to normalcy, more or less. Students in Santiago organized demonstrations against outrages by the dictatorship. These actions were met by beatings and arrests. An uproar would ensue and the students would be released. And so passed days and months.

The year 1953 was the hundredth anniversary of the birth

of José Martí. In Cuba he is known as the Apostle.

In Havana a group of young revolutionaries, organized and led by Fidel Castro, had become convinced that the only way we could get rid of the dictatorship was by force of arms. Other means had been exhausted. These young people became known as the Centenary Generation, since 1953 was, as I said, the hundredth anniversary of Martí's birth. Martí's ideas retained their full force.

With Martí as their inspiration, they carried out one of the boldest and most selfless acts of patriotism in the history of Cuba—the July 26 attack on the Moncada army garrison in Santiago de Cuba and the Carlos Manuel de Céspedes garrison in Bayamo. More than a third of the Moncada combatants were murdered in cold blood, many—like Abel Santamaría, one of the central leaders—after being brutally tortured.

The overwhelming majority of the people of Santiago de Cuba were appalled, but they felt powerless to stop the murderers. When they heard the rattle of machine-gun fire, they knew people were being hunted down.

In the wake of these horrors, Vilma, two other compañeras, and I decided to head to the Moncada garrison to see for ourselves if what people were saying was true. Rumors were flying that the bodies of young people who had been murdered had been dumped on the grass outside the garrison.[3] We got close but could go no further. A state of siege had been declared, and the soldiers were acting like wild animals.

Moncada left a mark on the consciousness and patriotism of the people of Santiago. A crime had been committed against the young combatants, in full view of all. The bodies were

3. The reports were true. Batista's troops placed bodies of murdered combatants inside and outside the garrison to give the appearance they had been killed in combat.

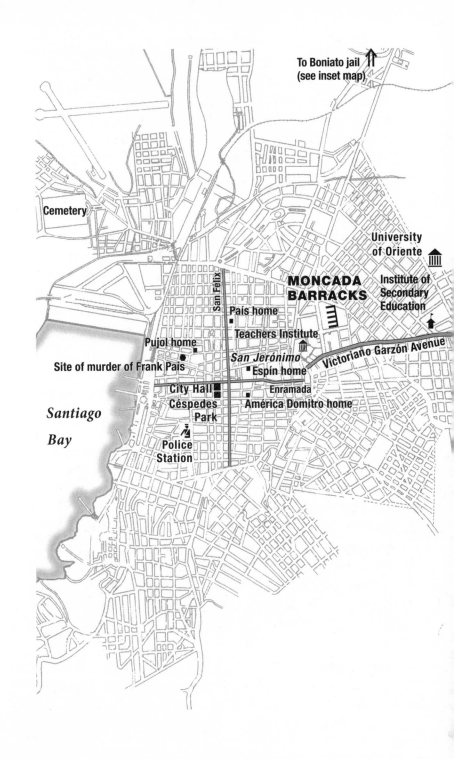

To Boniato jail
(see inset map)

Cemetery

University
of Oriente

San Felix

MONCADA
BARRACKS

Institute of
Secondary
Education

País home

Teachers Institute

Pujol home

San Jerónimo

Site of murder of Frank País

Espín home

Victoriano Garzón Avenue

Santiago
Bay

City Hall

Enramada

Céspedes
Park

América Domitro home

Police
Station

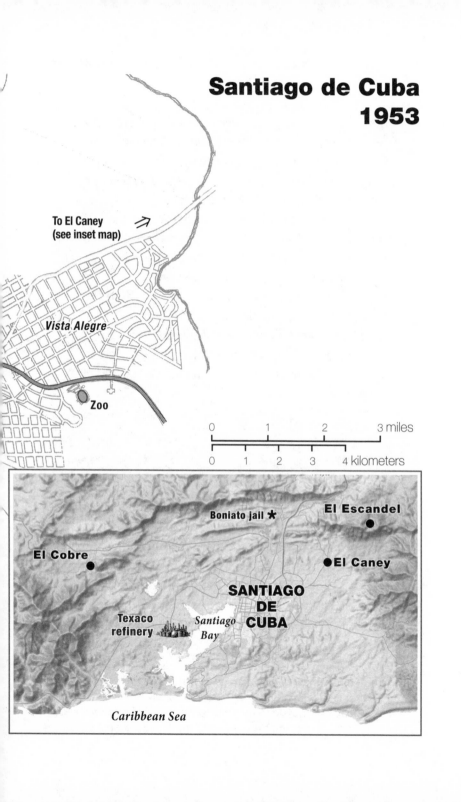

Santiago de Cuba
1953

To El Caney
(see inset map)

Vista Alegre

Zoo

0   1   2   3 miles

0   1   2   3   4 kilometers

Boniato jail ★   El Escandel ●

El Cobre ●

● El Caney

**SANTIAGO
DE
CUBA**

Texaco
refinery   *Santiago
Bay*

Caribbean Sea

> From the beginning [of the Moncada assault] we took numerous prisoners. . . . Those soldiers testified before the court, and without exception they all acknowledged that we treated them with absolute respect, that we did not subject them to even a single scoffing remark. . . .
>
> Our losses in the battle had been insignificant; 95 percent of our dead came from the army's cruelty and inhumanity when the battle was over. . . .
>
> Our men were killed not in the course of a minute, an hour, or a day. Rather, throughout an entire week the blows and tortures continued, men were thrown from rooftops and shot. All methods of extermination continued nonstop, practiced by well-skilled artisans of crime. The Moncada garrison was turned into a workshop of torture and death.[*]
>
> FIDEL CASTRO
>
> *History Will Absolve Me*
> 1953

thrown onto trucks and buried. Everybody knew about it.

Oriente province is where liberation struggles in Cuba have traditionally begun. Just as in the wars of 1868 and 1895 against Spanish colonial rule, Oriente was also where, in 1956, the final stage of the struggle for genuine independence began, led by Fidel Castro. This history has a lot to do with the political and patriotic consciousness of the people of Oriente.

[*] *History Will Absolve Me*, Fidel Castro's reconstruction of his courtroom defense speech, was smuggled out of prison, printed, and circulated clandestinely throughout the island in late 1954. Moncada combatants Haydée Santamaría and Melba Hernández were instrumental in leading the campaign for its wide distribution.

WATERS: Had you heard of Fidel Castro before Moncada?
DE LOS SANTOS: No. The Moncada attack was the first time I
heard his name. Elsewhere there had been talk about a young
lawyer from Havana, Fidel Castro Ruz—although he wasn't
actually from Havana. He was from Oriente province. Fidel's history was beginning to be known by people: from the
time he entered the University of Havana in 1945; his days as
a young revolutionary who, as a student, wanted to clean up
the university, drive out politics-as-usual; his later actions in
solidarity with the people of the Dominican Republic.[4]

But in Santiago, people knew nothing about Fidel. It was
through Moncada that we learned of him.

Moncada was a defining moment for the group of young
people I was part of. That's when we decided to organize
ourselves. Along with Vilma, Frank País, and several other
young people who wanted to fight the dictatorship. I contributed to the work of Oriente Revolutionary Action even
though I wasn't a member. The ARO was one of the groups
that came together to form the July 26 Movement when it was
founded two years later.

For the most part, the July 26 Movement was made up of
young people. This included students who, as a generation,
made a patriotic commitment to break with all the old structures that represented the political past. From the outset we
saw all politicians as crooks. We were determined to break

4. In July 1947 Fidel Castro enlisted in an expedition to overthrow
    the US-backed dictatorship of Rafael Trujillo in the Dominican
    Republic. The operation—known as the Cayo Confites expedi-
    tion, after the name of the small island off Cuba's northern coast
    where preparations took place—was funded and controlled by
    the Authentic Party government of Cuban president Ramón Grau
    San Martín. Under pressure from Washington, Grau San Martín
    pulled the plug on it in September 1947.

with the shameful conditions that existed in our country.

WATERS: Was that when you met Frank País?

DE LOS SANTOS: I met Frank at the university. I was in my last year, and he was starting his first.[5]

KOPPEL: What can you tell us about other political organizations that university students belonged to, such as the Orthodox Youth?

DE LOS SANTOS: The majority of students at the University of Oriente were sympathetic to Eduardo Chibás, the founding leader of the Cuban People's Party, or *ortodoxos*, the Orthodox Party, as they were known. There were also students who belonged to the Communist Party, organized at that time as the Popular Socialist Party. But most students, I'd say, didn't belong to a party.

At its founding in 1947, the Orthodox Party was viewed favorably by a majority of people. They saw it as offering solutions to many social problems. Chibás, the party's central leader, put forward a program of clean government. He promised to fight corruption and press for social measures that benefited ordinary people. He was famous for his constant stream of denunciations aimed at alerting people and mobilizing them. He was a leader who was revolutionary and nationalist and who won support, above all, among young people. Fidel, Abel Santamaría, and other revolutionaries belonged to the Orthodox Party.

Chibás shot himself in August 1951, at the end of his weekly Sunday radio program. This act was intended to demonstrate that his charges of corruption against the minister of education were true, even though he couldn't prove them in a court

5. País, formerly student body president at the Teachers Institute in Santiago, was teaching grade school in early 1954 and taking Saturday classes at the University of Oriente.

of law.[6] He wanted to salvage his reputation for truthfulness, his integrity and dignity.

Chibas's action had a big impact. Had the June 1952 elections been held, the majority would have voted for Orthodox Party candidates. Batista, in contrast, was the candidate of a party that represented only his own interests. He knew he couldn't become president through an election. So on March 10, 1952, he carried out a coup and canceled the elections.

After Batista was in power, he began political maneuvers to turn himself into an elected president. Fidel has said more than once that if Chibás had lived, Batista could not have succeeded. But the Orthodox Party had lost its political leader and, with him, its fighting spirit.

In August 1955, when Fidel was in Mexico preparing the expedition to Cuba, he sent a letter to the Orthodox Party. Fidel asked them to read and discuss the letter at the meeting later that month of the party leadership. He explained why it would be playing Batista's game to join together with those calling for local elections in 1956. Such elections, Fidel said, would be a fraud. The outcome had already been decided in favor of the dictator. Batista would use them to claim a legal basis to retain power.

Fidel's letter called on the party to take a position in support of insurrection, which he showed—based on facts and the existing situation—was the only way to get rid of the dictatorship. The majority of the Orthodox leadership didn't agree.

The patriotic and honest youth of Cuba did agree, however. They agreed with the political course of Fidel Castro and the

6. José Manuel Aléman was minister of education from 1946 to 1948. His successor, from 1948 to 1952, was Aurelio Sánchez Arango. Chibás accused both of being equally corrupt.

Cuba is at a crossroads. It will prostrate itself even more shamefully. . . . Or it will liberate itself gloriously once and for all from oppression.

One road leads to local elections, to making a deal with the tyranny, to recognizing the legitimacy of the regime, to unbridled ambition for municipal posts certified by election, to hunger, poverty, injustice, humiliation, to betrayal of the people, to criminally turning one's back on those who have died in the struggle.

The other road is revolution. The road of the people exercising their right to rebel against oppression; of historical continuity with the struggles of 1868, 1895, and 1933; of uncompromising intransigence in face of the treacherous coup of March [1952] and the shameful masquerade of November. The road leading to justice for the oppressed and hungry, to dignity, to selflessness and self-sacrifice, to loyalty toward those who gave their lives.[*]

FIDEL CASTRO

Letter to Orthodox Party
August 15, 1955

---

[*] Letter to National Congress of Orthodox Party Activists. Excerpts published in Heberto Norman Acosta, *La palabra empeñada* [I have given my word] (Havana: Publications Office of the Council of State, 2005), vol. 1, pp. 218–19. An English translation can be found in Rolando E. Bonachea and Nelson F. Valdés, *Selected Works of Fidel Castro: Revolutionary Struggle, 1947–1958* (Cambridge: MIT Press, 1972), pp. 271–77. "Shameful masquerade" refers to the November 1954 elections. See chronology and glossary for Cuban wars of independence (1868, 1895) and Revolution of 1933.

Centenary generation, who had launched an underground movement and armed struggle to overthrow the dictatorship.

When Fidel left prison in May 1955, freed by the strength of the amnesty campaign, he tried to remain in Havana and organize a revolutionary civic movement to create by legal means the conditions to overthrow Batista. That wasn't possible. The military set out to hunt down Fidel and kill him.

Fidel tried to communicate through the media, the radio. He tried to inform people, to tell them the truth about the situation. The regime responded by shutting down radio stations, television stations, and newspapers. And by pursuing Fidel.[7]

While still in Havana, Fidel organized the group that would become the national leadership of the movement. Revolutionaries from several groups came together. They decided to call the new organization the July 26 Revolutionary Movement.

Fidel and the other compañeros went to Mexico to prepare what became the *Granma* expedition. Those who stayed behind were responsible for revolutionary work in Cuba.

In 1956 we would either be free or be martyrs, as Fidel put it. That's what all of us thought.

Raúl Castro had to leave for Mexico sooner than planned. He had been framed on false charges of sabotage, part of an effort to arrest and perhaps kill him. In effect, the police were after all the young people who had been amnestied, seeking to kill some, arrest others.

In Santiago, while the Moncada combatants had been in prison, young revolutionaries—Frank País was an outstand-

7. Within weeks of Fidel Castro's release from prison, the Batista dictatorship banned him from speaking on the radio. On June 15, 1955, the Havana mass circulation daily *La calle* [The street] was ordered to stop printing articles by Castro; the following day the paper itself was shut down by police.

"A general amnesty is the cry of the entire citizenry. We students support it as well. . . . Not one of the noble fighters against the dictatorship should be behind bars!" —José Antonio Echeverría, president of the Federation of University Students (FEU), *Bohemia***, March 27, 1955.**

Joint meeting of Civic Front of Martí Women and FEU in Havana, October 1954, demanding amnesty for jailed Moncada combatants and other political prisoners. Many activists among Martí Women became founding members of Federation of Cuban Women.

ing example—organized actions, planned projects, and formed revolutionary groups to fight the dictatorship. Frank formed Oriente Revolutionary Action and gave it a national identity. ARO members, too, believed that armed struggle against the dictatorship was the only way to solve the problems of Cuba.

WATERS: So you joined the July 26 Movement when it was formed?

DE LOS SANTOS: Yes. It was formed in June 1955, after the amnesty. *History Will Absolve Me*, Fidel's defense speech at the Moncada trial, had been published, and supporters made sure it made its way all over the island. Fidel transformed himself from accused to accuser. From that moment on, I was won to the cause for good.

I began to work in the July 26 Movement alongside Vilma, alongside Frank, and alongside Haydée Santamaría and Armando Hart. The two of them had come to Santiago at the request of the movement's national leadership to strengthen the work there.

At first I was given small missions, which I carried out in a disciplined way. Then I was given tasks of a broader scope. But I didn't take on leadership responsibilities in the July 26 Movement.

Vilma, on the other hand, did—as a result of her leadership qualities, her personal integrity, her capacity and intelligence. Frank had great confidence in Vilma's capacities, in her sense of responsibility. She devoted herself full time to the insurrectional struggle but didn't have to go underground right away.

Vilma modestly claimed she was Frank País's driver. That's true, she did drive the car; it was hers. Sometimes she accompanied Frank to protect him. But above all she did so because she participated in leadership meetings herself and was increasingly taking on broader responsibilities.

As for me, my full participation began with the November 30, 1956, action in Santiago.

WATERS: Were you teaching at that time?

DE LOS SANTOS: Yes. I was both working as a teacher and carrying out assignments in the underground struggle.

WATERS: What kind of school?

DE LOS SANTOS: A primary school. I taught grades one through six. The school was in a rural area, in El Caney municipality. The job made my political work a lot more difficult.

As the date of what became the November 30 uprising neared and preparations increased for armed action, I asked for a leave and devoted myself full time to the insurrection. As I said, Fidel had already proclaimed that in 1956 they would come to the shores of Cuba to begin the armed struggle.

November 30 armed action

On November 30, 1956, beginning at 7:00 a.m., we carried out an armed action in Santiago de Cuba in support of the *Granma* landing, which we thought was going to be the same day. (They ended up landing two days later.) Combatants stopped cars in Santiago and told drivers that their cars were being taken over on behalf of the movement. We had no other means of transportation. Combatants took to the streets, in uniforms with armbands, chanting, "Down with Batista!" and "Long live Fidel!"

The fighting lasted until ten or eleven in the morning—Vilma describes it well in her account.[8] Three combatants were killed, Pepito Tey, Otto Parellada, and Tony Alomá. But several of the mission's objectives had been achieved. When the insurrectional forces retreated, the army began to emerge from the barracks, where they had been holed up.

8. See pages 139–45.

No one was arrested on the day of the action in Santiago itself, since the people protected us. People opened the doors to their houses.

"Come in here," they'd say.

"Put on these clothes."

"Leave by the door over there."

"Store your weapons here."

The people knew what had been done to the Moncada combatants could happen again. It still fills me with emotion to talk about it. I'm not telling you something I heard from others. I lived through it.

To me it seemed something unheard of—people not yet involved in the movement protecting youth who had gone out in the streets ready to die, ready to sacrifice their lives.

I'll give you an example. Sometimes the houses the movement used, and out of which we organized the November 30 action, were the homes of families. Other times we rented houses. Neighbors would quickly catch on that something unusual was going on—people and cars coming and going—and they'd be on the lookout to protect us. Someone would knock on the door and say, "Watch out, a strange guy just went by." They thought these might be informers, people who spied for the regime and who would report a young person or a house to the authorities. A protective atmosphere was created.

WATERS: When did you go underground?

DE LOS SANTOS: I never went underground. Vilma did. Her house was the headquarters, and Batista's forces raided it and began to hunt for her. So she went underground. But this being Santiago, the authorities never could get her. People protected her and she managed to escape. We always tried to choose houses with more than one way to get out, including by rooftop if need be.

I'll tell you a wonderful story. One day, after an informer

tipped off the cops, they came to the house where Vilma was staying. She managed to jump from the roof of her house to the adjoining house, which had a peaked roof. As she was climbing the neighbor's roof, a woman in the backyard saw a head appear, then a body, then a woman. She thought it was an apparition.

"A miracle!" she cried. "It's the Virgin Mary!"

Vilma managed to escape, climbing down the other side and jumping into the backyard. After the cops left, she returned over the same roof and went back to the house. But the most dramatic part of the story is that Haydée Santamaría was the one who took Batista's cops through the rooms to show them no one was there, that nothing subversive was going on! Events like these, no matter how nerve-wracking at the time, became an inside joke among all of us who were part of them.

Like me, Haydée also never went underground. She moved around Santiago de Cuba with impunity, even though the police were actively looking for her. Haydée had the ability to transform her appearance depending on the circumstances. When she put on a scarf and walked in such and such a way, she looked like a peasant woman. When she dressed well, she looked like a bourgeois.

Haydée even visited Armando Hart in Santiago's Boniato jail. The cops were on the lookout for Haydée, desperately searching for her. Yet here she calmly goes to the jail with another compañera. They identified themselves to the jailers as family or whatever.

"What are you *doing* here?" Armando said as soon as he saw her. He got very nervous.

"Relax. Don't worry," she answered.

At the time, Haydée was just about to leave Santiago to go abroad. She had been named July 26 Movement delegate in the United States, and she needed to get some information to Armando before she left. But she didn't want to send anyone else to do it. That shows the degree of her daring. Not to mention luck.[9]

As I said, I never went underground either. My house was never reported to the police. I was able to move around without being discovered.

WATERS: You've mentioned on other occasions the important place of women in the underground struggle. What were some of the things they did?

DE LOS SANTOS: Cuban women have a tradition of struggle, from the *mambises* in the nineteenth century wars of independence to today. That tradition is an important political element in our socialist revolution.

With a historical leap, we find ourselves in 1953, the beginning of the struggle for genuine independence—I'm referring here to the attack on Moncada—and the heroic examples of Melba Hernández and Haydée Santamaría, who participated in that action.

As the struggle continued, more and more women became part of it.

Fidel's course of building a mass revolutionary movement capable of sustaining and supporting the armed struggle enabled both men and women to be integrated.

Women joined the ranks of the Rebel Army. In the Sierra Maestra there was a platoon of women fighters known as the Marianas,[10] named after Mariana Grajales, the mother of the

9. For Armando Hart's account of the visit in May 1958, see his book *Aldabonazo: Inside the Cuban Revolutionary Underground* (Pathfinder, 2004), p. 283 [2010 printing].

10. For a firsthand account of the formation and experiences of this unit, see Teté Puebla, *Marianas in Combat: Teté Puebla and the Mari-*

eight Maceo brothers, all of whom fought for independence from Spain. She was one of the great heroes of the war for independence.

In the underground we did whatever was necessary. We sewed uniforms and armbands for the Rebel Army. We helped provide cover for moving weapons and young combatants. We found families who would house revolutionary fighters who had gone underground. We secured medicine. We served as messengers between different revolutionary fronts. We distributed subversive propaganda and collected supplies.

In short, women worked on every front in the underground struggle.

This included tasks that were even more dangerous. In Miami, for example, there was a delegate of the July 26 Movement who was responsible for collecting weapons, provisions, money, and so on to be sent to Cuba in various ways. A group of young women would leave Miami with small weapons, bullets, messages, letters, you name it, hidden under the full skirts that were fashionable then.

One time there were three of us on a trip. We were running late for the plane in Miami. I put four or five pistols in pouches, which we placed under our skirts. We simply basted them in. When we arrived at the airport in Varadero and I got up from my seat, I suddenly felt something rip. I called over a compañera who was traveling with me—we were already standing in the aisle, waiting to get off the plane.

"Whatever happens, you don't know me and I don't know you," I said.

To stop the gun from banging, I started limping, like I'd just

---

ana Grajales Women's Platoon in Cuba's Revolutionary War (Pathfinder, 2003).

had surgery. Somehow we got out.

There's a photo in the Museum of the Second Front in Mayarí Arriba with a caption that says, "The compañeras carried weapons under their skirts." It's a photo of us on one of these trips, taken by a soldier. We gave him the camera to take our picture, and we flirted with him to draw attention away from what we were concealing. We then went through immigration and on to Havana, where we delivered the guns.

In all, I made nine trips from Miami to Havana, Camagüey, or Varadero.

WATERS: Nine trips is a lot.

DE LOS SANTOS: Once in the Havana airport they set a trap using a compañera from Santiago as bait. I had something under my skirt, and I saw her walking between two men. "Something's not right here," I said to myself, and kept on going. It turned out they were using this compañera to try to catch anyone greeting or making contact with her.

You develop an instinct after a while, as well as an ability to remain calm in face of danger. That's what protects you. At the beginning I was scared. After some experience, I lost that fear. That's the truth.

The women in the underground struggle were very serious. The compañeros had great respect and admiration for us, and they protected us.

A young woman like Vilma, who came from a well-off family, was willing to give her life. That's just one example. There were others.

The seriousness of women in the movement helped our mothers have confidence that the struggle we were involved in was genuine. Think what it meant when a mother knew that her daughter—sometimes very young—was involved in underground activity, yet the family raised no objections. Most of the time the family was not an obstacle to young

"As the revolutionary struggle deepened in Cuba, women saw greater possibilities opening up, even before the victory. . . . When a deepgoing revolution takes place, women, who have been oppressed for millenia, want to take part."—Asela de los Santos

Workers from Calixto García hospital in Havana greet Rebel Army's Freedom Caravan, January 8, 1959, as it enters city after eight-day march across island from Santiago de Cuba.

women and men being able to join the struggle. That had tremendous significance.

Women became increasingly involved in Santiago de Cuba
and in the rest of the country.

WATERS: Participating in this kind of struggle must have
given women confidence, a sense of accomplishment and
liberation. It wasn't so easy to do.

DE LOS SANTOS: That's right. In other conditions this
wouldn't have been possible. Girls would have studied in order to get a job, as they normally had.

I'm talking about the middle class—the upper class is
something else. But for women of the professional middle
class, and from poor families, the hope was to get ahead by
getting an education and a job.

As the struggle deepened, women saw greater possibilities
opening up. There were many important things to do. The
revolution offered them this opportunity. And I'm talking
about even before the victory.

When a deepgoing revolution takes place, women, who
have been oppressed for centuries, for millennia, want to
take part.

You asked me if working in the underground was a liber-
ating experience for a woman. Yes, it was. No one could stop
the women.

WATERS: It gave you a sense of worth . . .

DE LOS SANTOS: . . . of worth as a human being, as part of
the people.

WATERS: For me this is a very significant element of the Cuban Revolution. Your generation in Cuba was in the vanguard
of the historic changes in women's economic and social status, as we were drawn out of the home and into social labor
to a previously unprecedented degree, something that began
during the Second World War.

In no other socialist revolution have there been so many leaders who were women: Vilma Espín, Celia Sánchez, Haydée Santamaría, Melba Hernández, to name but a few of the best known. Their leadership was indispensable. It's one of the elements of Cuba's revolutionary history that needs to be better known and better understood.

With regard to yourself, what kind of family did you grow up in? As a young woman coming of age, how did you see your future?

DE LOS SANTOS: My father had retired very young from the armed forces, around 1935. He was a lieutenant. My mother was a housewife. I had one brother and two sisters. From the time we were little, our family's economic situation was tight, since we lived on my father's pension. As we grew up, we began preparing for the professions we wanted to study. All of us went to school. I was able to go to the university. It wasn't cheap, but we could afford it. You could say we were lower middle class.

My parents were very concerned that the children be educated, above all the daughters. My father said he wanted his daughters to be educated and trained in a profession, so we could be economically independent. That way we wouldn't be dependent on a husband.

Our parents worked hard so we could go to school. One of my sisters studied to be a preschool teacher—it was called kindergarten then—and she got a job. I took education courses and got a position too, as I said. My other sister, when she was in high school, had planned to study law, but she landed a job at the telephone company as an operator. That made her economically independent.

At home I didn't feel inferior because I was a girl. To the contrary, in my house the women were always the privileged ones.

The murder of Frank País

WATERS: In the six months after the November 30 action, the struggle in Santiago de Cuba intensified, culminating in the events surrounding the murder of Frank País. What was the atmosphere like then?

DE LOS SANTOS: The majority of people in Santiago de Cuba became involved, since it got more and more common to find the body of a tortured youth thrown into the street, almost always right outside the city limits. Many young people died under torture. Many young women were arrested, some were raped and tortured.

People not only rejected and hated the tyrannical regime. They also protected and defended the revolutionaries.

WATERS: Were you in Santiago de Cuba on July 30 1957, when Frank País was murdered?

DE LOS SANTOS: Yes. Lucía Parada and I were in a car on the way to pick up uniforms at the home of some seamstresses when it happened. We heard the rattle of automatic weapons. That always gave me a start—I wondered, "Which one of our compañeros has fallen?"

I didn't imagine it could be Frank. I thought Frank was immortal, that he could get out of anything. Many times he had escaped right out of the hands of Batista's thugs. Then we saw a compañero named Luis Felipe Rosel driving toward us in his car.

"They're saying Frank's been killed," he told us. He had tears in his eyes.

"It can't be."

"Where?"

"Over by Raúl Pujol's house."

I knew where that was. So I said to Lucía, "Let's go."

When we got there, the cops had surrounded the area and

In July 1957 a tragic event occurred in Santiago de Cuba—the murder of Frank País. It marked a turning point for the entire revolutionary movement.

The people of Santiago took to the streets spontaneously, making the first attempt at a political general strike. Though leaderless, the strike totally paralyzed Oriente province and had a similar impact in Camagüey and Las Villas. The dictatorship throttled this movement that had emerged with neither preparation nor revolutionary guidance.

This action by the masses, however, made us realize that the struggle for the liberation of Cuba had to incorporate the social power of the working class. We immediately began clandestine work in the unions to prepare a general strike that would help the Rebel Army seize power.[*]

ERNESTO CHE GUEVARA
JANUARY 29, 1959

set up roadblocks.

"Where are you going?" they asked.

"We live here, we're scared." And all the other things you learned to say to survive in that environment.

The police had set up a big outer roadblock, with a smaller

[*] Ernesto Che Guevara, "Proyecciones sociales del Ejército Rebelde" [Social ideals of the Rebel Army], speech given January 29, 1959. In José Bell and others, *Documentos de la revolución cubana, 1959* [Documents of the Cuban Revolution, 1959] (Havana: Ciencias Sociales, 2008), p. 32. Much of this speech was incorporated into an interview by two Chinese journalists who interviewed Guevara on April 18, 1959. See "A New Old Interview" in *Che Guevara Speaks* (Pathfinder, 1967, 2000), p. 15–21 [2011 printing].

"The people of Santiago de Cuba took to the streets spontaneously, making the first attempt at a political general strike. Though leaderless, the strike totally paralyzed Oriente province and had a similar impact in Camagüey and Las Villas."—Ernesto Che Guevara

Santiago de Cuba, July 31, 1957. Sixty thousand, one-third of the city's population, joined funeral march for July 26 Movement leader Frank País, murdered by Batista's cops the day before.

one inside it, then a very small innermost circle. We got through the first police line but couldn't get past the inner ones. Frank and his compañero Raúl Pujol had been murdered. Photographers were there from the press. A pistol had been planted by Frank's side. We left right away.

I telephoned Vilma.

"It's true, it's true," she told me.

"OK. You, Lucía, and the other compañeras, try to see Frank's mother, Rosario," Vilma said. "Because they have to hand over the body." Vilma gave the same instructions to other compañeros, so we all knew what we had to do.

We went to see Rosario. The police had the body in the morgue at Santa Ifigenia cemetery with plans to immediately bury it. Our idea was to mobilize people to go there, along the main street, and to demand they turn over the body. As we did so, people began joining us.

"Where are you going?" they asked.

"To find Frank, to find Frank."

When we were almost there, someone told us, "Frank's body has been taken to his home." His body was indeed there, in a coffin. His mother, Doña Rosario, was sitting beside the coffin, grief-stricken but displaying great calm.

Once again Vilma made contact with us. She said to move Frank's body to the house of his girlfriend, América Domitro, which was in a central location. We wanted the funeral march to move through all of Santiago.

We took Frank's body to América's, and from there our group of compañeros prepared everything. The people of Santiago started coming to see Frank's body. No one wanted to believe they'd killed him.

At two in the morning we had to organize all the coming and going, since so many people wanted to see him.

What did Batista's forces do while all this was happening?

They confined their troops to the barracks.

We dressed Frank in his olive green uniform, with a beret and a white flower honoring José Martí. It was Frank who had designed the uniform and proposed it to Fidel in Mexico. Frank was an extraordinary young man, capable of doing things both big and small—of designing a uniform down to the smallest detail, as well as working out a strategy for struggle. For him, no detail was insignificant.

Tens of thousands in Santiago accompanied Frank's body on the funeral procession. They shouted their hatred for Batista, for his henchmen, for [José María] Salas Cañizares, the officer who killed Frank. Inflamed by what had been done, people shouted curses at the murderers. They sang the July 26 Hymn and the national anthem. As the hearse went by, they threw flowers from balconies.

No one had to call for a general strike, but one took place nonetheless. All business establishments closed.

Even today in Santiago de Cuba, many people can't talk much about Frank without being overcome with emotion. It's like with Che's death, which was very painful for all of us. Because you recognize the loss represented by the death of someone who was young, someone who would have contributed greatly to the revolutionary process and had every right to see the victory. Frank was only twenty-two years old!

But that's the way it is. That's the price we sometimes have to pay to win dignity and freedom.

The Rebel Army's Second Front

WATERS: What were the tasks of the urban underground as the revolutionary war led by Fidel from the Sierra advanced?

DE LOS SANTOS: The urban underground movement was an important part of the war against the dictatorship. It supported and supplied the Rebel Army with revolutionary cadres as well as equipment and resources. It got out the word about what was happening in the mountains, the insurgency in towns and cities, what Fidel was leading. It explained the movement's slogans, helping to win people over to the armed struggle.

These were all important aspects of the urban underground's work.

It became harder to get weapons to the mountains, but some were delivered by various means. They were used to strengthen the first reinforcements that Fidel received. Everyone in that first group, in March 1957, brought their own weapons.

WATERS: You're referring to the group known as the *Marabúzaleros?*

DE LOS SANTOS: Yes, the ones who assembled and hid out in the *marabú* patch.[11] That was the work of Celia [Sánchez]. She chose a spot that was inaccessible. Somewhere no one would suspect fifty young people would be camped out waiting to join the struggle in the Sierra.[12]

Celia was one of the main leaders of the July 26 Movement in Manzanillo, which organized the urban network that provided supplies to the Rebel Army in the mountains. Working with Frank País, she helped young recruits get through to the rebel forces. She became the first woman combatant in the Sierra Maestra and part of the Rebel Army's general staff.

---

11. *Marabú* is a dense, thorny shrub that grows wild on uncultivated land in Cuba.

12. For an firsthand account by a member of the initial group of reinforcements, see Luis Alfonso Zayas, *Soldier of the Cuban Revolution: From the Cane Fields of Oriente to General of the Revolutionary Armed Forces* (Pathfinder, 2011), pp. 66–75.

The majority of the Rebel Army's weapons were seized from Batista's army. The Rebel Army increased its weaponry primarily through direct combat. They armed themselves with weapons taken from the enemy. That's the truth. But the underground was also key to supplying weapons, uniforms, boots, medicine, and combatants, both male and female. When reinforcements were sent, we helped make sure they were well equipped. The urban underground was an indispensable political force, a creator of consciousness, a force capable of maintaining a combative, revolutionary, and patriotic spirit in the cities.

By early August 1958 the "encircle and annihilate offensive" by Batista's forces, aimed at wiping out the rebels in the Sierra Maestra, had been defeated, and the Rebel Army had gone on the counteroffensive.[13]

The Frank País Second Eastern Front had been opened in eastern Oriente province five months earlier, in March 1958, under Raúl Castro's command.

In the area around Santiago de Cuba, the Mario Muñoz Third Front had also begun operation in March, under Juan Almeida's command.

The Simón Bolívar Fourth Front, led by Delio Gómez Ochoa, was operating in the area west of Holguín.

13. For Fidel Castro's account of how in 74 days of battle in the summer of 1958, 300 revolutionary fighters—with the support of workers and peasants across Cuba—defeated Batista's 10,000-strong "final offensive," see *La victoria estratégica: Por todos los caminos de la Sierra* [The strategic victory: on every road through the Sierras] (Havana: Publication Office of the Council of State, 2010). For his account of the Rebel Army's subsequent 147-day counteroffensive that brought down the dictatorship, see *La contraofensiva estratégica: De la Sierra Maestra a Santiago de Cuba* [The strategic counteroffensive: from the Sierra Maestra to Santiago de Cuba] (Havana: Publication Office of the Council of State, 2010).

Eastern fronts 1958

First front established December 1956, Cmdr. Fidel Castro.
Second front established March 1958, Cmdr. Raúl Castro.
Third front established March 1958, Cmdr. Juan Almeida.
Fourth front established October 1958, Cmdr. Delio Gómez Ochoa.

1, 2, 3, 4 *FRONTS*

Front boundaries

CENTRAL HIGHWAY

Smaller roads

Country roads

Railroad tracks

Provincial boundary

⊛ *Provincial capital*

● *Larger city*

◉ *All other cities, towns and villages*

⚑ *Rebel Army command center*

✕ *Nickel mine*

🏭 *Sugar mill*

◆ *Place mentioned in text or pictured*

★ *Headquarters of Second Front*

Banes

Atlantic Ocean

Mayarí   Nicaro   Moa

SIERRA CRISTAL

◆ Tumba Siete
★ Mayarí Arriba

Miranda   *SAGUA BARACOA MOUNTAINS*   Baracoa

2

Palma Soriano   San Luis   Ermita

TRA   Guantánamo

⊛ SANTIAGO DE CUBA   Caimanera

Siboney

U.S. NAVAL BASE   *Caribbean Sea*

| 0 | 20 | 40 miles |
| 0 | 30 | 60 kilometers |

At the end of August, the invasion columns of Che and Camilo had set off for Las Villas and Pinar del Río, and in November the Camagüey Front was organized.

By that time, the urban underground no longer played such a weighty role, and the Civic Resistance came to the fore.[14] Most of the urban underground cadres joined different Rebel Army fronts, where they took on important responsibilities.

WATERS: When did you join the Rebel Army's Second Eastern Front?

DE LOS SANTOS: I remained in Santiago through 1957 and part of 1958. In August 1958 I was transferred to the Second Front. Vilma was already there; she had been sent to the Sierra in July. It had become too dangerous for her to stay in the underground. Vilma had told Raúl I could take over the organization of schools throughout the entire Second Front, and of literacy classes for the combatants there.

WATERS: You had made a trip to the Second Front once before, hadn't you? Coming back from one of your Miami runs?

DE LOS SANTOS: Yes, on one of my trips I was telling you about, to bring weapons back to Cuba, I also brought with me a message for Raúl. That's why I made my way up to the Second Front. When I got there, Raúl asked me when I was going to come and stay for good. As far as I was concerned, I told him, I'd stay right then and there. But I had to return to Santiago to carry out some tasks, I said.

I did that, and after my work was done I returned to the Second Front and stayed.

14. The Civic Resistance incorporated broad middle-class and even some bourgeois sectors, including religious figures and professionals, who collaborated with the July 26 Movement to free the country of the Batista dictatorship.

I was greatly relieved. It was very different from living under conditions of repression, where every time you heard car tires screech, you thought Batista's thugs might be arriving. That's how we lived in the cities, in a never-ending state of tremendous tension.

When I got to the Second Front . . . ay, what a feeling! It was free territory at last! None of those things happened. There were no criminals, torturers, thugs.

WATERS: In the territory of the Second Front, as Vilma proposed, you were given responsibility for the entire education system established by the Rebel Army there. It was one element of civil life organized by the revolutionary forces, in continuity with the future transformation of the rest of Cuban society. This experience is hardly known outside of Cuba.

DE LOS SANTOS: That's true. It was in the Sierra Maestra that preparations began on a large scale to teach literacy to Rebel Army combatants. It was in the Sierra Maestra that Fidel made sure teachers were assigned to all the tiny rural schools that had been closed by the tyranny.

From the moment the Second Front was established, Raúl had the same concern. He issued instructions stating that in all the camps, combatants who were illiterate had to be taught how to read and write. And he ordered the reopening of every small rural school that had been closed because of the war.

Carrying this out was the assignment I was given when I arrived in August.

Within the first months of the establishment of the Second Front, a wide swath of territory was liberated. After the defeat of Batista's "encircle and annihilate offensive" by early August, those areas were largely free of Batista's ground forces, making it possible to open more than four hundred small schools, old and new. This was also due to Raúl's organizational capacities and to his insistence—whatever the demands of war—that there would be no neglect of something so important to the lives of the fighters and children as education.

How was this possible?

The Second Front had both mountains and plains. The topography, and the gathering together of people in small settlements, helped in setting up schools.

But most important was the region's social composition—above all, the large exploited rural population. This was a territory of large estates, of landowners who possessed enormous tracts of land. Many US corporations owned mills and plantations there, as well as nickel, manganese, and cobalt mines.

All these things together made it possible to advance. That experience became the forerunner. It showed us what needed to be done once victory was won. The growing determination of the rural population to make sure their children had schools was a big help in turning those ideas into a reality.

Raúl arrived in the area of the Second Front on March 11, 1958, with seventy-six men. They were the founders. They're also known as the *crossers*, because they crossed the Central Highway that divided the region of Fidel's Column 1 and Almeida's Column 3 from the Second Front.

Once he was there, Raúl immediately toured the area and did two things. First, he created the initial military structure. Second, he met with the peasants—peasant leaders, peasant families—to draw them into the struggle and win their support.

Alongside the military structure, a military-governmental structure was also built to aid the functioning and development of the armed struggle. Seven departments were established, one of them being Education. The others were Agriculture, Construction and Communications, Finances, Health,

Justice, and Propaganda.

How did they function? I'll give you an example: Finances.

No one in the Rebel Army could confiscate anything from the peasants. Everything was bought and paid for. The peasants were respected. That was part of the ethical standard set by the Rebel Army. So Raúl created a group to manage finances, to manage the small amount of economic resources we had at the beginning. Out of this came a financial plan to support the expanding war.

There were also sugar plantations and mills in the area governed by the Second Front. Fidel, as commander in chief in the Sierra, ordered that for each 250-pound bag of sugar produced, the plantations had to pay 10 centavos to the movement in that territory. This was managed through the Finances Department.

Other funds were collected in the form of taxes formerly paid by the landlords and businessmen to the state. Since they were now within the territory of the Second Front, these tax payments were collected by the Front's Finances Department.

We also had a Construction and Communications Department. When it rained, roads sometimes became impassable. So this department repaired them, and opened new ones.

I don't know how, but from the beginning in the Second Front we had bulldozers. I say this tongue-in-cheek. I *do* know how. They "appeared" because compañeros in the July 26 Movement took them and brought them up as supplies. Ramón Castro, Fidel's older brother, who lived in the Birán area, supplied a lot of equipment to the Second Front, for example.

This machinery was a big help in road repairs. It helped in waging the war, enabling us to improve the mobility of our troops. And it provided a service for the population, which

"The Rebel Army never confiscated anything from the peasants. Everything was bought and paid for. The peasants were respected. . . . To support the expanding war, the commander in chief, Fidel, ordered that for each 250-pound bag of sugar produced, plantation owners had to pay 10 centavos to the movement in the Second Front. These funds were managed through the front's Finances Department."—Asela de los Santos

Above: Combatants at coffee depot where similar tax on coffee was collected, Sierra Maestra, 1958. **Below:** Fidel Castro with Pastora Núñez, Rebel Army combatant in Column 1 responsible for collecting the sugar tax, at La Plata headquarters in Sierra Maestra, October 1958.

benefited from the improved roads.

There was also the Health Department, headed by José Machado Ventura, who is today first vice president of the Council of State and Council of Ministers. We organized hospitals and medical units. Medicine was supplied by the July 26 Movement in the cities. These units even performed surgery.

The Health Department provided health care to the population, peasants and combatants, without distinction, including wounded enemy soldiers.

For the most part, people living in the area of the Second Front had never had the chance to see a doctor before. Many had that opportunity only when the Second Front was established. For the first time they were treated like human beings.

That was the Health Department.

Another department was Propaganda. It was important politically, because we had a radio station that could be heard throughout the country. It reached as far as Venezuela. Through its transmitters, the radio station broadcast news and advanced the struggle. It refuted all the lies being spread to demoralize the Rebel Army and the people. It was also a way of communicating with the other fronts.

Then there was the Justice Department. It performed marriages and settled disputes among people in the area. It also regulated legal matters in the camps. There were even trials for misconduct. Some combatants were expelled from the Rebel Army. Discipline and order reigned in the life of the camps.

And finally there was the Education Department.

In *History Will Absolve Me*, Fidel denounced the existence in Cuba of widespread illiteracy. Illiteracy is a tool in the hands of the exploiters. If you are ignorant, if you don't know how to read or write, you're not free. Not knowing even how to sign your name makes people feel inferior.

"Rebel hospitals provided health care to the population, peasants and combatants, without distinction, including wounded enemy soldiers."—Asela de los Santos

Waiting to see doctor at field hospital near Fidel Castro's headquarters at La Plata, in Sierra Maestra, late 1958. This hospital is named after Mario Muñoz, doctor and combatant killed in 1953 attack on Moncada garrison.

The rural population in the Second Front was poor, exploited, hungry. Many young people joined the Rebel Army, so the number of combatants who were illiterate grew. And this was a challenge.

That's how the education effort started. Raúl issued orders that we teach all these young combatants to read and write.

"You know how to read," the head of the camp would say to someone. "Teach so-and-so here, who doesn't."

But it's not so simple.

A person trained as a teacher can teach someone to read and write even without an instruction book. They know the methods. They know how to do it. Good teaching makes use of phonics, analysis, and synthesis. Phonics is important, since language enters through your ears. You have to pronounce the letters. These are methods a teacher learns.

For someone who isn't a teacher, it's harder. We began to realize in the Second Front that to teach the troops to read and write, it was important to use people with more training. That's where the idea of creating the Education Department came from.

I was a teacher—I had a doctorate in education—and they put me in charge. The number-two person was Zoila Ibarra, a woman who had come to the Second Front with her husband, an engineer. I remember her with deep affection and gratitude. She was older than I was. With her greater maturity, she taught me a lot about many things and helped establish the department.

We tried to find teachers among the rural population, or people with a high enough education level that they could teach. But many teachers had abandoned their schools. Raúl saw these abandoned schoolhouses during his tour of the territory of the Second Front, and he ordered the department to reopen them for the children.

So we set about teaching both Rebel Army combatants who were illiterate and school-age children. When peasants heard and saw what we were doing, they became interested. They asked about it. We told them that if they found the facilities, it was possible to organize small schools. So people started to look for sites, to find chairs, and to organize schools. Schools expanded at an incredible pace. In fact, we had to slow down the process. Before authorizing a new one, we organized a census to see how many school-age children there were in the area.

The Education Department adopted the same military structure as our columns and companies. On the company level, we assigned a person in each area to be responsible for education, someone who would be the contact with the department. That person dealt with the teachers, overseeing books and resources. We held a meeting of all the teachers in the front, where we read out the assignments. That gave us a chance to find out how many teachers and schools we had. It also let us meet the teachers in person and explain some technical things. Then we told each one to do what was humanly possible within the limitations.

I want to emphasize the help Raúl gave us. When we arrived, Raúl provided a jeep and a driver so we could get around through all that territory. He supported us with orders and instructions to the heads of the military units.

There was even a military order, number 50, which set down all the functions of the Education Department.[15]

WATERS: Did parents resist sending their children to study?

DE LOS SANTOS: No, just the opposite. There was a desire to learn how to read. Many campesinos were convinced that

15. For the text of Military Order no. 50, see pp. 117–20.

if their children learned to read and write, if they went to school, they wouldn't go through everything their parents had suffered.

So the campesinos helped open schools in locations they themselves found. After the triumph of the revolution, those new little schools remained.

In wartime you can sometimes achieve things that in normal times can't be done so easily. In the Second Front, change was in the air. There was very little resistance there.

It's true that in the old rural schools peasants often kept their children back. There was a high rate of absenteeism. One reason was that children went to work in the fields with their parents to sustain family income. There were other reasons also: distances that were too long, lack of shoes and clothing, and health problems.

But the new political motivation, the new hope, had a decisive influence not only on the willingness to build little schoolhouses, to make benches and improvise blackboards, but also on school attendance. This despite the danger from bombing runs by the dictatorship, which at times directly targeted civilians in murderous raids.

WATERS: In addition to children, were women studying too?

DE LOS SANTOS: The classes we organized were for children and for combatants who were illiterate. In the evenings some teachers taught classes to the adult civilian population. But that wasn't generalized.

WATERS: The teachers were mostly women?

DE LOS SANTOS: Yes. Many were from the area, and others came from Santiago or Guantánamo.

WATERS: And you say four hundred schools were opened in the Second Front?

DE LOS SANTOS: Yes, we set up more than four hundred. In

VISIÓN DE FUTURO

"At first many of those selected for the school didn't want to attend. They thought they wouldn't be allowed to fight any more. Some even thought it was a punishment. These misconceptions were laid to rest when Raúl explained why they had to study and pass on what they had learned, without ceasing to be combatants."—Asela de los Santos

Students in first class of José Martí School for Teachers of Combatants, Second Front, November 1958. Standing at back, with beret, is Zoila Ibarra.

my book *Visión de futuro* there's a list of the schools, organized by the military columns they were linked to, and the names of the teachers at each school.[16]

WATERS: How were you able to establish so many schools in so little time, less than six months?

DE LOS SANTOS: We went through several stages. It might help if I sketched what they were.

The first went from March 11, 1958, when the front was established, until late May, when Batista's "encircle and annihilate offensive" began in the Sierra Maestra. The focus then was on establishing and expanding the front. Only a few schools and literacy groups were organized.

The second period, from late May to August 1958, saw a big increase in attacks against the enemy. The rebel forces were reorganized, new columns and companies were formed, and the front was strengthened. We set up departments to work with peasants and workers, and to do political education. More schools and literacy groups were organized.

The first two stages were marked by a significant increase in recruitment to the ranks of the Rebel Army. Most new recruits were young and poor—workers, peasants, students, men and women of the exploited masses who supported the revolutionary cause. Many had little schooling. Some were illiterate or semiliterate.

In the third stage, which I was part of, from August to December 31, 1958, we set up the Education Department and several others. More schools and literacy groups got started, and they were better organized.

We organized study groups in the camps and began to set up rural schools with the teachers available to us. The liber-

16. Asela de los Santos, *Visión de futuro* [Vision of the future] (Havana: Ediciones Verde Olivo, 2001), pp. 158–77.

ated zone was already taking on a certain stability. The leadership gave priority to teaching and to instilling the social, moral, and political values that inspired the revolutionary process.

To capture this dual function—fighting both ignorance, and the existing social order—these educators were called *rebel teachers*.

Just try to imagine the conditions in which these teachers worked, in the midst of armed struggle and extreme poverty. Many began without the most minimal of elements— uniforms, boots, teaching materials, sometimes even a place to stay.

Their prior training varied widely, ranging from university graduates who had specialized in education to those who had completed no more than the fifth grade. But they all had something in common—a love of their country and the determination with which they undertook the task. They set a valuable example for our entire education system.

It's also important to understand the degree of political heterogeneity at the time, given the breadth of the popular movement against Batista, a movement the ranks of the Rebel Army were part of. This was evident in the political confusion—you might almost say "intoxication"—that reigned among the majority of combatants and officers. It registered the widespread anticommunist and anti–Soviet Union propaganda in the mass media.

These were the circumstances under which we set up our first teacher training school—the José Martí School for Teachers of Combatants. The school began in November 1958 in Tumba Siete, where the Department of Education was based. That course ran until November 30 and had thirteen students. The second course, in December, had thirty-two.

At first many of those selected for the school didn't want to

As the insurrectional struggle against the hated regime deepens, we have to increase political education. . . .

Understanding that many of our combatants do not have a deep grasp of the true motivation that impels us forward, yet despite this have not ceased to demonstrate courage, valor, sacrifice, selflessness, and a high degree of patriotism on every front.

Knowing that there is much disorientation, along with erroneous conceptions that multiply different opinions.

Seeing that it is an urgent necessity that all that has united us as brothers in this struggle also brings together our discordant views, so that we may enter the phase of the revolutionary seizure of power with a way of thinking that is both uniform and aimed at attaining a country that is happy, free, independent, united, strong, democratic, and progressive.

For these reasons, the José Martí School for Teachers of Combatants has been created to train the greatest possible number of compañeros to provide the troops with a minimum program of education, help them understand the historical process through which we are living, and prepare them for what is to come.[*]

ASELA DE LOS SANTOS
JOSÉ CAUSSE PÉREZ
RAÚL CASTRO RUZ
NOVEMBER 29, 1958

[*] From circular on establishment of the José Martí School for Teachers of Combatants. In *Visión de futuro*, pp. 149–50.

attend. They thought once they graduated they wouldn't be allowed to fight any more, that they'd just be teachers. Some even thought being sent to the school was a punishment. These misconceptions were laid to rest when, at the opening of the school, they heard Raúl explain why they had to study and pass on what they had learned—without ceasing to be combatants.

As for the number of schools, remember, the Second Front covered a territory of twelve thousand square kilometers.[17] Four hundred schools was a drop in the bucket. The bulk of the schoolhouses were already there. Fortunately, many even had a textbook for teachers on how to teach reading and writing. It was written by an eminent professor of education, Carlos de la Torre.

WATERS: What about the rural clinics? Did they already exist?

DE LOS SANTOS: No. The clinics and field hospitals in the Second Front had to be built. I think there were seventeen, possibly nineteen. They provided services to the population in very isolated areas.

WATERS: Yet you did this all in the middle of a war, despite air raids by Batista's forces and everything else.

DE LOS SANTOS: With regard to the bombing, Raúl ordered trenches to be dug at every school. And the combatants did so at each of them. When the planes flew over, you knew they were coming. You could hear them. Everyone ran for the trenches. You put a stick in your mouth, so your eardrums wouldn't burst from the air compression after the explosion.

Raúl also ordered that no vehicles be parked in front of schools. The Second Front had a few cars, and when the pilots saw one, they'd open fire.

The first time I experienced a bombing raid, I heard some-

17. That is, about 4,700 square miles.

one yell, "Plane!" And *voom!* everyone ran for the trenches. But I wasn't trained.

"Plane?" I said. "What's going on? Where's the plane?"

I didn't know what to do. I saw everyone else running, but I straggled behind. I was out in the open, and the plane started strafing.

"Down on the ground!" they shouted to me. "Get down!"

So I threw myself down.

"Curl up in a ball!"

So I curled up in a ball. Fortunately I wasn't hit.

The next time I reacted like a track star. I knew where to go. I knew where the trench was.

At first a plane is terrifying. But in Mayarí Arriba, the headquarters of the Second Front, every day dawns with a heavy cloud cover. Until ten in the morning, nothing can be seen from a plane. So those were the times we'd move around.

The strafing runs were part of our lives. Toward the end of the war there weren't so many. By then there was a lot of demoralization in Batista's army. They kept fighting, but what cause were they fighting for? The soldiers had learned the Rebel Army wouldn't mistreat prisoners, that it would give them food, that they'd be treated if they were wounded and later released. All of this was becoming known in the ranks of Batista's army.

WATERS: You mentioned the Second Front's political work with the peasants. How was the Education Department involved in this work?

DE LOS SANTOS: We began to do political work with the peasants, so they'd understand the possibilities that would open up when the revolution triumphed.

Some campesinos were already politicized and organized. Their own leaders and cells strongly supported our education work. If a teacher didn't have a place to live, the peasant cell would help them find somewhere to sleep, and somewhere to eat. The Rebel Army gave teachers a uniform and boots. But sometimes the schools were separated from the encampments, and the peasants helped the teachers a great deal.

The campesinos also carried out intelligence work for the Rebel Army.

A peasant congress was held in September 1958.[18] Questions of the future were discussed, a future that was imminent—things like the right to land, the guarantee that the land belonged to those who worked it. In fact, following the triumph of the revolution, one of the first acts was the agrarian reform. More than 100,000 peasant families received titles to the land they worked.

WATERS: How were the experiences of the Second Front used more broadly?

DE LOS SANTOS: The Second Front organized a military structure and, alongside it, a governmental structure. Departments began to deal with the large landed estates and the use of the land. They began to deal with industry, such as the nickel, iron ore, chrome, and cobalt mines and related processing plants, almost all of which were in foreign hands. With the sugar plantations and mills—the one-crop agriculture that had made us so dependent and caused so much harm. With education and health care.

These were issues that had been very clear to us ever since *History Will Absolve Me*. The Moncada program—Fidel's speech at the trial of the Moncada defendants—addressed all of them.

The Second Front experience was extremely important, because it set a precedent for much of what came afterward.

18. See glossary, Congress of Peasants in Arms.

"In the Second Front, when we experienced how the peasants lived, we increasingly came to realize that the changes would have to be very big. We found ourselves, little by little, on the road to Marxism, without even discussing it."—Vilma Espín

Delegates representing 84 local peasant committees at Congress of Peasants in Arms, held in Soledad de Mayarí near headquarters of the Second Front in Mayarí Arriba, September 21, 1958.

"Agrarian reform was one of the first actions taken after the triumph of the revolution. More than 100,000 peasants received titles to the land they worked."

—Asela de los Santos

Right: "Fidel signs first title" reads banner headline of December 10, 1959, issue of July 26 Movement's newspaper *Revolución*. First on list of peasants to receive a deed was Engracia Blet, from Baracoa in Oriente province. **Left:** Blet, with copy of *Revolución* reporting that event.

Handwritten note below masthead, signed by Ernesto Che Guevara, one of the drafters of the May 1959 agrarian reform law, reads: "Today a death certificate was signed for large landed estates. I never thought I would put my name with such pride and satisfaction to the death notice of a patient I helped 'treat.'"

Many cadres of the Second Front later shouldered important responsibilities in different sectors.

Of course, the same was true of cadres from the First Front, the Third Front, and others.

In Fidel's strategic conception, the Third Front in the Sierra Maestra was very important. It was the containment front. After the defeat of Batista's offensive in July, the Third Front allowed the First Front—which was under Fidel's command—to organize the counteroffensive.

The slogan of the Third Front was, *"No pasarán!"*—They shall not pass! And they did not pass.

Fidel kept only a small group of carefully selected combatants for the First Front, or Column 1. His strategy was to expand the guerrilla force throughout Oriente and the country as a whole, using more experienced combatants to form the Second, Third, and Fourth Fronts, as well as the columns that would march to the center of the country under the command of Camilo and Che.

So you can't equate the opportunities the different fronts had. Each operated in a given territory, with specific missions. Raúl's mission in the Second Front was to secure this territory and expand it. That area couldn't be lost. It was strategic. It encompassed the entire north and south coast of Oriente, extending as far east as Baracoa. It was a territory that had been stabilized.

At the triumph of the revolution, the goals we were fighting for were very clear. The most tested and courageous cadres in each front took on different tasks and responsibilities.

The Second Front's experience was relevant, but its relevance above all was in the many cadres it was forging. As to the implementation of the ideas we had in the Second Front, those had already been clearly laid out by Fidel and the whole leadership of the revolution.

I recall that in December 1957, at a place known as Balcón de La Habanita, we [Raúl Castro and Fidel] had a long talk, and Fidel explained to me that as soon as the Sierra Maestra front was consolidated, he would set up new columns and send them to different parts of the country. He mentioned at that time the Sierra Cristal area and the region east of the Sierra Maestra, near the city of Santiago de Cuba. But what surprised me most was when he said he would also send rebel columns to the central region of the country and Pinar del Río [Cuba's westernmost province]. I couldn't imagine at that time how he was going to do this.

Fidel was convinced—and this was how things turned out—that the First Front would be where the cadres and fighters would be forged and that they would gradually leave the mother column, as Che called it, to take the war to other territories, thereby multiplying the Rebel Army and forcing the enemy to divide its forces, thus becoming weaker and more vulnerable.[*]

RAÚL CASTRO
MARCH 1988

WATERS: What happened to the Education Department and the structures you had created in the Second Front?

DE LOS SANTOS: After the victory of the revolution, Raúl told all these teachers, all those young women from the Second Front, that they would be given scholarships to continue

[*] Interview with Raúl Castro, *Bohemia*, March 11, 1988. An English translation was run in *Granma Weekly Review*, March 15, 1988, and reprinted in the socialist newsweekly the *Militant*, February 12, 1996.

their education. And all those who wanted to remain teachers could do so.

In 1961 we launched a literacy campaign across the country. Before the revolution, 23 percent of the population was illiterate—more than 40 percent in the countryside. The goal was to eliminate this backwardness in a single year. The experience in the Second Front was a big help in the nationwide campaign. The campaign to wipe out illiteracy ended with a gigantic scholarship program that gave all young people continued access to study at higher levels.

As for the Rebel Army's Education Department, it continued to function in Santiago de Cuba throughout 1959. This was deliberate—to make sure that at the moment of victory, we didn't forsake the commitments we'd made on education. Subsequently the Education Department was merged into INRA, the National Institute of Agrarian Reform, as a section within it.

I did not continue in the department myself, since Raúl sent me to head up education for Oriente province as a whole, as provincial superintendent. You can just imagine—the only thing I'd been in my life was a teacher. All of a sudden in 1959 I became responsible for education in the whole province, which at that time encompassed what today are five provinces.[19]

When I took that assignment, Zoila Ibarra, assistant head of the Rebel Army's Education Department, replaced me as head of the department. I used to call her "old lady"—Zoila was then about forty-five. Today when I see someone that age, or even sixty, they seem very young!

19. In 1976 Oriente, as part of a broader reorganization of provinces in Cuba, was divided into five provinces: Holguín, Las Tunas, Granma, Guantánamo, and Santiago de Cuba.

Building a women's movement

WATERS: After the revolution's triumph, you were involved in the founding of the Federation of Cuban Women, the FMC?

DE LOS SANTOS: I always worked very closely with Vilma in the assignments she carried out. She knew she could count on me.

When the initial idea was raised of creating an organized women's movement, I was still working in education, the assignment Raúl had given me. But Vilma thought I could help, and she was right.

So my assignment was changed, and I worked six years with her in the Federation of Cuban Women.

WATERS: How was the FMC created?

DE LOS SANTOS: The women's movement began to take shape in the first months after the victory of the revolution.

Several organizations already existed. There was the Unidad Femenina Revolucionaria (United Revolutionary Women). This was an organization of left-wing women—not necessarily Communist but women with progressive ideas.

Within the Popular Socialist Party, both women and men were organized around specific assignments.

Catholic women were organized in a movement called Con la Cruz y con la Patria (With Cross and Country).

And there were the women who had participated in the underground struggle as part of the July 26 Movement and the Revolutionary Directorate.[20] The July 26 Movement never had a separate women's section. It was a movement that included both men and women, young and old, students, intellectuals, workers, campesinos.

With the victory of the revolution, many women felt their

---

20. See glossary, United Revolutionary Women, With Cross and Country, Revolutionary Directorate.

place was no longer limited to the home, that they didn't have to go back to being housewives alone, isolated from a broader social, political, and economic life. There was a whole field of action, of work, of struggle, they intended to be part of.

These organized groups of women, above all women from the July 26 Movement, saw Vilma as the person who could lead them. She was famous in the underground struggle. She became a kind of folk hero, since Batista's forces had tried to hunt her down many times and she kept escaping. Someone who popped up here, disappeared, then popped up somewhere else. Vilma became a legendary figure in the underground, just as Frank did.

Vilma's personal qualities helped a lot too. She was very direct and straightforward, well mannered, I would say refined—not artificially so, but naturally. That's how she always was. Very concerned about others. At the university she didn't choose her friends for their social standing but for their qualities as individuals. She would just as likely be the friend of a student from a poor family, enrolled at a teachers school, as of a young woman from the upper class. What mattered was that they shared Vilma's values and goals.

Later she proved herself in the Sierra Maestra, and in the Second Front.

By the time the revolution triumphed, Vilma was recognized among women as a heroine. Everyone admired the very attractive young woman who combined many qualities— above all, that of being revolutionary but not at all sectarian. That was important. All the groups accepted her. She was recognized as a person who could lead, who could bring people together, around whom people could unite.

There was a growing consciousness among women, as well as in the leadership of the revolution, that it was necessary to organize a women's movement. It was necessary to do political work among women, because they were at the bottom, the most exploited. We didn't speak in terms of women's equality at that time. We talked about women being housewives, confined to work in the home, overlooked and discriminated against. We talked about the need to integrate women into society and the workplace.

The various women's groups and associations sought Vilma's help to bring them all into one organization. They began to pressure her.

Vilma was trained as an engineer. She thought she could help in industrializing the country. Perhaps that was her dream initially. But this pressure from the women's groups undoubtedly made her think, and she began taking the first steps toward creating such an organization. Fidel welcomed the idea. He had already given some thought to it and believed Vilma would be the best person to lead it.

This is how United Revolutionary Women, other organizations, and the July 26 Movement women came together. A unification process began. But it wasn't a rose-strewn path. You can imagine all the things dividing one group from the other. It's not surprising there would be initial misunderstandings and divisions, snubs: this one's labeled communist, that one's bourgeois, whatever.

But Vilma was able to develop cadres around her—people she gave assignments to, who were responsible to oversee the work that had to get done. She was able to lead in the creation of an initial structure.

Although she confronted many challenges, Vilma was highly respected. She was listened to and was very convincing. She said what had to be said, but did so with tact and diplomacy. A women's organization would have been created no matter what—even if someone else had led it. But

Vilma's presence at the founding of the federation was crucial to ensure that varying opinions were heard, listened to, and respected.

Vilma stressed the need to incorporate the revolutionary capacities of women in the work of building a new society—a source of strength that was very important.

At the same time, the unfolding revolution itself increasingly helped women grasp their place in it. It helped them develop a consciousness of the need to take part in socially useful work outside the home. It helped them develop a consciousness that they had as many rights as men.

The federation set itself the goal of defending women, without bringing on a confrontation with men.

It wasn't called the Federation of Cuban Women at first. It was called the Congress of Cuban Women for the Liberation of Latin America. Vilma was president. The vice president was a well-known woman in Cuba named Delia Echeverría, who had been the fiancée of Antonio Guiteras and had fought alongside him against the Machado dictatorship in the early 1930s. There was another vice president, from the Communist Party, Dr. Elsa Gutiérrez, as well as Lula Horstman from the Catholic group, With Cross and Country. Vilma helped put together an initial leadership with the most capable people from all these groups.

A regional congress of the Women's International Democratic Federation was held in Chile in November 1959. We went to it as Cuban women revolutionaries, as part of a united Latin American front. By the time we returned, the structure was already growing in Cuba. Women were being organized.

So the question was posed: "What are we going to call ourselves?" Different names were proposed. Fidel wanted to meet with the women to discuss the organization's broad perspectives, the work we would carry out. On August 23, 1960, Vilma organized a packed meeting at the Lázaro Peña auditorium in the headquarters of the Confederation of Cuban Workers. Fidel explained fundamental aspects of the revolution and women's place in it. That's when we named ourselves the Federation of Cuban Women.

At this founding meeting, Fidel stressed the importance of organizing women as a powerful force of support for the revolution, one with broad social implications because of women's influence on their children and husbands. That's how the Federation of Cuban Women arose, with a thought-out structure and initial program of struggle.

The integration of women into the workforce was the centerpiece. It was the watchword. There were varying reactions.

"My wife doesn't need to work," some said. "I'm supporting her."

"Who will do the cooking?"

"Who will do the cleaning?"

"Who will wash the clothes and care for the children?"

We'd answer, "But your wife has a right to join the workforce."

This was a battle for the consciousness of men and women, a battle the federation waged and won, step by step.

To avoid making their husbands look bad, women would often come up with excuses. A woman would say she was sick. Or that her mother had some problem and needed care. Or whatever. Anything to avoid saying her husband wouldn't let her work. It was embarrassing for a woman to say that. This was a tough battle.

In keeping with his pledge, Fidel gave the FMC important work to carry out. He gave the federation the responsibility to bring peasant women from the mountains of Oriente, the Es-

"I saw Batista's March 1952 coup as an act of brutality. The university shut its doors in protest."

ASELA DE LOS SANTOS

UNIVERSIDAD DE LA HABANA

ABAJO la DICTADURA

Above: April 6, 1952. Students at University of Havana protest suspension of 1940 constitution. Banner says, "Down with the dictatorship."

Below: Youth in Santiago de Cuba protest Batista dictatorship, Céspedes Park, 1950s.

> **"Before the revolution, the great majority faced increasingly intolerable economic, political, and social conditions. Cuba was dominated by big landowners. Few peasants had access to land."**
>
> ASELA DE LOS SANTOS

Above: The hated Rural Guards evict peasant family, 1940s. Following 1952 Batista coup, eviction of peasants by plantation owners, enforced by troops, increased sharply. **Below:** Mansion of sugar mill boss, United Fruit's Preston plantation, Oriente province.

Above: Batista police occupy and sack University of Havana, April 21, 1956; in front, with uniform and sunglasses, is notorious murderer Rafael Salas Cañizares.

Inset: A wall at University of Havana, April 1958, demands "Down with tyrant Batista." Signs were written with charcoal and paraffin. "The more the police scrubbed them," said Vilma Espín, "the more they showed up."

Below: Santo Domingo, central Cuba, during December 1955 nationwide strike by 200,000 sugar workers. Strikers took over towns in Las Villas province, pushing back a pay cut and dealing political blow to Batista regime.

"The attack on the Moncada garrison was a defining moment for revolutionary-minded youth. After Moncada, we decided to organize."

ASELA DE LOS SANTOS

On July 26, 1953, under leadership of Fidel Castro, 160 revolutionaries attacked garrisons in Santiago de Cuba and Bayamo, launching armed struggle against dictatorship.

Above: Future Moncada combatants outside Havana at farm used for military training. Clockwise from back row, Antonio "Ñico" López, Abel Santamaría, Fidel Castro, unidentified, José Luis Tasende, Ernesto Tizol, unidentified. Santamaría and Tasende were among 56 combatants captured and brutally murdered. **Below:** Bodies of revolutionary combatants, executed and then thrown on ground to appear as if killed in battle.

Above: Moncada combatants Melba Hernández and Haydée Santamaría (third and fourth from left) leaving Guanajay women's prison February 1954 after serving seven-month sentences.

Below: Moncada combatants released from prison, May 1955, following amnesty. Left, Juan Almeida; from right, Armando Mestre, Fidel Castro, Raúl Castro. At center, two other political prisoners, Agustín Díaz Cartaya (obscured), Mario Chanes. **Inset:** *History Will Absolve Me*. Based on Fidel Castro's trial testimony, document was smuggled out of prison and circulated across Cuba beginning in October 1954.

"Between 1945 and 1957, more than 1.2 billion human beings conquered political independence in Asia and Africa."

SECOND DECLARATION OF HAVANA

Anti-imperialist battles by peoples of Asia, Africa, and Latin America accelerated during and after World War II.

Above: Vietnamese liberation fighters guard captured French soldiers after victory at Battle of Dien Bien Phu, May 1954.

Inset: Throng in Cairo, Egypt, July 1956, celebrates nationalization of Suez Canal, formerly controlled by imperialist interests in United Kingdom and France. President Gamal Abdel Nasser at center with arms raised.

Above: Montgomery, Alabama, 1955. First mass meeting supporting boycott of city transit system that forced Blacks to sit at back of the bus. A movement that grew to millions ended Jim Crow system of state-sanctioned racial segregation in US South.

Below: Future *Granma* expeditionaries in courtyard of immigration prison, Mexico City, July 1956. They were detained for a month by Mexican government. Standing with sunglasses is Fidel Castro; next to him is María Antonia González, Cuban living in Mexico who aided combatants. Front row at left, Calixto García; from right, Ernesto Che Guevara, Ramiro Valdés, Juan Almeida, Ciro Redondo.

"On November 30, 1956, some 360 July 26 combatants carried out an armed action in Santiago de Cuba in support of the *Granma* landing."

ASELA DE LOS SANTOS

Above: Police station in Santiago de Cuba, hated bastion of tyranny, in flames November 30, 1956. Three combatants died in assault on station.

Below: Frank País (second from left), national organizer of July 26 urban underground, with Léster Rodríguez (left) and Antonio Darío López (right) at April 1957 trial of 73 participants in November 30 action and 22 captured *Granma* expeditionaries. Hatred of Batista's crimes made it possible to win release of País and most November 30 combatants. *Granma* combatants were convicted and imprisoned.

"One of the biggest blows to the revolutionary struggle took place July 30, 1957, when Frank País was captured and murdered," Fidel Castro said. "Frank's death set off a spontaneous reaction of such scope that it virtually paralyzed Santiago for several days."

Above: Morning of funeral, women demanding end to US support to Batista confront US ambassador Earl Smith.

Below: People in Santiago escort País's hearse to cemetery. "No one had to call a general strike," Asela de los Santos recounts, "but one took place nonetheless."

> **"Frank País's attitude toward women made it possible for female combatants to work as equals with men. He made no distinction between men and women in making assignments."**
>
> VILMA ESPÍN

Left: Women were part of leadership vanguard of the revolutionary struggle from the beginning. Melba Hernández (left) and Haydée Santamaría in Santiago jail after being taken prisoner during attack on Moncada garrison, July 26, 1953.

Right: Mothers march in Santiago de Cuba, January 1957, condemns police murder of 15-year-old July 26 Movement member William Soler. Soler's mother is at center in white jacket. Banner reads, "Stop murdering our children. Cuban mothers."

Above: First leadership meeting of July 26 Movement held in Sierra Maestra, February 1957. Among meeting participants were (from left), *Granma* expeditionary Ciro Redondo, Vilma Espín, Fidel Castro, Haydée Santamaría, Celia Sánchez. Espín and Sánchez, working with Frank País, organized urban recruitment and supply network for Rebel Army. Espín became movement's coordinator for Oriente province.

Inset: Rebel Army messenger Lidia Doce (right) and Ramón "Mongo" Pérez, peasant who provided shelter to Fidel Castro and other combatants in early December 1956. Doce was later captured, brutally tortured, and murdered by Batista police.

"In September 1958, Fidel formed the Mariana Grajales Platoon, the first female combat unit of the Rebel Army.... It was an extraordinary moment in the history of women's participation in the revolution."

VILMA ESPÍN

COURTESY OF TETÉ PUEBLA

GRANMA

Above: Fidel Castro and Celia Sánchez, at Rebel Army general command in La Plata with fighters of the Mariana Grajales Women's Platoon, September 1958, as they left on first combat mission. From left: Lola Feria, Edemis Tamayo, Teté Puebla, Castro, Isabel Rielo, Sánchez, Lilia Rielo. Far left and right: Fidel Vargas and Marcelo Verdecia.

Below: Women's platoon members after participating in victorious 10-day Battle of Guisa, November 1958: Angelina Antolín, Ada Bella Acosta, Rita García, and (kneeling) Eva Palma, with Hipólito Prieto.

COUNCIL OF STATE OFFICE OF HISTORICAL AFFAIRS

FEDERATION OF CUBAN WOMEN

"It has been proved that it is not only men who can fight. In Cuba women fight, too," Fidel Castro proclaimed January 1, 1959.

Above: Rebel Army combatants on march, April 1957. Haydée Santamaría, followed by Celia Sánchez and Universo Sánchez. **Below:** Vilma Espín with Fidel Castro, 1958.

"Combatants in the Second Front created not only a military structure but a governmental one as well.... Seven departments were established—education, health, agriculture, justice, construction and communications, finances, and propaganda."

ASELA DE LOS SANTOS

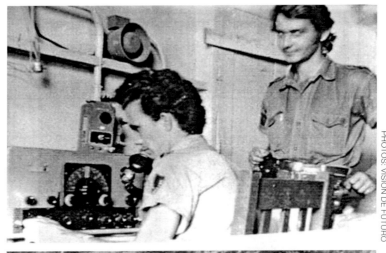

Above: Rebel radio transmitter for communication within Second Front. **Below:** Roads were opened or improved using bulldozers and other heavy equipment captured by rebel supporters. "The Second Front was a model of organization and efficiency and played an extraordinarily important strategic role in our war," Fidel Castro said in 1985. "Once it was established, you could say the rebel armed forces were unbeatable."

Above: 200 delegates from 84 peasant committees met near head-quarters of Second Front, September 1958, to support Rebel Army and program for distribution of land to those who worked it. From left: Jorge Serguera, sitting, Raúl Castro speaking, Augusto Martínez, by pole behind Castro, Vilma Espín, and peasant leaders Pepe Ramírez, standing at right, and Teodoro Pereira, sitting.

Inset: Deed issued to peasant family by Rebel Army Second Eastern Front, December 1958. **Below:** Field hospital in Second Eastern Front, late 1958. Rebel Army provided medical care to all—peasants, combatants, and wounded enemy soldiers.

> ## "The Second Front became a veritable 'republic.' Four hundred schools for the children, and night schools for the combatants and for peasants. That was the first literacy campaign."
>
> VILMA ESPÍN

VISIÓN DE FUTURO

Above: René Fraga Revolutionary Night School no. 3, where combatants learned to read and write. "Most new recruits to Rebel Army in Second Front were young, poor, and had little schooling," said Asela de los Santos. "So we organized literacy groups in the camps and began to set up rural schools with the teachers available to us. The liberated zone was already taking on a certain stability."

Inset: Form used to conduct census of school-age children in rebel-commanded Second Front.

Above: Primary school abandoned by dictatorship, reopened by Rebel Army Second Front. **Below:** Julio López Miera at printing press where educational materials were produced.

> **"Fidel's strategy was to expand the guerrilla force throughout Oriente and the country as a whole, using more experienced combatants to form the Second, Third, and Fourth Fronts, and for the columns that would march to the center of the country under the command of Camilo and Che."**
>
> ASELA DE LOS SANTOS

After defeating tyranny's 10,000-strong "encircle and annihilate offensive" in Sierra Maestra, August 1958, Rebel Army launched counteroffensive. By December 31 Batista's regime collapsed in face of liberation of Santa Clara, capital of Las Villas province in central Cuba, and imminence of fall of Santiago de Cuba.

Above: New recruits to Rebel Army, mostly peasants from Oriente, train at Minas del Frío camp in Sierras in last months of war.

Above: Rebel Army combatants and supporters celebrate liberation of Santa Clara in Las Villas province, January 1, 1959.

Below: Batista troops surrender in Palma Soriano, north of Santiago, in one of last battles of revolutionary war, December 27, 1958.

"On January 1, 1959, Batista fled Cuba.... The entry of the Rebel Army into Santiago was tremendous."

VILMA ESPÍN

Above: Raúl Castro addresses Batista troops at Moncada garrison in Santiago January 1, following surrender. At left with cigar, Colonel José Rego Rubido, former commander of Batista forces in Oriente province. At right, with automatic rifle, Raúl "Maro" Guerra, sole combatant accompanying Raúl Castro.

Below: Fidel Castro enters Santiago, January 1, 1959. Behind him, to left, is Archbishop of Santiago, Enrique Pérez Serantes. At far left is Juan Almeida.

cambray, and Pinar del Río to Havana for the famous Ana Betancourt School, for example. Thousands of peasant women passed through it. Dr. Elsa Gutiérrez and Alicia Imperatori led the program, which lasted several years.[21]

Women in the Ana Betancourt School stayed in houses abandoned by the bourgeoisie. These buildings were seized and turned into boarding houses as well as classrooms. Young women, primarily peasant women, came there to learn how to sew. Those who were illiterate learned to read and write, and those who could already do so joined the program to reach the sixth-grade level. They received dental and medical care.

The women returned to their homes with a sewing machine they earned upon graduation, and with tremendous prestige. Many developed into leaders of the agricultural production programs and other work.

They became part of society.

There were other programs, too, such as the one for former prostitutes. They took training courses, learned skills, and were placed in jobs. Women who formerly worked as domestic servants graduated as taxi drivers and bank workers.

Vilma also started the child care centers. Women who wanted to work now had a place where their children would be cared for, fed, and protected. Fidel gave this task to the Federation of Cuban Women. The child care centers were born in the federation.

WATERS: What did you do when you left the FMC leadership?

DE LOS SANTOS: I went into the Ministry of the Revolutionary Armed Forces in 1966, to serve as director of the education section. All young men did two years of military service,

21. See pp. 237–45.

Heroic were those two compañeras of ours, Lidia [Doce] and Clodomira [Acosta], cowardly murdered by thugs of [Havana police chief] Esteban Ventura. Lidia had been a formidable collaborator from the very first moments. Clodomira was a young, poor peasant woman with great natural intelligence and a courage that had met every test.

Around the beginning of April 1958, when communications along the Manzanillo-to-Bayamo road had been cut, it was necessary to send an urgent message to the city. No one was driving; the people had complied with the movement's call for no travel; furthermore it was dangerous. Clodomira volunteered to take the message. She had the boldness to go to the camp of the dictator's troops and say that because of a family emergency she had to get to Manzanillo. She asked them to take her in a combat vehicle. And the unsuspecting soldiers of the tyranny did it.

She always solved problems. To do so, she often took risks, entering and leaving the Sierra until she was arrested, together with Lidia, tortured, and murdered, without revealing a single secret, without saying a single word to the enemy.[*]

FIDEL CASTRO
AUGUST 23, 1960

and recruits were required to study two hours a day in a general program aimed at raising everyone's level of education.

Later on I worked in the creation of the Camilo Cienfuegos

---

[*] Speech at founding meeting of Federation of Cuban Women, August 23, 1960. In *Mujeres y Revolución*, p. 35.

Military Schools—the Camilitos, as we called them. These were established in 1966, just as I went to work in the teaching section of the armed forces. The first students were war orphans; they got an education and job training. The schools were soon expanded and became vocational high schools training military cadres for the armed forces.

The struggle to keep our independence and sovereignty continues. The risks are the same, although the circumstances have changed.

The victory of the revolution produced overwhelming joy among the people. It put an end to a blood-soaked tyranny. It was the triumph of a revolution with native roots, for which generations of Cubans had fought since the wars of independence against Spanish colonial rule from 1868 to 1895. It was a struggle that had been thwarted by US military intervention in 1898, when we became a neocolony of the United States.

The Cuban Revolution ended more than fifty years of neo-colonialism. It redeemed the struggles of our forebears for independence and freedom.

For me, I'm a Cuban woman like others of my generation, those who lived and those, like Lidia and Clodomira—who Fidel paid tribute to at the founding of the FMC—who didn't have the good fortune to see the triumph of the revolution.

I'm just one more person. In all of them, I recognize myself.

BOHEMIA

"I am a Cuban woman like others of my generation, those who lived and those, like Lidia and Clodomira, who didn't have the good fortune to see the triumph of the revolution. . . . In all of them, I recognize myself."
—**Asela de los Santos**

From left, Clodomira Acosta, Rebel Army messenger arrested, tortured, and murdered by Batista's police in Havana, September 1958; Pilar Fernández, teacher who collaborated with underground movement in Manzanillo, later assigned to work with Celia Sánchez (in doorway) at Rebel Army's general command center. Photo is from early 1958, Guayabal de Nagua, Sierra Maestra mountains; others are unidentified.

Military Order no. 50

DECREE ESTABLISHING
DEPARTMENT OF EDUCATION
IN SECOND FRONT

NOVEMBER 2, 1958

ARTICLE 1. The Department of Education is a body of a technical character among the cadres of the July 26 Revolutionary Army in the Frank País Second Eastern Front. It is empowered to carry out the functions conferred on it by this military order.[22]

ARTICLE 2. Primary education shall be mandatory and free. School materials shall likewise be free.

ARTICLE 3. Consistent with Article 49, Title V, Section 2 of the [1940] Constitution of the Republic, the July 26 Revolutionary movement will create and maintain a system of rural and urban schools for children and adult civilians, for the purpose of eradicating and preventing illiteracy.

ARTICLE 5. The Department of Education will be made up of the following personnel:

a) A department director
b) An assistant director
c) Individuals responsible for education
d) Teachers
e) The necessary auxiliary personnel

ARTICLE 6. The director of the Department of Education

22. In *Visión de futuro*, pp. 139–43. There is no Article 4 in the original document

has the following duties and powers:

a) To lead the Department of Education, serving as its highest authority.

b) To supervise the guidelines for education, implementation of educational systems, preparation of programs, establishment of schools, and any other measures of an educational nature that may be necessary.

c) To issue resolutions, circulars, and any other documents needed to best perform the responsibilities that have been conferred on it.

d) To propose to the Central Command through the Interdepartmental Leadership all appointments of personnel to the department, and to request, accept, or reject any transfers and resignations considered advisable.

e) To maintain discipline and ethical conduct by the personnel who constitute the department.

f) To report to the Central Command through the Interdepartmental Leadership the following information:

1) Weekly: reports on the teaching and administrative performance of the department and the state of its personnel.

2) Monthly: a summary of the weekly reports.

g) Any other duty or power assigned by higher authorities.

ARTICLE 7. In order to provide a more complete education, the Department of Education will establish the following sections:

a) General Culture
b) Indoctrination of Troops
c) Short Courses for Teachers
d) Directed Instruction
e) Program Preparation
f) Teachers Bulletin

g) Artistic

h) Labor

ARTICLE 8. The director of the Department of Education may provisionally appoint teachers, directors of education, and other auxiliary personnel as required.

ARTICLE 9. The teachers for combatants will be chosen from among the most qualified combatants.

ARTICLE 10. Given the distances that must be traveled, the directors of education shall serve as liaisons between teachers and the Department of Education. They will attend to the needs of schools in their areas, investigate where it may be necessary to create new classrooms, and report this to the head of the department for approval.

ARTICLE 11. The directors of education will provide orientation to teachers when necessary. Their work is to assist, not punish. They will preferably be chosen from among the certified teachers available.

ARTICLE 12. Civilian teachers will be chosen from among the best-educated volunteers available, if there are not sufficient certified teachers.

ARTICLE 13. The teacher is required to provide the type of education determined by the department, to strive for the best development of the student, and to conserve the resources of the school.

ARTICLE 14. Teachers without degrees will be replaced by certified teachers as soon as circumstances allow.

ARTICLE 15. When teachers without a degree wish to obtain certification, they will be given every opportunity to do so as soon as the rule of law is once again established in the nation.

ARTICLE 16. Certified teachers who have schools on properties within the territories occupied and liberated by the rebel forces of the Frank País Second Eastern Front will be called upon to fulfill their responsibilities. Should they refuse, the school will be taken over and another teacher assigned to it, with the previous teacher losing all rights to the same.

ARTICLE 17. Teachers and directors of education shall carry out a census of the school population.

ARTICLE 18. The Department of Education in the Frank País Second Eastern Front shall use the Basic Primary School as the means to fully carry out its educational responsibilities.

ARTICLE 19. This law is retroactive with respect to what has been done by Department of Education officials prior to its enactment.

ARTICLE 20. Appointments made before the enactment of this law, whatever their origin, shall be null and void. Such appointments will revert to the department for replacement by official appointments.

FINAL DISPOSITION

SOLE CLAUSE. All laws, military orders, and other dispositions contrary to the fulfillment of this military order are revoked. This order will be in effect from the time of its publication in the *Legislative Bulletin* of the Frank País Second Eastern Front.

Issued in the Free Territory of Cuba of the Frank País Second Eastern Front, on the twelfth day of the month of November, nineteen hundred fifty-eight.

Freedom or death.

Raúl Castro Ruz
Commander in Chief
Frank País Second Eastern Front

Débora

INTERVIEW WITH VILMA ESPÍN

QUESTION: Can you tell us about the early days of the University of Oriente and the first political struggles students took part in there?

VILMA ESPÍN: We didn't even have a building! It was a university in formation. It had been operating for a year when I enrolled in 1948 and had very few students. It was in its embryonic stages really, and had plenty of problems. But those early years were very interesting because, in effect, we were actually creating the university.

Students and professors went to Havana to fight for official recognition. That was the beginning of a number of struggles. I remember we sang some verses José Luis Galbe had written and set to Spanish music, cursing the government because it hadn't given the university official status.[1]

We were really squeezed for space until they gave us an old, decrepit military hospital that stood where the present campus is. Until then we had used rooms at the School of Commerce, where it was very difficult for the chemical engineering students to work. There just wasn't enough space.

Published in the June–September 1975 issue of *Santiago*, magazine of the University of Oriente. "Débora" was the nom de guerre used by Vilma Espín during much of the revolutionary war.

FEDERATION OF CUBAN WOMEN

"It was a wonderful pioneer stage, very attractive, that allowed us to begin a struggle right there, creating a university."—Vilma Espín

Sports event at University of Oriente, 1949, the year students and faculty won national recognition and funding for the university. Vilma Espín, at center, carrying Cuban flag, was captain of women's volleyball team and a leader of the fight for recognition. At the time in Latin America, sports as part of the university curriculum was unusual. It was one of progressive measures fought for in founding of university.

I remember taking mops and buckets out to Quintero Hill in the little red convertible of an engineering professor. We cleaned things up and began to work there. We put in the plumbing ourselves—there was no running water or anything else. The school didn't even have a bell. We set up makeshift laboratories and vented gases through tubes that ran out a window.

It was a wonderful pioneer stage, very attractive, that allowed us to begin a struggle right there, creating a university. Those of us studying chemical engineering were pioneers, too, because that course of study was completely new in Cuba. The program was so grueling that it had to be modified later on. We had to study morning, noon, and night.

After that came a whole number of steps to expand the university, cultural activities, and compulsory participation in sports—ideas that were very progressive for their time compared to the University of Havana, for instance. The atmosphere at this school was quite different. Advanced ideas were in the air.

José Luis Galbe taught there; later, so did López Rendueles, Chabás, Almendros, Griñán, and Portuondo.[2] They helped make the university a progressive place. They had to fight hard for this, since not everybody held such advanced ideas. You have to remember that the US embassy was continually trying to influence the university by any means possible, including by infiltrating professors of its choosing. We had a university rector who was purely a puppet, a farce, as well as

---

1. See glossary, José Luis Galbe. The university admitted its first students in October 1947 but did not receive recognition and funding from the government in Havana until March 1949.

2. See glossary, Julio López Rendueles, Juan Chabás, Herminio Almendros, Leonardo Griñán, José Antonio Portuondo.

a lot of very weak people.[3]

At the time only a minority of students had enough political consciousness to see the extent to which the United States controlled Cuba, the extent of its economic and political domination, its maneuvers. But a certain anti-Yankee feeling had always existed. It made us dislike those we considered "Americanized"—we had an Americanized professor from Colombia, for example. We took a dim view of these people because of their foreign ways, but we didn't realize the depth and scope of the problem. Our first struggles, as I said, were for official recognition, to help the university expand.

After March 10, of course, we could see real pressure from the US embassy. Professors who belonged to the Spanish or Cuban Communist Party, or people who held leftist ideas, were persecuted.

QUESTION: Is that what happened with Chabás?

ESPÍN: Yes, Chabás was one of those persecuted, because he was a leader of the Spanish [Communist] Party. He died shortly afterward. Galbe was another—he had a big dispute with [Batista supporter] Otto Meruelo. López Rendueles was harassed, and so were other professors who held leftist views or belonged to the Communist Party.

QUESTION: Tell us about your personal experiences after March 10.

ESPÍN: At the time of the coup, I had very little political experience. I knew very little about the real situation in the country. I viewed corruption with a good deal of cynicism—I felt there was nothing I could do to change it. I was old

3. A July 26, 1954, cable from the US Consulate in Santiago de Cuba reports that "in view of the situation existing at the university," and "to counteract . . . the adverse attitude of members of the staff," discussions were under way with Rector Felipe Salcines about hiring the US vice consul as a professor.

enough to vote that year, but I wasn't interested in registering. "Why vote? They're all the same!"—that was how I felt. I
was very skeptical. I didn't think I could do much more than
make some kind of contribution, through my profession, to
the country's development in technology.

I can thank Batista, though, for the explosive impact March
10, 1952, had on me. I didn't know much about what was going on in the world, but I did make a firm decision that day to
put an end to what was happening in Cuba. I saw the coup as
a violation of the legality of "representative democracy," and
I took it almost as a personal offense. It was the straw that
broke the camel's back. It may well have been what decisively
crystallized a spirit of rebellion in me.

Someone came to our house around 7 a.m. that day saying,
"Listen, they say Batista has carried out a coup." A brother of
one of my professors was a candidate for the House of Representatives, and when the professor heard the news he said,
"If that's the case, it's time to rise up in arms."

It seemed to me he had voiced the best idea anyone could've
had. I took him very seriously. Right then and there I decided
there had to be an uprising. I began to jump for joy at the idea
of taking up arms.

Of course, it's normal to have romantic dreams of being
able to take part in heroic struggles such as the wars of independence, the struggles against the Machado dictatorship in
the 1930s, and so forth. At the time, it seemed to me that such
an uprising was exactly what was needed. I was as happy as
a lark, as if I were on my way to a party. I wanted to grab a
rifle and go fight right then.

We went to downtown Santiago, to Céspedes Park. People
were holding lightning meetings everywhere, milling around
to hear what one or another political figure of the day had to
say. Laureano Ibarra (who, only a few hours later, declared

"Batista's the man") had climbed up on a lamppost in the park. He was waving an old .45 cowboy revolver and shouting, "Let's go to the barracks! We can't let this happen!" So we set off for the barracks, where the commander hadn't wanted to give in to the coup.[4] But when we were halfway there, we learned that del Río Chaviano had already taken command of the barracks, so we went to the university instead.

Soldiers began showing up at the university that morning. We were all acting purely on our impetuousness. I was so furious I began taunting the soldiers to provoke them. Some compañeros erected barricades, using sacks of cement left over from construction. Then we set up loudspeakers and played a record with Guillén's poem, "I don't know why, soldier, you think I hate you. . . ."[5] The most progressive and militant people from the university were there. Everyone was indignant about the soldiers' presence on campus. We spent the whole day making speeches and shouting slogans.

The University Council had been meeting upstairs when the soldiers arrived. Asela de los Santos and I were sitting downstairs alone when they came in. They looked embarrassed and scared, poor things. We immediately lit into them for setting foot on university soil.

"You, what do you want?" I demanded, and began arguing with one of the soldiers.

Then somebody reported I was fighting with a soldier, which was false, of course—I was only talking to him—but the entire Council tore downstairs. The soldier, poor devil,

4. Colonel Francisco Álvarez Margolles, until then commanding officer in Oriente province, was one of seventy-seven officers Batista dismissed from the army the day of the coup.

5. From the poem "No sé por qué piensas tú" [I don't know why you think], 1937. See glossary, Nicolás Guillén.

was so shaken that he left and nothing happened. That was the first time I really had to make a choice about what to do. The first time I adopted a rebellious stance.

At 4 p.m. I was in one of the offices listening to Batista's speech on the radio. I felt I was going to blow up right there. When he finished, I was spoiling for action. Thinking the professor who had talked about rising up might have some plan, I went to him and asked:

"Well, what do we do?"

"What do you want me to do, send a thunderbolt to kill Batista?" he replied, as he burst out laughing.

That disappointed me so much, made me so angry, that tears streamed down my cheeks and I left. The man had let me down. I thought he had been talking seriously. But, well, that was the first experience. . .

After that we students began to write fliers ourselves and mimeographed them with the help of some of the attendants at the university—Salas, Justino, and Grandma Evelia. At lunch, while everyone was gone, we'd print the fliers on the school mimeograph machine. Then, naively, we distributed them door to door in Santiago de Cuba, as if they were movie programs.

The first time we did this kind of broad leafleting it was well organized. A group of us met in my house that night. We got a map and divided the city into areas, with two compañeras assigned to each one. Nilsa [Espín], Leyla Vázquez, and Asela de los Santos were among those who took part. At first we had women do all the leafleting, thinking it would be easier for us since we could hide the fliers under our skirts.

That very first time, Cowley arrested Asela, Leyla, and two or three other women.[6] They were taken to the military post

6.   See glossary, Fermín Cowley.

and then to the university. We had run off a small flier with some of Heredia's patriotic verses,[7] adding a brief commentary on the current situation and a call for struggle. The political content wasn't very deep, but it was very rebellious.

Cowley brought the flier with him to the university. I was sitting at a window where I could hear him talking to one of the professors.

"No, no, no," Cowley was saying, "what I want to know is who wrote this."

When the professor answered, "Heredia," Cowley yelled, "No, no, no, the other things!"

Those were our first struggles: running off fliers in secret, with the help of university attendants.

Then the street demonstrations began. I think the first one was in February 1953, after they had killed Rubén Batista in Havana.[8] We had a symbolic funeral for him in Santiago that turned into a real battle. The idea was to take flowers to the cemetery, but we wound up inside the coffee houses, throwing sugar bowls at the police.

Later came the issue of the "Vía Cuba Canal."[9] We worked hard to stop that. There were demonstrations, commotion, and

---

7. See glossary, José María Heredia.

8. See glossary, Rubén Batista.

9. In August 1954 Batista authorized construction of a fifty-mile canal cutting the island in two. This would have separated eastern Cuba from the rest of the country. The project had Washington's backing, since it would shorten trade routes to South America. The estimated cost of the canal was $700 million (nearly $5 billion in 2011 dollars). It would have allowed the dictator's cronies to seize thousands of acres of land, rule the canal zone, reap its profits for ninety-nine years, and exempt themselves from any taxes. Protests deriding the project as the "Break-Cuba Canal" embarrassed the government into shelving it.

a great deal of activity at the university. After March 10, we also held Oath to the Constitution actions against Batista's new constitution. Much later I learned that Raúl had taken part in a similar demonstration at the University of Havana.[10] By 1953 I was looking for a more effective way to oppose the regime, to do something more. At the time, a number of organizations of politicians from the past were trying to get back into power. The main ones were Prío's people—the Authentic Organization—and the Aureliano group—the Triple A.[11] They were trying to recruit young people still in the country (their own two leaders had gone into voluntary exile). They were looking for cannon fodder, in other words. I was approached by a number of people from these groups, first the Triple A, then the Authentic Organization.

Rafael García Bárcena, a professor in Havana, had established a group called the Revolutionary National Movement, which became widely known because of a little manifesto they issued.[12] If you read it today, you'd consider it very weak, but at that time I was impressed by its words: "There must be an end to March 10 and to March 9." In other words, there must be an end to that entire era of politics as usual.

The MNR's program seemed more serious to me than the others, and their ideas were fairly close to mine. So I joined the students in Santiago who began organizing around this

10. In April 1952 students organized a movement to swear allegiance to the 1940 constitution Batista had overturned a month earlier. These actions were the first demonstrations against the dictatorship. Raúl Castro, carrying the Cuban flag, was a prominent participant in the April 6, 1952, Havana action (see cover photo of *Aldabonazo* by Armando Hart, published by Pathfinder in 2004).

11. See glossary, Carlos Prío Socarrás, Authentic Organization, Aureliano Sánchez Arango, Triple A.

12. See glossary, Rafael García Bárcena, MNR.

group, among them Frank País—every one of whom later became part of the July 26 Movement. A number of professors
who had taken part in various actions joined along with us.
We set up an MNR propaganda group, a group on finances,
an action group, and others. Frank País was the action coordinator.

QUESTION: Although there was something spontaneous in
all this, you already had concerns and political ideas that
went beyond just overthrowing Batista.

ESPÍN: That's true. Without a doubt, many compañeros held
fairly advanced ideas, but we all wanted to end the corruption and stealing and create a more progressive situation. We
talked about things like agrarian reform but, at least for my
part, I had never read any Marxist literature. I had read a few
articles about Marx in magazines here and there. I admired
his ideas, but they seemed far off, utopian—something wonderful but completely unreal in terms of what people were
thinking in that political climate and period. I hadn't read
anything about what was going on in the Soviet Union either, except for the massive anticommunist propaganda that
always left you thinking some of it might be true and some
of it might be lies, but I had no way of knowing.

The MNR lasted only a few months. In 1953 it burst like a
soap bubble when forty members and leaders were arrested
in Havana.[13]

When the MNR leadership disappeared from the scene, a

13. MNR founder Rafael García Bárcena and thirty-nine others were
    arrested in April 1953 when an informer leaked plans of a con-
    spiracy involving military personnel as well as civilians to seize
    Camp Columbia in Havana, Batista's largest military base. Recent
    law school graduate Armando Hart acted as García Bárcena's de-
    fense attorney. For a contemporary account of the trial in the Cu-
    ban newsmagazine *Bohemia*, see *Aldabonazo*, pp. 73–76.

group of people who supported the MNR stayed in Santiago, functioning more or less as a nucleus. Armando Hart suggested to me that we maintain this movement on a national level. I discussed this with Frank [País]. Frank was already organizing Oriente Revolutionary Action, with very concrete ideas on action—above all, preparing for an uprising, gathering weapons, and attacking explosives depots to assemble stockpiles of dynamite.

A group was organized in this way. My sister Nilsa and Rafael Rivero were very active working with Frank, who in turn had begun to establish ties with Armando Hart, Faustino Pérez, and a group of compañeros from Havana. Several of them, including Faustino, were arrested. But in Oriente, under Frank's leadership, the movement continued to grow. The name was changed to Action for Liberty—there are still some guns around marked ALN. We kept in touch with Armando in Havana, but we were in fact an independent movement in Oriente, led by Frank. We even had our own finances section, which is where I worked at the time.

By the time of the attack on Moncada in July 1953, the MNR had fallen apart. I was working with Frank, and we kept the name MNR for several more months. We were in touch with Armando and other compañeros in Havana. That was the stage we were at on July 26, 1953.

QUESTION: What was your reaction that day?

ESPÍN: I was at home, in the San Jerónimo neighborhood, which was fairly close to the barracks. A little after 5 a.m. I could hear shots as if they were coming from my yard. I jumped out of bed, yelling that the Moncada had been attacked. That made my father think I had something to do with it, since I was so sure.

I didn't know who, but someone had attacked the Moncada. That Sunday we couldn't find out what had happened. First they said it was Pedraza,[14] then that it was a struggle between two military groups killing each other. There was confusion all day. I recall that Nilsa and one of the young men from the neighborhood went up near the archdiocese. From there they could see the bodies strewn in front of the hospital, but we still knew nothing about them.

The next morning, I went to the university, and still nobody knew who they were. Then, on an impulse, I said to Asela, "Well, let's go over there."

"Where?" Asela asked.

"Let's go to the garrison. Let's find out what's happening."

So Asela, two young women from Bayamo who were part-time students, and I took the bus by way of Garzón Avenue. But everything was surrounded by soldiers. Guard posts had been set up everywhere. Finally, we entered through the back, where the military hospital was located. We got right up to the door, Asela and I in front, the two women from Bayamo behind.

Then something really absurd happened. The guard on duty said, politely enough, "Yes, can I help you?"

But we were all worked up, since we now realized they had murdered a lot of young men. So I answered: "We've come to see the wounded."

"What wounded?"

"Who do you think?" I went on. "We've come to see the heroes! We've come to see the revolutionaries!"

As soon as I said that, of course, we realized we'd better get out of there. Asela and I began walking away as quickly as possible, but the women from Bayamo were frightened and tried to pretend they weren't with us.

"No, no," they told the soldier, "we've come to see the bugler

14. See glossary, José Eleuterio Pedraza.

corporal. He's our cousin."

That gave Asela and me time to get away, but it was all over for the two women who'd been with us. They were arrested on the spot. Asela and I walked rapidly, and just as we were approaching Garzón, a bus driver named Colás came over and said, "Listen, there's an order out for your arrest." We ran, jumped on a bus, and managed to escape. We didn't know what had happened to the two women from Bayamo. We checked and found that they were released the next day. Imagine! We were outraged. We didn't know what to do. We didn't know who had attacked the Moncada. In the next few days the news came out. But I didn't have the faintest idea who Fidel Castro was. I'd never heard of him. He had been in the Orthodox Party, however, and some people knew him, so that made a difference. At first, when I heard his name, I thought, "Well, so he's a student."

The day we went to the barracks, while we were waiting at San Felix and Enramadas for the bus to Garzón, we noticed that people were shouting. They were shouting so loud that the cops—who were out in force—wouldn't look them in the face. People were in a rebellious, angry mood.

Later, we helped some of the compañeros who had been wounded at the hospital,[15] and we hid a compañero who was fleeing—just as many other people in Santiago did.

But I had no direct ties with the July 26 Movement as such. I continued in our own movement there, with Frank. In 1954 I graduated. I had promised my father I would do postgradu-

15. One group of the Moncada combatants, under the command of Abel Santamaría, had been assigned to occupy an adjacent civilian hospital, which overlooked the rear of the barracks. They planned to use it to tend to the wounded as well. Many of the combatants in the group that took the hospital were among those captured, tortured, and murdered.

ate work, beginning the next September, at a university in the United States. I was working with Frank to collect money for the movement, but it was a slow year. There didn't seem to be any prospects for the immediate future, and I didn't know exactly what to do.

After the attack on Moncada, *History Will Absolve Me* made a tremendous impact. It was an assurance to us of something new. I remember I was in the laboratory when someone gave me a copy, and I stopped to read it right there. We were all fascinated. It spoke a new language. It set out a clear program around which we could all come together in struggle, an advanced program that was attractive to young people. Fidel was still in prison on the Isle of Pines, but from then on I completely identified with him and what he was fighting for.

In 1955 Frank led the attack on the police station in El Caney and helped organize the December 7 demonstration in Santiago.[16] He had been arrested after El Caney, but they hadn't been able to prove anything. I had washed his hands with a formula that produced excellent results. No traces of gunpowder showed up in the paraffin tests, but it almost ruined the poor guy's hands.

At that stage I was somewhat skeptical it was possible to do anything. It seemed to me it would be a long time before people were really ready to make a revolution. I discussed this with Dr. López Rendueles, a man of extraordinary principles. I was preparing my thesis with him, and of course, my relations with him were those of a student doing scientific research under the guidance of a professor.

16. On July 24, 1955, País led a predawn raid on the police station in El Caney, a few miles north of Santiago, capturing a rifle and a pistol. On December 7, 1955, the fifty-ninth anniversary of the death in combat of independence leader Antonio Maceo, opponents of the Batista dictatorship organized demonstrations in several cities.

Why were we sure of the people's support? When we speak of the people, we are not referring to the wealthy and conservative sectors of the nation, who welcome any oppressive regime. . . .

We are referring to the struggle of the great unredeemed masses, those to whom everyone makes promises yet who are deceived and betrayed by all . . . the 600,000 Cubans without work, who want to earn their daily bread honestly . . . the 500,000 farm workers who live in miserable shacks, who work four months of the year and starve the rest . . . who don't have an inch of land to till . . . the 400,000 industrial workers and common laborers . . . whose future is a pay reduction and layoff . . . the 100,000 small farmers who live and die working land that is not theirs . . . the 20,000 small store owners and vendors weighed down by debts, ruined by the crisis . . . the 10,000 young professionals . . . anxious to work and full of hope, only to find themselves at a dead end. . . .

This is the people—those who know misfortune and are therefore capable of fighting with limitless courage! To these people, whose desperate roads through life have been paved with the bricks of betrayal and false promises, we were not going to say: "We will give you . . ." but rather: "Here it is, now fight for it with everything you have, so that liberty and happiness may be yours!"

FIDEL CASTRO

History Will Absolve Me
1953

"Doctor, do you think socialism can be attained with people the way they are?" I asked him one day. I'd never spoken to him in such a direct way before.

He looked at me a moment and then said, "I'm going to tell you something. There were gypsies in Andalusia [in southern Spain] who carried out incredible robberies. But after the triumph of the revolution there and the talk of revolutionary changes, of a new system, people even raised rabbits in the public parks of Andalusia. Nobody stole them. And the people were hungry!"

I remember he told me that story, without saying anything more.

QUESTION: The Spanish republican professors undoubtedly had a big political influence on all of you, or at least those of you in the university.

ESPÍN: Yes, we admired them a great deal. There were also some Cubans such as José Antonio Portuondo, who gave seminars that were in fact anti-imperialist talks. He gave a series of talks about the Americans in Caimanera, and made it very clear to us what the situation was.[17]

So, while it's true, as I said, that we didn't have a clear awareness of what could be done, we did have anti-imperialist feelings, a spirit of rebellion against the system in power. We talked about agrarian reform and about socialism. We discussed Guillén. But we had no Marxist education. There were a few members of the Juventud Socialista [Socialist Youth, youth group of the PSP] around. They had studied Marxist literature, but the vast majority of young people at the uni-

17. That is, the situation with the US naval base at Guantánamo, imposed on Cuba in 1903 under the terms of the Platt Amendment. The base, which Washington claims the right to hold forever, occupies about one-third of the Cuban municipality of Caimanera.

versity knew very little about these things.

QUESTION: Was any activity organized around the Moncada trial?

ESPÍN: Yes, but the main thing was that Armando and Frank made contact with Fidel when he was in prison on the Isle of Pines. They began talking about uniting all the genuinely revolutionary forces into a single movement. By September 1954—eight or nine months before the amnesty—things were already solidifying, and the name of the movement was under discussion. That was really when the best revolutionary forces joined together. Frank, who led actions throughout Oriente province, had a great deal of influence in the rest of the island as well. Fidel was the leader of the movement nationally.

When I got to Havana in July 1955, Fidel had left for Mexico.[18] I remember that Haydée Santamaría said, "What a shame that you didn't talk to Fidel, that you didn't meet him."

Then I went to the United States to study. That was a year of experiencing what the United States was like. At the same time, I was restless since I didn't know what was happening in Cuba.

Some time around May 1956 I received a letter from one of the compañeros who had fought at Moncada, saying he had arrived in Mexico. I immediately wrote him and told him to let me know everything that had happened during the seven months I'd been away. He gave me a report on a lot of things that had happened, things I hadn't heard about. I wrote back saying I'd be returning to Cuba in July and to let me know whether to go through Mexico.

Fidel had to send a great many letters, and he wanted to ask Frank for a lot of data and maps to be used for the landing.

18. Fidel Castro left Cuba for Mexico July 7, 1955.

So I was told to come. As it happened, I got the letter after I'd given up hearing from them and was packing up to leave for home. I went to New York and spent four days trying to get plane tickets to Mexico. It was nearly impossible because of the number of tourists going there. Finally, on the fourth day, I booked a flight to Kansas and from there to Mexico.

When I arrived, Fidel, Raúl, and three or four other compañeros were waiting for me at the airport. That was a moment I'll never forget! I spent two and a half days there. One night, Fidel explained to me in detail everything he wanted me to take to Cuba. I asked him how Frank was.

"Frank is like those movie characters who do a million things without anything ever happening to them," Fidel told me. "When you see Santiago, you're going to be surprised."

Compañeros had just organized a campaign to spread the name July 26 Movement all over Santiago. They used charcoal pencils to write on all the walls, and the pencils were wonderful—the more the police scrubbed the messages, the more they showed up. The compañeros made the pencils by dissolving charcoal in a paraffin formula, so we found all of Santiago de Cuba well covered. Fidel talked a great deal that night about what Frank was doing, what a difference it made, how actively he was working, how important his work was.

The moment I reached Cuba I went to Las Villas, since many of the letters were for compañeros there. When I got there, I found out that the compañero I was bringing the letters to had been arrested. I was almost arrested too, but I managed to make contact with others and return to Havana. There I got in touch with Armando. We met in a park with Montané and Melba—I had letters for them—and so I continued to make contacts until I left for Oriente.[19]

19. See glossary, Armando Hart, Melba Hernández, Jesús Montané.

Once in Santiago, I placed myself under Frank's direction again. I didn't know exactly what was going to happen. I knew there was to be a landing, but nothing else. "We're going back this year," Fidel had said, and that's the basis on which we had begun to work.

At home we had a jeep and another vehicle I drove. We used them both to go out to a farm near San Luis for target practice with the three guns we had. We also hid the weapons at the farm.

Frank put me in charge of preparing several emergency medical stations to be put into operation during our actions. I talked with several doctors and nurses, and we organized first aid courses for a group of young women. We asked people to let us use their houses, and eventually we had nine first aid stations across the city. We called them "medicine chests." Each had a doctor and a nurse, or a nurse and a group of first aid trainees. Nilda Ferrer, the Atala sisters, Fe Carbonell, Asela, and others worked on this.

I also helped transport materials and compañeros, especially after Armando and Haydée arrived in mid-November. I would accompany them all day, taking them from one place to another. We had to keep changing where they stayed, since they were very well-known—they, along with Frank, were national leaders of the movement—and the police were looking for them.

QUESTION: Is that when the November 30 action took place?

ESPÍN: Yes, but when Arturo received the confirming telegram,[20] I didn't know specifically what it was about. A

---

20. Arturo Duque de Estrada received a telegram November 27, 1956, confirming the *Granma* expedition had set out from Mexico. Delayed by storms, the *Granma* did not reach Cuba until December 2, two days later than planned.

meeting had been called for November 28, but I didn't give it much importance. It was just one more meeting, I thought. But it turned out to be preparations of all the action groups for November 30. On the morning of the 29th, Frank told me the boat had left Mexico, so we were to have everything ready for the early morning hours of the 30th.

I had many things to do, including giving the action groups the addresses of the "medicine chests." All the arrangements were last minute. Things were done in a big hurry, but the secret was tightly kept right up to the very moment of the action.

Everyone had been informed it was a trial run, a test. But at 6 a.m. we were all told, "This is not a drill. The boat has already left, and it should land today." It was scheduled to arrive at 7 a.m., and that's when all the events of November 30 began.

I was to stay home in order to give a tape we'd recorded the night before to a man who was going to play it on national radio through a telephone hookup. The tape reported Fidel's arrival and called on the people to rise up in revolt.

But the tape was never broadcast, since the man who was supposed to do it was so scared he burned it . . . Well, there are always some who fail. But almost everything else was carried out exactly as planned. My job was to deliver the tape, and let compañero Carlos Amat at the telephone company know, so he could make arrangements with the person who was supposed to broadcast it, as planned. Then I was to go to the house at San Felix and Santa Lucía, where Frank and other compañeros of the general staff were meeting. I spent the morning there. Our instructions were to go there as soon as we finished our part in the action.

We didn't know whether the landing had actually taken place. Maybe they had landed somewhere else, or had been detained in port before leaving. Maybe the ship had sunk and everyone had drowned. There was even talk of taking a truck and leaving for the Sierra. But what prevailed was the need to maintain the link between the two actions. So in the end we decided to wait until we knew where the expedition had landed and then try to make contact.

Meanwhile, somebody said the house was being surrounded. A doctor I knew lived next door. His house had a big wooden attic, and I wanted to stow all the weapons, uniforms, and everything else we had up there, so we wouldn't lose anything when we left. I told Frank, and then I went over to the house. When I got outside, I discovered we weren't surrounded. But the compañeros who were arriving thought they were being followed, that the whole block was surrounded. That made sense, and in fact it's exactly what did happen two hours later.

But I still didn't want to leave without taking the weapons next door. So I went over there and told the family, in the most abrupt manner possible, "Go to the house across the street right away. Everyone is coming through here, and you'll be accused of something later if you stay." They all went running across the street, one of them so terrified she took off in her housecoat.

When I went back to get the weapons, everyone except Armando and Haydée had left. Frank had told them I was to leave too, that there was no longer any need to stay. Everyone should go home. The weapons, it's true, were almost worthless and were never used. But there were lots of other things that I didn't want to leave lying around. Armando and Yeyé [Haydée] said Frank had left orders that I was to go at once.

I made up a story that I had left my purse with my ID card next door, so Haydée and I made one more trip. When we got there, we realized we'd left the two domestic servants who worked in the house locked up in a room the whole time we'd been there, so we let them out.

Frank had given instructions that anyone who got separated should try to make contact with me at home the next day. Some did so that same day—four or five of the youngest members of the action groups. I went to Agustín Navarrete's house and found that his whole family had been arrested. We went to the homes of others too, but the police were after them, so I didn't find anyone around.

I learned later that Frank had been in an exchange of gunfire at the Teachers Institute. We had placed a mortar on its roof to bombard the Moncada. As it turned out, however, Josué and Léster,[21] who were responsible for the action, were arrested on the way there, so they couldn't set off the mortar. Frank went to see what had happened. He got up to the roof and exchanged shots with the guards. Then he left quickly through the rear of the building.

The day after the actions, Frank immediately began planning what to do next and how to find out about Fidel. We still didn't know what had happened to the expedition. In fact, Fidel landed the next day, December 2. Meanwhile, there had been several other armed actions in Oriente, as planned—at Nicaro; at Ermita, led by Julio Camacho; and at various other points. In Oriente, the plans were carried out very well.[22]

QUESTION: What was the connection between Frank and Pepito Tey?

ESPÍN: Pepito and Frank knew each other from their student days. When they were both in the Teachers Institute, they ran against each other for student government president.

21. See glossary, Josué País, Léster Rodríguez.

22. For an account by Alfonso Zayas of one such action, see *Soldier of the Cuban Revolution*, pp. 60–64.

As Frank organized this or that movement, Pepito was always his second in command. He was a student at the university and worked on the railroad. The fact that he worked on the railroad was very important, because in addition to access to telephones, we needed a way to transport our propaganda. Pepito would send messages with co-workers as well as with interprovincial bus drivers. In 1953 he had started to organize a strong nucleus of left-wing railroad workers in Guantánamo. Many workers in our movement were from the railroad.

Pepito was very different from Frank. Frank would sometimes joke around and tease Armando Hart. Generally, however, he was introverted, quiet, and serious. From the very beginning, he was the leader who thought things out. Pepito was the one who led the actions. He was very popular at the university, partly because of his native wit and natural charm.

I believe Pepito thought he was going to die in the November 30 action. He took a lot of risks. As head of the group, he stayed to the end, making it possible for his compañeros to escape, and he was killed. He knew it was a dangerous and difficult attack, and that the odds were against his coming out of it alive.[23] But the action was carried out successfully.

Pepito even said goodbye to the compañeros the night before. All he wanted was a white rose, he said. He called me at 7 a.m. to leave a message for Frank, but really to say goodbye to everyone. He thought he was going to die, but he was convinced the action was necessary. He was a small, wiry, ner-

---

23. Pepito Tey headed the squad that attacked the police headquarters in Santiago on November 30 and set it on fire. The other two revolutionaries killed that day—Tony Alomá and Otto Parellada—also fell during the assault on the police headquarters.

"Pepito and Frank knew each other from their student days. As Frank organized this or that movement, Pepito was always his second in command. He worked on the railroad, which made it possible to transport propaganda and messages with the help of his co-workers. Many workers in our movement were from the railroad."—Vilma Espín

Pepito Tey, killed in combat November 30, 1956, during action in Santiago de Cuba to support landing of *Granma* expedition.

vous fellow, but highly motivated and intensely passionate.
QUESTION: How long was it before you had news of the compañeros on the *Granma*?
ESPÍN: Not until about December 20. That's when we finally
got word. A peasant from the area told us Fidel was alive,
confirming everything we believed. We had been sure all the
rumors about Fidel's death were just lies. This peasant also
brought a list of things they had requested. That's when we
began sending supplies to the Sierra Maestra.
We also learned that one of the compañeros would come
down from the Sierra to see us. It turned out to be Faustino,
who arrived December 24.[24] We took him to a house on the
outskirts of town that belonged to my relatives. Faustino was
surprised, since every time we went by a guard post, they
would search all of us. They frisked Frank without knowing
who he was. Frank climbed back into the car, we stopped
at the next guard post, they checked us all again. The same
thing happened on our way back. Faustino couldn't believe
we could get away with it.
After Faustino went to Havana, he kept in touch with us.
We began to send boots, uniforms, all sorts of things to the
Sierra. Then, in February, Faustino said that *New York Times*
journalist Herbert Matthews[25] wanted to come interview Fi-

24. A *Granma* expeditionary, Faustino Pérez headed the July 26 underground in Havana until April 1958, when he was assigned to
return to the Sierra Maestra following the failed call for a general
strike on April 9.

25. The article appeared on the front page of the February 24, 1957,
New York Times, under the headline "Cuban Rebel Is Visited in
Hideout: Castro Is Still Alive and Still Fighting in Mountains."
Javier Pazos, a member of the July 26 Movement in Havana, ar-
ranged the interview at the request of the Rebel Army leadership.
Pazos contacted Matthews in Havana, where he and his wife Nan-

Fidel Castro, the rebel leader of Cuba's youth, is alive and fighting hard and successfully in the rugged, almost impenetrable fastnesses of the Sierra Maestra at the southern tip of the island.

President Fulgencio Batista has the cream of his Army around the area, but the Army men are fighting a thus-far losing battle to destroy the most dangerous enemy General Batista has yet faced in a long and adventurous career as a Cuban leader and dictator.

This is the first sure news that Fidel Castro is still alive and still in Cuba. . . .

This account, among other things, will break the tightest censorship in the history of the Cuban Republic. The Province of Oriente, with its 2,000,000 inhabitants, its flourishing cities such as Santiago, Holguín and Manzanillo, is shut off from Havana as surely as if it were another country. Havana does not and cannot know that thousands of men and women are heart and soul with Fidel Castro and the new deal for which they think he stands. . . .

"We have been fighting for seventy-nine days now and are stronger than ever," Señor Castro said. "The soldiers are fighting badly; their morale is low and ours could not be higher. We are killing many, but when we take prisoners they are never shot. We question them, talk kindly to them, take their arms and equipment, and then set them free.

"I know that they are always arrested afterward and we heard some were shot as examples to the others, but they don't want to fight, and they don't know how to fight this kind of mountain warfare. We do."

> "The Cuban people hear on the radio all about Algeria, but they never hear a word about us or read a word, thanks to the censorship. You will be the first to tell them. I have followers all over the island. All the best elements, especially all the youth, are with us. The Cuban people will stand anything but oppression."
>
> HERBERT MATTHEWS
>
> New York Times
> February 24, 1957

del. There were reports everywhere that Fidel was dead, and Matthews wanted to confirm he was alive.

Before that, a meeting took place in the Sierra, the first that Fidel held with all the members of the national leadership of the July 26 Movement to work out plans for the following months. At the time, none of us had been to the Sierra before.

---

cie were on vacation. Matthews later recounted that he jumped at the offer to interview Fidel Castro in the Sierras and that he and Nancie traveled as tourists by car to Manzanillo in Oriente province. Pazos was with them in the car, along with two other Cubans he was introduced to as "Luis" and "Marta." Matthews later learned they were Faustino Pérez—as noted earlier a *Granma* expeditionary and organizer of the Havana underground—and Liliam Mesa, a supporter of the movement from Havana. According to Matthews, from Manzanillo Pérez went ahead of them to the Sierra, and Pazos and July 26 Movement cadre Guerrito Sánchez took him (Matthews) by jeep into the mountains. Matthews and Pazos completed the trip on foot, accompanied by Rebel Army combatant and *Granma* expeditionary Universo Sánchez. Pazos served as the interpreter for the interview. When Matthews returned from the mountains, his wife Nancie carried his seven pages of notes— each page signed by Castro—back with her on the return flight to the United States.

The New York Times.

© 1957, by The New York Times Company.

NEW YORK, SUNDAY, FEBRUARY 24, 1957.   TWENTY.

Cuban Rebel Is Visited in Hideout

Castro Is Still Alive and Still Fighting in Mountains

This is the first of three articles by a correspondent of The New York Times who has just returned from a visit to Cuba.

By HERBERT L. MATTHEWS

Fidel Castro, the rebel leader of Cuba's youth, is alive and fighting hard and successfully in the rugged, almost impenetrable fastnesses of the Sierra Maestra, at the southern tip of the island.

President Fulgencio Batista has the cream of his Army around the area, but the Army men are fighting a thus-far losing battle to destroy the most dangerous enemy General Batista has yet faced in a long and adventurous career as a Cuban leader and dictator.

This is the first sure news that Fidel Castro is still alive and still in Cuba. No one connected with the outside world, let alone with the press, has seen Señor Castro except this writer. No one in Havana, not even at the United States Embassy with all its resources for getting information, will know until this report is published that Fidel Castro is really in the Sierra Maestra.

This account, among other things, will break the tightest censorship in the history of the Cuban Republic. The Province of Oriente, with its 2,000,000 inhabitants, its flourishing cities such as Santiago, Holguin and Manzanillo, is shut off from Havana as surely as if it were another country. Havana does

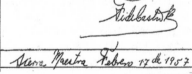

The New York Times

Fidel Castro at a heavily shaded outpost on Feb. 17. He gave the signature to the correspondent who visited him.

We stayed three days.

QUESTION: Were you there when Frank and Che Guevara met in the Sierra?

ESPÍN: Yes, that was in February 1957. Something happened at that meeting that impressed me greatly. "Frank gave us a quiet lesson in discipline," Che said when he later told the story—and a lesson in selflessness, I would add.

Here's what happened. I had on one of those full petticoats they wore back then, and when we arrived, I changed into pants. We went to another camp that day, and Frank stayed behind sleeping. It had rained in the Sierra, and it was very cold. He was already asleep but shivering, so I threw the petticoat over him and left. When he woke up, he took the petticoat, tore it into strips, and used them to clean guns during the two days we were there.[26]

For a brief moment, Frank hoped he'd be able to stay in the Sierra, since that was the kind of struggle that appealed to him, to his innermost wishes. But he couldn't stay. When we returned to the city, he said something to the effect—I can't quote it precisely—that our job was the other part of the struggle, the underground struggle.

QUESTION: What would it have meant to join the battle front in the Sierra?

ESPÍN: It meant you'd die fighting instead of being hunted down. To be hunted down was a terrible thought. Frank had always wanted to fight a guerilla war, and, as I mentioned, on November 30 we actually discussed leaving for the Sierra. That was Frank's dream. Going to the Sierra meant fighting the enemy face to face, without having to hide. It meant

26. Guevara's account of the incident appears in *Episodes of the Cuban Revolutionary War, 1956–58* (Pathfinder, 1996), p. 142 [2010 printing].

sleeping peacefully, regaining strength to work and fight the next day. It meant going up to the mountains, carrying your backpack, fighting in an open war. It was undoubtedly a more attractive battle front than the other, in the underground.

The first meeting with the compañeros in the Sierra was tremendously moving. We had been wondering where they were, what had happened to them, and now we were going to see them. We left from Manzanillo and arrived within a short time. It was dusk, almost nightfall. I looked up and saw the silhouette of a soldier, wearing a helmet. I jumped and threw myself down behind a bush. Then I realized I was mistaken—he was one of ours, Guillermo García.

García had been in the Sierra for about a month and a half, and his beard was already fairly full. Fidel's beard had grown somewhat, and Che's too, but Raúl only had long hair. Very few of them had uniforms anymore. They'd had a hard time of it since the landing, and everything that was left was ripped and torn. There were just over twenty men.

What a joy it was to see them there, full of life and toughened by the hard campaign existence. Fidel, as always, was full of optimism and confidence in the future, brimming over with energy and enthusiasm!

QUESTION: How was the mission to meet Matthews and take him to the Sierra carried out?

ESPÍN: I wasn't involved. Faustino took Matthews to Manzanillo.

As for Armando, Haydée, Frank, and me, we left from Santiago, with me driving, as always. We spent the night in Manzanillo, and the next day they took us to the camp. It was very close, right next to the plains, and there was really quite a risk.

QUESTION: Masetti was also in the Sierra? [27]

ESPÍN: Masetti came to Santiago several times, but that was the next year, in 1958. He spent some time at Che's camp, did some reporting there, and got the news out about the Rebel Army.

The government did the most absurd things imaginable during that period. After the *Granma* landing, Barrera's troops were sent to Santiago.[28] These were soldiers who knew absolutely no one in the city and went around wearing mesh on their helmets, as if they were in the field. They combed the streets by twos, one on each side. Frank was looking out the window one day and a soldier said to him: "Psst! Close the door, fellow!" That kind of thing.

You'd open your door and find a soldier standing there with his gun pointed at you. But the authorities hadn't the vaguest notion what was going on.

At first they made a lot of blind stabs. They spent a lot of money but they didn't fight.

At the meeting we held in the Sierra, Fidel wrote a manifesto explaining to the people what had happened, where the combatants were, and the reasons for the struggle. He explained what the July 26 Movement stood for and called on the people to join in the struggle. By then we had an entire apparatus set up—including propaganda, action, coordination, and sabotage—and we were able to distribute the manifesto all over the island.

The Rebel Army was still very small. It was made up of the initial group of just over twenty, plus the peasants who had joined them. At the meeting I mentioned, Fidel asked Frank to send up fifty compañeros most seasoned in the struggle in Santiago. As soon as we got back, we got the first group

27. See glossary, Jorge Masetti.

28. See glossary, Pedro Barrera.

The Sierra Maestra campaign has shown that the dictatorship, despite sending its best troops and most modern arms to the battle zone, is incapable of crushing the revolution. In contrast to this weakness, each day we have more arms, more men joining us, more experience in struggle, a broader field of action, more knowledge of the terrain, and more total support from the peasants. The regime's soldiers are weary of the exhausting, strenuous, and useless campaign. . . .

To the people of Cuba, the July 26 Revolutionary Movement proposes the following demands:

1. Intensify the burning of cane fields in the entire sugar-producing region, depriving the tyranny of the income it uses to pay the soldiers it sends to their deaths and to buy the planes and bombs with which it is murdering dozens of families. . . .

2. General sabotage of all public utilities and all means of communication and transport.

3. Direct and summary execution of all the thugs who torture and murder revolutionaries. . . .

4. Organization of civic resistance in all cities of Cuba.

5. Intensification of the financial campaign to meet the growing costs of the movement.

6. A revolutionary general strike as the culmination and final point of the struggle.[*]

FIDEL CASTRO
Manifesto to the People of Cuba
February 20, 1957

[*] Excerpted in Pedro Álvarez Tabío and Heberto Norman Acosta, *Diario de la guerra* [Diary of the war] (Havana: Office of Publications of the Council of State, 2010) vol. 1, pp. 362–64.

together in about ten days. We sent our finest compañeros—Furry; Jiménez; Nanito Díaz, who died at El Uvero; the photographer Domínguez; and some of those who had fought in the November 30 uprising and were known to the police.[29] It was time to get them out of the city.

That group was very well equipped. They all had uniforms, backpacks, and boots. We also sent up a complete set of clothes for each of the compañeros already in the Sierra. During that first month they had worn out their clothing, shoes and all.

The July 26 Movement continued to gain strength. We were able to publicize the actions that took place in the Sierra, so people would know Fidel was active. The interview by Matthews made the revolutionary struggle in Cuba known around the world.

In Santiago, we worked with Armando to establish what was called the Civic Resistance. This was a formation that included members of the bourgeoisie and the petty bourgeoisie who opposed the Batista regime and who collaborated with the July 26 Movement by contributing money, hiding compañeros, and providing medicine, clothing, armbands, and other things.

In a sense you could say the entire city of Santiago de Cuba began to play a part in the underground movement. In San Jerónimo, my neighborhood, all the families worked together. I wish you could talk with the men and women who took part in the struggle on a rank-and-file level, people who aren't well-known. They're the ones who can tell the really rich and fascinating story of the heroism displayed day in and day out

29. See glossary, Abelardo Colomé (Furry); Reynerto Jiménez; Emiliano Díaz (Nano, Nanito); El Uvero, battle of; Guillermo Domínguez.

Above: Frank País, Faustino Pérez, Fidel Castro, and Armando Hart at first meeting of July 26 Movement leadership—from both mountains and city—in the Sierra Maestra, February 17, 1957. Until then, said Ernesto Che Guevara, the Rebel Army's "nomadic and clandestine life had made it impossible to have any exchange between the two parts of the movement."

Below: Fidel Castro being interviewed by *New York Times* correspondent Herbert Matthews, same day. After Batista official claimed interview was faked, publication of photo caused sensation in Cuba, United States, and elsewhere.

by the ranks of the July 26 Movement in Santiago de Cuba. The Civic Resistance was a broad front, a support organization. The July 26 Movement was made up of militants who were part of the struggle, who engaged in action, who helped distribute our propaganda.

There was tremendous support from the population. We'd come out with a call for action, and people would observe it to the letter. There was a call that set a date for "lights out, radios off: dead city," for example. And at dusk that day Santiago de Cuba was completely dark and silent. "Don't go to the movies," we'd say, and we began to sabotage all social activities. After November 30, Santiago had virtually no social life. For a few months, some people still went to the movies. But by April and May 1957, everything was blacked out, as if there were a curfew. Nobody went anywhere at night.

The July 26 Movement continued to gain strength. Frank had built a very disciplined organization. He was a strong, intelligent person. He had all kinds of aptitudes, including for military matters, that he never had the opportunity to develop. He was very much the teacher, very much the soldier. Naturally, he developed very rapidly under the circumstances, not only as a fighter and leader but also politically. At the time he became active in the struggle, he was a Baptist, with strong ideas about changing society, a strong class feeling, and a deep-rooted sense of justice, discipline, and order. He was also very concerned about the peasantry, that is, about what the revolution should do to meet the peasants' needs.

Frank was very interested in political questions. He paid a lot of attention to increasing his knowledge in that area. His thinking evolved a great deal. In one of the last documents he wrote before his death, he outlined a number of ideas about the future of our country, including the question of socialism.

QUESTION: Was Frank concerned about the moral caliber, the

character of the compañeros who were recruited?

ESPÍN: Discipline was very strict, right from the beginning of the July 26 Movement. In cases of serious breaches of discipline—for example, an individual stealing a weapon from the movement, or selling one of the movement's weapons—the penalty was death. This level of discipline was maintained throughout the struggle.

In Santiago de Cuba, even in the early days of the MNR and ALN, it was understood that anyone capable of talking under torture or for any other reason had to die. "If you don't die there, you'll die later," went the saying. It was a deeply rooted understanding. People in the July 26 Movement knew you couldn't talk, and the population knew it too. You couldn't talk because it would cost others their lives. Discipline was very strong. Any moral failure had violent consequences.

The movement instilled and enforced moral standards in our combatants in every sense, including respect for the combatants who were women.

Frank himself was very highly respected. Everyone loved and admired him, but they respected him as well. At the beginning of the struggle, Frank was just a youngster; even later on, he had barely begun to shave. It used to amuse me—here was this rosy-cheeked youth, yet political fakers and people who went bad would tremble when he spoke.

When an action meting out justice to a torturer, murderer, or traitor had to be carried out, Frank spoke to the men beforehand, explaining why it was necessary. He tried to select the most conscious and mature compañeros for such a task.

We were always concerned about the trauma the youngest combatants would face. Life in the underground is very high-pressure, violent. It destroys some people. Compañeros would get very nervous. When somebody showed up unexpectedly, or slammed on the brakes, they'd jump. That was the difference between city life and life in the Sierra. In the Sierra you could say, "Well, if I'm killed, at least I'll die fighting." In the city, you felt like a hunted animal. Not only could you be cornered, with no way of getting out alive, but death would often come after prison and torture. It was very hard. There were many who wanted to go to the Sierra but couldn't, since we didn't have enough weapons. It was hard keeping up the morale of all those youth facing persecution, who had to hide behind closed doors.

Frank drew his political views from José Martí's ideas and he translated them into consciousness about discipline, struggle, and sacrifice. Before the November 30 uprising, I talked with him about the effect that carrying out actions that had to be taken against individuals could have on the morale of compañeros involved. In response, he worked with Pepito Tey to prepare a series of readings from Martí, from material on guerrilla warfare, and from the struggle against Nazism. Several books with such materials were circulated among members of the action groups.

Frank also rapidly became more conscious of what the struggle meant, what a revolution was, what the future could be. We had no way of discussing these things in Marxist terms, of course. At that time only a small minority of young people had any idea what Marxism, socialism, or communism meant. Our knowledge of the October [1917 Russian] Revolution was totally vague and distorted.

Frank told me I had to study hard and prepare myself for the future. The way he talked made me realize he didn't think he'd live to see the end of the struggle. Especially after his brother Josué was killed,[30] Frank seemed to think his time

---

30. Josué País, Frank's younger brother, was murdered in Santiago by Batista's forces on June 30, 1957, one month before Frank was gunned down.

VILMA ESPÍN: In terms of social questions, by 1957 Frank's views had begun to change. He spoke of the need for major social changes, that without this there would be no revolution. Although he still didn't have a clear idea of what these changes would be, he raised ideas that, I would say, converged with Marxism.

Something similar happened to the rest of us. I hadn't read the Communist Manifesto, but I expressed ideas about social justice that one can find in the Manifesto. Frank spoke in a similar vein. He had a very strong class consciousness. He came from a modest background and was outraged at the differences between classes. It angered him that there was a class of rich people and a class of poor people.

SZULC: You're saying, it seems, that many young people arrived independently at conclusions that later would be Marxist . . .

ESPÍN: Exactly, and in my case as well. I knew very little of the fundamentals of Marxism. But over time I began to realize that I agreed with Marxist ideas—especially as we found ourselves, through struggle, more in contact with the peasants of the Second Front.

I'd say that for the big majority of us—those who came from the university as I did, and even those who were illiterate, as were many of the peasants—we gradually moved in that direction out of pure necessity.

SZULC: Due to a lack of alternatives?

ESPÍN: No, because it was the utter truth that things had to be changed. And even more so when I was in the Second Front, the last six months of the war, when we experienced even more harshly how people there

lived. They had no medical care, no education. They
lived in terrible conditions. The region was rich in coffee, but the peasants were tremendously poor. In addition, their land was taken. Their huts were burned. They
were killed. And all this went unpunished.

As we learned more of this history, we increasingly
came to realize that the changes would have to be very
big. We found ourselves, little by little, on the road to
Marxism without even discussing it.*

VILMA ESPÍN
MAY 15, 1985

was almost up. Even in letters to Fidel, he would say, "If they
give me a little more time, I'll be able to do such and such."
He said it quite consciously, of course. "Things are very tight.
I'm going to try to gain a little time." A little more time to live
is what he meant. He was in a great rush to write down his
ideas about military and political organization, about agrarian reform and what it should be like. He wrote about some
of the same things Fidel had taken up in *History Will Absolve
Me.*

Frank was very bold and daring. He demanded that actions be conducted that way, without taking unnecessary
risks based on emotions. He had fought Josué hard on that
score, because Josué was passionate and impetuous. Frank
had even urged Agustín Navarrete to use his close friend-
ship with Josué to try to exercise some control over him, to
rein him in a bit. Because Josué wouldn't listen to anyone

* Interview with *New York Times* correspondent Tad Szulc, tran-
scribed by Cuban Council of State. In Cuban Heritage Collection,
University of Miami.

else. Frank admired Josué a great deal. He admired the very qualities he knew were defects in the long run, but that also showed a very strong, firm character.

At home Frank had been very disciplined, while Josué was very rebellious. And Frank admired Josué's rebelliousness because the rest of the family was so introverted and quiet. When we were hiding out in the house in San Jerónimo, Frank composed a song called *Melancholy*, which he played on the piano. The melody stayed with me for many years, but I've forgotten it now. What a shame it wasn't written down. Frank was very sensitive about artistic things, the beauty of nature, of women.

He greatly admired his mother. Her life had been a hard one. She was a strong-willed woman, and he was always extremely gentle with her. He asked me to buy an orchid on Mother's Day and send it to her, since he couldn't go see her.

In my opinion, it was Frank's attitude toward women that made it possible for us to work as complete equals with men in the July 26 Movement. Even though he had a little bit of a tendency to protect women from danger, he made no distinction between men and women in terms of assignments except for those that were demanding physically.

Of course, you always think of how much Frank—like so many other compañeros who died—could have contributed after the victory of the revolution.

QUESTION: When you first went to the Sierra in February 1957, were you already underground?

ESPÍN: No, not yet. And I still had all the people in my house in Santiago. That's where we made all the contacts, where we kept the dynamite until we sent it to the Sierra, where we did everything. The uniforms were sent from there to Manzanillo and from Manzanillo to the Sierra. Everything was done from that house, and, of course, it was dangerous. Many of the people in the house were being hunted. To get them out, we'd have to take them to neighbors' houses at night. In fact, the whole neighborhood worked with the underground. Then came a period of harsh repression. That was the only time the authorities caught me, but they didn't manage to haul me to the garrison. Three of them surprised me in the lab where I was working—two assassins from the SIM [Military Investigation Service], who were tried and executed in January 1959, and one from the Secret Service, who was higher-ranking. I had a packet of photos with me taken in the Sierra in February, in which Fidel, Frank, Raúl, Armando, Yeyé, and I appeared. I had to put on quite an act so they wouldn't get the photos—finally slipping them, almost like a pickpocket, into the lab doctor's pocket. He was an old man and almost fainted, since he thought it was a pistol. Actually it was worse.

The Secret Service man tried to make a deal with me. When he finally decided I wasn't a serious case, he said he wanted to speak to me alone in the doctor's office.

"What's this all about?" I asked

"Listen," he said, "they tell me I'm on the blacklist of the underground."

I looked at him without saying a word, and he went on:

"I didn't do anything. I know Josué País and Pepito Tey. I picked them up, and I didn't even slap them. I have a daughter"—a little sob caught in his throat—"and I'm going to leave the Secret Service. I'm going to work for Texaco."

"From what you're telling me," I said, "you seem to think I belong to an underground movement with a blacklist that includes your name. Do I understand you correctly? And you think I may be able to take your name off that list."

"I'm not a coward," he said.

"No," I replied, "but you do seem worried."

By then, as far as the Secret Service agent was concerned, I knew I was in a strong position. And I'd fooled the SIM agents by slipping the photos to the doctor right in front of them, without their knowing it. The whole chain of events had left me a little shaken. But they had nothing on me. They'd already searched my house. They were convinced I was mixed up in something, since they'd seen me at a demonstration—an action by the mothers of Santiago to protest the murders of revolutionaries. Frank had expressly prohibited me from going, since the action was in early January 1957 and everybody was hiding out in my house. None of us were supposed to go. But I was worried the demonstrators would be attacked by surprise and broken up. It wasn't that I doubted the resolve of the mothers, but you never knew what the soldiers would do.

Everyone in the demonstration was dressed in mourning. So I put on a jacket that was red, picked up my camera, and told Frank I was just going out for awhile to take some pictures. At San Felix and Enramadas, the demonstrators were stopped by army troops in a jeep. The mothers hesitated for a minute, and I yelled, "Let's sing the national anthem!" We began to sing, louder and louder. Then I went to the front of the demonstration. An army corporal, the one who recognized me and had come to arrest me at the laboratory, started arguing with me. The next day my picture appeared on the front page of *Diario de Cuba*.

Frank reprimanded me severely for that breach of discipline.

After that, I had to be more careful. Until then I had always been Frank's driver. People notice the driver, not the passenger—that was my theory. "Always sit in front," I said, "and look at a magazine. They won't be so apt to see you." That's exactly how it went.

Santiago de Cuba, January 6, 1957. March to protest cop murder five days earlier of William Soler, a fifteen-year-old member of July 26 Movement. Espín (in circle) had been instructed by Frank País not to take part. Her picture, arguing from sidelines with soldier trying to disperse demonstration, ended up on front page of local newspaper the next day.

"Frank País reprimanded me severely for that breach of discipline," Espín said.

But the day they questioned me in the lab, Frank ended that. "If you continue to drive for me I'll be a marked man," he said, "because they just questioned you." So he drove himself and was doing so when they caught him in early March 1957. They arrested him without knowing who he was.

When Frank didn't show up the next day, I talked with his mother and the girls. I asked them to go to the garrison and make a scene, so the police wouldn't kill him. We also got in touch with the civic forces, the archdiocese, the embassies—we urged everyone to raise a hue and cry. By that time the authorities realized they had Frank, but they couldn't kill him because of the public pressure.

The prosecutors brought the *Granma* landing into the trial.[31] But with the Civic Resistance behind us, we put enough pressure on the lawyers and the court to win the release of those we needed most, especially the younger people, the people who could best carry out actions. The others were eventually taken to prison on the Isle of Pines.

Frank was released in May 1957, and we began to prepare a number of actions, because that was when Masferrer[32] began to hold political meetings. From then on, Frank didn't want me to participate in anything like this, since I was very easily identifiable. I stayed underground for several months.

Then came the terrible days of June and July 1957. On June

31. In May 1957 *Granma* expeditionaries who had been captured by Batista's forces and a number of November 30 combatants were put on trial in a Santiago courtroom. On May 10, the 22 *Granma* expeditionaries were convicted and sentenced to up to nine years in prison. Frank País—who had been picked up in March, under the circumstances Espín describes above—and others arrested in connection with the November 30 Santiago action were acquitted and released.

32. See glossary, Rolando Masferrer.

30, Masferrer held a meeting in Santiago. We planted dynamite to blow it up, but the firing device didn't work. Then
something awful happened: Josué became desperate, went
out into the street, and was killed.

The day as a whole was terrible. The action in Santiago
failed. An action elsewhere in Oriente designed to launch a
second front was defeated. Everyone was arrested, one combatant killed, and the weapons captured.[33] Those were dark
days! We spent all of July recovering from them. One Sunday
late that month I went to see Frank. We talked about Josué's
death—Frank had already written the poem to him.

While we were talking, Frank said he had to take on major organizational responsibilities and asked me to take over
coordinating the movement's work in the province. Frank
was not only the leader of the July 26 Movement in Oriente
province. He was also responsible for coordinating actions
on a national level. He was under tremendous pressure; they
were hunting for him everywhere. At the same time, he was
trying to create the foundations for what would become the
militias. He sent Fidel several proposals on the military structure of the Rebel Army and of the leadership of the militias
nationally.

Frank also drew up the oath militia volunteers took. When
compañeros joined an action cell, they signed a powerful but
very beautiful oath. It was outstanding! The commitment was
a very serious one.

These oaths were kept in a bank we secretly used. We had
a file there listing compañeros' real names. It was extremely

33. In an initial effort to open a second front to take pressure off combatants in the Sierra Maestra, an attack was planned for June 30,
1957, on army barracks near the Miranda sugar mill in northeast
Oriente province. The police, informed in advance, arrested the
combatants before they could begin the attack.

dangerous, but the list never fell into enemy hands. It was kept among the bank papers, and nobody ever knew a thing about it. It was kept by a compañero who maintained a low profile. His assignment was precisely to do what he did, although he would have liked to have been active. I'm talking about Ortega, Francesa's husband, a fine, brave, and discreet person who always carried out his work well. We hid an entire action group at his place for a long time.

QUESTION: In the "cave"?

ESPÍN: Yes, the "cave," as we called it.[34] Actually many families gave the July 26 Movement tremendous support, including participating in activities themselves.

QUESTION: You were speaking earlier about July 20, ten days before Frank's death . . .

ESPÍN: Yes. Ten days before Frank's death, he asked me to take responsibility for coordinating work in the province, so he could concentrate on national work and have some time to write and study.

That day, at Frank's house, was the last time I saw him. After that I was in touch with him only by telephone. He had moved to another house, but the young woman who lived there was pregnant and got nervous he'd be captured there. Frank was concerned about this and went to another house, one he himself had previously vetoed because the police had gone there once to arrest someone. The compañero had managed to escape, but the problem was that the house had no back exit. It belonged to a very trusted person, Raúl Pujol, but it was a mousetrap.

A few days before he moved, Frank called to ask me to make an important contact for an operation that involved

---

34. The "cave" was the basement of the apartment building in Santiago where Claudia Rosés (La Francesa) and Carlos Ortega lived.

sending a compañero abroad to get weapons. When I called back, he was no longer at the original house. He didn't return my call, either that day or the next. That surprised me, since in the past he had always called to reestablish contact as soon as he changed houses.

On July 30 I was hiding in a house in Vista Alegre, near the zoo. About 4 p.m. I got a call saying there had been some kind of commotion in the area where Pujol lived. I didn't know Frank was there, however. He had just called me twice. The first time, I asked why he hadn't phoned before and began to tell him the results of the assignment he'd given me. I talked very fast. It's possible he was about to tell me something and I didn't give him a chance. He listened until I finished and hung up.

About ten minutes later he called again, but I don't recall what he said—I think it had something to do with that same assignment. He was on the way out of the house, but he didn't say anything about what was happening.

Then a compañero we knew at the telephone company called to say there had been a shootout (I had heard some distant shots) and that the police were chasing somebody over the roofs. I said I'd tell everyone to get over there and see if they could help. We were able to use the telephones since Carlos Amat, the compañero who worked at the phone company, would keep us informed of what section of the city we could call freely. Even on local calls, I'd ask him whether I could call such and such a neighborhood, and he'd say yes I could, or no, that the board showed taps on phones in that area.

Just then, Amat called to ask whether I'd like to listen in on a call from Salas Cañizares to Tabernilla.[35] I took it and

35. See glossary, José María Salas Cañizares and Francisco Tabernilla Dolz.

In early 1957, we consolidated our guerrilla force in the mountains. At the same time, the underground apparatus of the July 26 Movement was being organized in the cities. Increasingly important actions were carried out under the leadership of Frank País who, from Santiago de Cuba, served as national action coordinator and, later, as de facto leader of the underground. . . .

One of the priorities during the final weeks of his life was to help provide leadership to the workers section. In our view of how to make a revolution, as exemplified in the attack on the Moncada garrison, workers would deliver the final thrust to the tyranny after we rose up and armed the city of Santiago de Cuba. War in the mountains was the alternative if the strike failed to materialize.

One of the biggest blows to the July 26 Movement and the revolutionary struggle in Cuba took place July 30, 1957, when Frank País was captured in Santiago and murdered right on the street. Frank's death set off a spontaneous reaction of such scope that it virtually paralyzed the city for several days.

The funeral march for the young combatant became the most massive demonstration of rebellion Santiago had ever witnessed. It was an eloquent expression of generalized rejection of the regime, of the spirit of rebellion of the people of Santiago.[*]

FIDEL CASTRO
2010

---

[*] In Fidel Castro, *La victoria estratégica: Por todos los caminos de la Sierra*, pp. 2–3.

heard one of them say: "Hey, chief, I'm going to let you talk to the winner," and on he went with some vulgarity I don't recall. "Here's Sariol, the guy who did it." Then Sariol came on and said, "Do I get the 3,000, chief? We just killed Frank País." Right then and there, Amat cut me off for fear I'd say something and they'd hear me. It was an awful moment.

I began calling around to get details. René Ramos Latour (Daniel) had been with Frank shortly before to coordinate some work, and found him very depressed over Josué's death a month earlier. They talked awhile and Daniel left.

Commander Villa (Demetrio Montseny) had driven up in a van and tried to get Frank to come with him, since the area was already being surrounded. But Frank had made plans with Pujol to pick him up on the corner in a rented car. "No, it's better for me to go with Pujol," Frank said. "He's on his way, so you go ahead." Pujol wasn't underground.

When Pujol arrived, he went in the house to look for Frank. When they came out, they were arrested.

I more or less reconstructed what had happened from talking to Pujol's wife, Ñeña, and his son, Raulito, who was thirteen years old at the time. They had witnessed the whole thing. Frank and Raúl had been beaten and thrown in a car, they said. Ñeña went running after the car, screaming, and the whole neighborhood followed. Apparently the police realized they'd better kill Frank and Raúl right away. Otherwise, they wouldn't be able to, since they'd face the same kind of public pressure they had before. So when they got to an alley two and a half blocks away, the police pulled them out of the car and killed them right there.

That same afternoon we found out who had tipped off the police. It was Laureano Ibarra's mistress, who had seen Frank entering Pujol's house. They got her out of Ibarra's house in a hurry and sent her to the home of a young woman I'd known at the university, the daughter of a man known as "Black" Martínez, one of Ibarra's thugs. They then quickly put her on a ship that was in port and sent her straight to Santo Domingo.

When the woman had first reported seeing Frank, they also brought someone over to the house who'd been his classmate at the Teachers Institute—and had identified him once before, at the garrison—to verify it was really him. As soon as this person—Randich[36]—did so, they surrounded the house. Later we took care of Randich.

What an afternoon for all of us. I immediately called Frank's mother, Doña Rosario, and his girlfriend, América Domitro, to come claim the body before they disposed of it.

Frank's body was lying in the middle of the street. Lots of people were milling around, so they cordoned the area off. The reaction was tremendous. Frank was dead, and Santiago de Cuba was at the boiling point. That afternoon, shop owners and members of Civic Resistance began calling me to say that people wanted to close up and go on strike—the bosses, the workers, everybody. Everyone agreed, and shops began to close.

Finally I got Rosario on the telephone. "You have to go and make some kind of a scene until they give you Frank's body," I told her. She went right over, with tremendous courage, ready to do whatever was necessary.

When she arrived, the authorities had already taken the body to the morgue. People had been trying to get to the body, and there were incidents with the police. People's reaction was spontaneous and powerful. The entire city stopped, as people headed to where Frank's body had been taken. The authorities released the body. They were also intelligent

36. See glossary, Luis Mariano Randich.

enough to call in all their forces and keep them in the barracks while a crowd gathered around América's house, where we took the body.

There we dressed Frank in his uniform. Of his two very clear vocations—that of the soldier and that of the teacher—I would say the military took precedence. I insisted he be dressed in his uniform, with his beret on his chest, because he loved the beret and had worn it for ages. A white rose and the July 26 armband were placed on the beret. He was given a three-star rank, according to the nine-rank plan he had been drawing up to send Fidel.

The funeral was truly a people's demonstration.[37] Workplaces shut down. No police were anywhere in sight. The whole city was taken over by the people. Those who didn't go to the cemetery threw flowers as the casket passed. A group of navy men awaiting the funeral procession stood at attention as it went by. They turned out to be the group that, just a bit more than a month later, took part in the action at Cienfuegos.[38]

I wanted desperately to participate in that popular homage to Frank, but I had strict orders not to—orders that Frank himself had given when he criticized me for participating in the mothers' demonstration. Discipline with regard to public action was very strict, but it was awfully hard for me to comply on that occasion.

QUESTION: There was a demonstration the day after Frank was killed, the day of the funeral?

37. It's estimated that 60,000 people participated, more than a third of the population of Santiago de Cuba at the time.

38. On September 5, 1957, anti-Batista forces in the navy joined with July 26 combatants to seize the Cienfuegos naval base, distribute weapons, and take the city of Cienfuegos. Simultaneous actions at other naval bases, which had been part of the plan, never took place. The Cienfuegos uprising was crushed the next day.

ESPÍN: Yes. US ambassador Earl Smith had arrived that morning. I don't remember why. I think the visit by him and his wife was supposed to convey an appearance of normalcy on the island, or something of the sort.

We immediately organized a demonstration of women in mourning to go to Céspedes Park, in front of city hall, and make a commotion. Everyone dressed in black. There was a run-in with the police, and Gloria Cuadras bit Salas Cañizares's finger so hard she almost severed it.[39] The police turned fire hoses on the demonstrators, and Nuria García[40] was beaten. Most demonstrators weren't able to attend the funeral since they were arrested, but they did manage to create quite a scandal. The ambassador's wife was distressed at seeing such things at firsthand. She wasn't accustomed to the sight of police beating women as they screamed "Murderers!" at them.[41]

The funeral was that afternoon. Emotions were running high and everyone was outraged. Frank really had tremendous prestige. He was in command of actions not just for Oriente but for the entire island.

QUESTION: Who replaced Frank?

ESPÍN: We were in a bind at that time, since Haydée,

39. See glossary, Gloria Cuadras.

40. Nuria García was a combatant in the July 26 underground in Santiago.

41. In a dispatch from Santiago the day of the action, the *New York Times* reported "200 women demonstrated against the Government at the City Hall" as "United States Ambassador Earl E.T. Smith received the keys to the city." Police tried to break up the demonstration, "soldiers were called out and a fire truck brought to the scene began drenching the women with water." When the women stood firm against the attack, "they were cheered by several thousand persons who gathered on nearby sidewalks and balconies."

"The morning after Frank's murder, US ambassador Earl Smith arrived in Santiago. We organized a demonstration in front of city hall of women in mourning. . . . The police turned fire hoses on them and some were beaten. The ambassador's wife was distressed. She wasn't accustomed to seeing police beating women who were screaming 'Murderers!' at them."—Vilma Espín

July 31, 1957, Santiago de Cuba. Women stand their ground despite police assault with water cannon.

Armando, Faustino Pérez, all the compañeros in the national leadership were somewhere else. Faustino was in overall charge of national coordination, but Frank was responsible for organizing the actions themselves. And Faustino, since he was in Havana, was very isolated.

René Ramos Latour, or Daniel, as we called him, had been coordinating a number of actions with Frank. So that afternoon I suggested he take over that front. He didn't know what to say.

"How can I? . . . Imagine . . . Frank!"

"I'm not suggesting you take over the entire leadership," I said, "just the action part, at least.

"In any case," I told him, "I'm not the one to decide. Go to Havana, talk to Haydée, discuss it with the compañeros in the movement there, and come to a decision."

So that's what happened. Daniel became national head of action, and Fidel later ratified the decision.

We called Daniel "the man from Nicaro." He was very serious, one of our best. Through him, we got lots of supplies in Nicaro. He was a great organizer and always carried out his assignment.

Frank had been thinking about sending Daniel to the Sierra. It had become very dangerous for him to remain in the city, and he was a very stable, serious person as well. A compañero said he once carried Daniel's backpack in the Sierra and it weighed a ton because it was filled with books. He loved to study politics, but of course there wasn't much time to study just then. He also respected and admired Che a great deal.

QUESTION: What effect did Frank's death have on the movement's strategy in the struggle?

ESPÍN: In addition to the sorrow we all felt, Frank's death created a number of problems. He was the one in direct contact with the navy people in Cienfuegos, for instance. That action was still a deep secret, and he hadn't reported the details to others. We had to reinitiate the contacts ourselves. Something like that is always difficult, but we finally managed to do it.

Fidel was in the Sierra. But the organization in the cities needed a leader like Frank, because Fidel couldn't lead things in the cities from the mountains. At the same time, Frank had a deep interest in military discipline, strategy, and organization. He had made preparations for the underground struggle that others put into practice. The organization of the militias, for instance, was his idea. He laid the basis for it, and Daniel was able to take it from there, using what Frank had prepared.

Armando was given responsibility for coordination. He went to the Sierra and talked to Fidel. Together they worked out a plan, but Armando was captured on the way back and sent to prison. Haydée went to see him there, but they didn't have a chance to talk everything over. Since we didn't know what decisions Fidel and Armando had made, we had to send someone else to the Sierra. It was very complicated.

QUESTION: What responsibilities did Agustín Navarrete have in the July 26 Movement?

ESPÍN: Tin, as we called him, was head of action in Oriente province when Frank was killed. He had spent every day that month with Frank. But when Frank moved to Pujol's house, which was very small, they separated. He was in the other house when Frank was killed.

Then we had to send Tin to Camagüey, because the movement was very weak there at the time. After that, many compañeros had to be sent to different provinces. Julio Camacho had been in Las Villas with a group of compañeros since the action in Cienfuegos. Matanzas was not very strong. In Havana, so many compañeros had been killed that another group had to be sent there from Oriente. Later, compañeros went from the Sierra to Pinar del Río to help with the armed action that was to take place there. To strengthen Matanzas, we sent people from Havana and Las Villas; Enrique Hart went there and that's where he was killed. We lost a lot of compañeros that year.

We had to carry out a national campaign to make clear that informers could not act with impunity, especially after Frank was informed on. Eleven were brought to justice in one week in Santiago, among them Randich. This had a very positive effect—informing was fairly rare after that.

I was in considerable danger in the city. So in February 1958 I left Santiago and spent a month and a half in the Sierra. While I was there, Raúl left to establish the Second Front. I saw him for a few days at Che's camp at La Mesa. In the first days of March, we saw off Raúl's column as well as Almeida's column, which was leaving to establish the Third Front.[42] Three actions were carried out at the same time so Raúl's forces could cross the Central Highway without incident.

In early March a national meeting was held in the Sierra to define future strategy.[43] A revolutionary fervor was stirring among the people. Press censorship had been temporarily lifted, so more news was getting out. In addition, we had been through the experience of the spontaneous strike in Santiago at the time of Frank's death. We discussed the pos-

42. For a map of these fronts, see p. 84.

43. A meeting of the National Directorate of the July 26 Movement was held in the Sierra Maestra March 6–9, 1958. Present were Fidel Castro, José Aguilera Maceira, Luis Buch, Vilma Espín, Marcelo Fernández, Faustino Pérez, René Ramos Latour, David Salvador, Celia Sánchez, and Haydée Santamaría.

sibility of a national strike, and it was agreed that the forces in the Sierra would support it by closing off the highways and preparing for whatever else might come. Raúl was already at the Second Front, and Daniel went there to coordinate strike actions with him.

The April 1958 strike in Oriente was very solid. We carried out many actions in support of it. Rebel combatants came down from the mountains, and action groups took up positions all along the highways leading to the cities. We were on the highest state of alert. In Oriente we did what we said we'd do.

But the repressive forces, too, had learned from what happened in the days after Frank's death. The strike didn't surprise them. They were prepared for something of that kind. In Havana, for example, they killed a great many compañeros as soon as it started. There was tremendous repression, so much so that, except in Oriente, the strike was only partially effective.

In early May we met again in the Sierra to assess the situation—the positive and negative aspects of the strike, and where we should go from there. We made a number of decisions about future strategy. The military fronts had become stronger, and a different approach was outlined.

Fidel proposed that the national leaders of the July 26 Movement come to the Sierra, so a broad leadership could be established there. Many compañeros in the militias had already gone to the Second Front, since they were known to the authorities in the cities. The urban groups decreased in size but continued carrying out actions. The November 1958 elections were approaching, and it was important to maintain a constant climate of agitation through September. We lost many compañeros in Santiago in these actions.

This is when Batista's army launched a major offensive

Various concrete problems of the movement were finally clarified [at the Altos de Mompié meeting on May 3, 1958]. In the first place, the war would be led militarily and politically by Fidel in his dual role as commander in chief of all forces and as general secretary of the organization. The line of the Sierra would be followed, that of direct armed struggle, extending it to other regions and in that way taking control of the country.

We did away with various naive illusions about attempted revolutionary general strikes when the situation had not matured sufficiently to bring about such an explosion, and without having laid the necessary groundwork for an event of that magnitude. In addition the leadership lay in the Sierra, which objectively eliminated some practical decision-making problems that had prevented Fidel from actually exercising the authority he had earned.

In fact, this did nothing more than register a reality: the political predominance of those in the Sierra, a consequence of the fact that their positions were correct and their interpretation of events was accurate.[*]

ERNESTO CHE GUEVARA
NOVEMBER 22, 1964

[*] "A Decisive Meeting," in Ernesto Che Guevara, *Episodes of the Cuban Revolutionary War, 1956–58* (Pathfinder, 1996), pp. 353–54 [2010 printing]. Present at the May 3, 1958, meeting were Fidel Castro, Luis Buch, Vilma Espín, Marcelo Fernández, Ernesto Che Guevara, Enzo Infante, Faustino Pérez, René Ramos Latour, David Salvador, Celia Sánchez, Haydée Santamaría, and Ñico Torres.

against Fidel's column in the Sierra Maestra and against the Second Front.[44]

QUESTION: What was the "Antiaircraft Operation" on the Second Front?

ESPÍN: The Antiaircraft Operation was Raúl's capture of a group of Americans.[45] Its name came from the fact that Batista's air force was carrying out intensive bombardment of the civilian population as a reprisal for guerrilla actions. The bombings stopped as soon as the Americans were seized. Then, for a whole month, Raúl took advantage of that breath-

44. In wake of the failure of the April 9, 1958, call for a general strike and the sharp setback it entailed for the revolutionary movement, Batista sent 10,000 troops to the Sierras to "encircle and annihilate" the Rebel Army. In ten weeks of fierce combat, Batista's forces were defeated. In August 1958 the Rebel Army and July 26 Movement were again able to take the offensive.

45. On June 28, 1958, in the midst of Batista's offensive in the Sierra, combatants under Raúl Castro's command in the Second Front captured twenty-nine US marines returning to their base at Guantánamo. They—along with twenty US and Canadian civilians captured at different times from Moa Bay Mining Company, United Fruit, and other US-owned companies—were held until Fidel Castro received a report of the action in early July and ordered their release.

"Fidel was critical of what we had done," Raúl wrote later, in a June 1963 article, "and he was completely right. Just as he had said before Batista opened the offensive, Batista was finished; the offensive was his last hope, and, once it was defeated by the Rebel Army, which is what happened, Batista and his regime had no chance. In this situation the United States could have used the detention of the Americans as a pretext for military intervention in Cuba to save Batista, which would have made the situation worse, more dangerous." Raúl Castro, "Operación antiaérea en el Segundo Frente 'Frank País,' en junio de 1958" [Antiaircraft operation in the "Frank País" Second Front in June 1958] in Raúl Castro, Selección de discursos y artículos, 1959–1974 [Selected speeches and articles, 1959–1974] (Havana: Editora Política, 1988), pp. 132–33.

"Fidel was critical of what we had done and he was completely right. . . . The US could have used the detention of the Americans as a pretext for military intervention to try to save Batista."—Raúl Castro

Negotiations with US consular officials Park Wollam (back to camera) and Robert Wiecha (right) in July 1958 over return of 49 US and Canadian citizens—including 29 marines—detained by Second Front combatants under command of Raúl Castro. Vilma Espín, at left end of table, next to Raúl Castro, is translating.

ing space to organize and extend the Second Front. The front became a veritable "republic," as we called it then. Leadership structures for Communications, Transportation, and Education were set up, among others. We contacted Miami to have Asela de los Santos come and set up schools for the peasantry, the children, and the combatants. That was the first literacy campaign. Compañero Machado Ventura organized the Public Health Department to provide medical care for the population. Then, with support from the cities, we sent out a call for notebooks, pencils, and medicine. We brought teachers in from Santiago, Guantánamo, and all the nearby cities. Many women members of the July 26 Movement came to help out. They worked intensively on a number of projects in July, while we were negotiating the return of the captured Americans. The talks were stretched out to buy time to strengthen the front.

In late July, when I had been with the Second Front for a month, we talked about the need for me go back to Santiago. After discussing the question at length, we finally decided I would stay in the Sierra. Batista's police were hunting for me all over the city. I was too well-known there.

By then we had decided how the July 26 Movement would function in the cities under these conditions. Its basic responsibility would be to provision the fronts, provide a line of communication, and support their actions. That is, the plan of action was different. The character of the actions we foresaw was not the same as before.

Until then, the July 26 Movement in Santiago had organized the urban struggle in Oriente. From now on, it was the Second Front that held that responsibility. Other cities and towns near the Sierra Maestra came under the leadership of the First and Third Fronts.

So Santiago became the supply zone and also maintained

contact with the rest of the island. The national leaders of the movement were all in the Sierra.

The guerrilla situation had changed a great deal. The battle of El Jigüe, which ended July 21 in the victory of our forces, and the legendary campaigns of Che and Camilo [Cienfuegos, establishing operations in Las Villas province] were well under way. The war was nearly over.[46]

QUESTION: Before the victory, how was the political education of the Rebel Army approached in the Second Front?

ESPÍN: By September 1958, we were already operating our political school for officers at Tumba Siete, the José Martí School for Teachers of Combatants. As part of the effort to raise the educational level of the combatants, we set up a school for young officers who showed the most military promise, the most leadership.

I remember that Risquet gave one class, Juanito Escalona gave another, and Causse a third.[47] I was asked to teach political geography. Of course, I hadn't studied anything of the

46. In the battle of El Jigüe, July 11–21, 1958, forces commanded by Fidel Castro broke the back of the Batista dictatorship's "encircle and annihilate offensive," capturing the last major outpost in Oriente and more than two hundred forty of the dictatorship's troops. Fighting continued until August 6, when the final units of Batista's armed forces withdrew following their defeat at Las Mercedes.

On August 21, combatants under the command of Camilo Cienfuegos set out to cross Cuba. In a change of plans they established a zone of operations in northern Las Villas province. On August 31 a separate column of combatants under the command of Ernesto Che Guevara also set out on a westward march. After a grueling forty-seven days they reached the Escambray mountains of Las Villas province, where they established a front and Che took command of all forces there.

47. See glossary, Jorge Risquet, Juan Escalona, José N. Causse Pérez.

In the course of the nine months of the Second Front, an enormous effort was made to reopen schools shut down by the dictatorship and, at the same time, to create many more. . . .

The first literacy campaign carried out there was organized by our Department of Education. It was a massive undertaking because it included both Rebel Army combatants and men and women who until then had lived in the most profound ignorance. That department was led by compañera Asela de los Santos. . . .

The rebel teachers not only raised the cultural level of the combatants and the peasantry. They also helped them understand clearly why this struggle was taking place—why profound political, economic, and social change was an urgent necessity.

From time to time these educators, like our doctors, after completing their obligations in teaching or in health care, took part in missions of a military character. It was an instructive example for the peasants— this image of the future represented by the teacher-combatant or physician-combatant with a rifle in one hand and book or medical bag in the other.[*]

RAÚL CASTRO
MARCH 11, 1988

kind. My field was chemical engineering. I said it would be a bit difficult for me, explaining how I thought the subject might be taught. "Yes, that's exactly what you should do," they told me.

[*] Interview on thirtieth anniversary of Second Front, in *Bohemia*, March 11, 1988.

I got hold of books by Levi Marrero and Núñez Jiménez, as well as some pamphlets Risquet found for me—and proved to be very helpful—about the Realengo 18 struggle.[48] I didn't know anything about that struggle, but many compañeros in our columns had known people at Realengo, since those battles were fairly recent. I went through Cuban history from Hatuey to the present, explaining the US penetration and how they had crushed all the revolutionary movements.[49]

The classes were interesting. I made them fairly short and encouraged discussion. Every class was conducted that way, and it turned out to be quite fruitful. The officers who stood out in those discussions were the ones interested in learning, the ones who wanted to know more and more. Actually, these classes planted the seed that took root in many of the compañeros who later taught combatants the most advanced political courses.

QUESTION: What was the situation right before January 1?

ESPÍN: A joint attack on Guantánamo and Santiago de Cuba on January 1 was being planned. All the combatants in Fidel's column, in Almeida's column, and in the Second Front had converged.

At 6 a.m., we were in Ermita waiting to go with the troops to Guantánamo, when the woman whose house we were staying in told us Batista had fled. We immediately took off for where Fidel was staying and met up with him on the road before we got there. Right there, it was decided what we would do. We advanced toward Santiago, stopping in El Escandel.

It was decided that Raúl would go to Santiago to accept the surrender of the Moncada garrison. Three compañeros went into the city by jeep—just three. Almeida's combatants

48. See glossary, Levi Marrero, Antonio Núñez Jiménez, Realengo 18.

49. See glossary, Hatuey.

VISIÓN DE FUTURO

"As part of the effort to raise the educational level of the
combatants, we set up a school for young officers who
showed the most military promise, those who showed
leadership. We called it the José Martí School for
Teachers of Combatants."—Vilma Espín

Raúl Castro (left) with three of the instructors: Vilma Espín,
Jorge Risquet, and José Causse Pérez, Second Eastern Front,
late 1958.

had already begun to enter Santiago from Marimón, that is, from El Cobre.

After the surrender of the Moncada garrison, Raúl spoke to the troops and returned to his own forces. Fidel had already talked to the officers in the navy. That night we all went into the city.

The entry into Santiago was tremendous. We came in by way of Vista Alegre, along the highway from El Caney. Women ran out into the street in groups, and men, in their pajamas, ran after the jeeps. It was really something.

I was dead tired since I hadn't slept for days, so I went right to bed. Pretty soon someone called me and said, "Fidel's already at city hall. He's going to speak." When I got there, I saw quite a scene. The police chief, Haza, was there wearing a July 26 armband, and the mothers of the martyrs were furious.[50]

Fidel departed immediately for Havana, leaving Raúl in command of the garrison in Santiago, giving Fidel time to get to Havana. Raúl remained at the garrison with those men and all their arms until, finally, they were sent to Havana, where Batista's army was demobilized.

The first few days, the mothers of the martyrs went to talk with Raúl.

"Do you have confidence in us?" Raúl asked them.

They said yes.

"Then don't worry," he told them.

Very soon, right after the final trial, revolutionary justice was meted out to the most notorious thugs and murderers.

QUESTION: In the underground you used a nom de guerre . . .

ESPÍN: I had several. While Frank was leading the general staff out of my house and I was making the telephone con-

---

50. Bonifacio Haza, chief of police in Santiago de Cuba, was tried, convicted, and executed for his crimes in January 1959.

**"On January 1, when we learned Batista had fled, we met
up with Fidel and advanced toward Santiago, stopping in
El Escandel. . . . The entry into Santiago was tremendous.
Women ran into the streets and men, in their pajamas,
ran after the jeeps. . . . Fidel left immediately for Havana,
leaving Raúl in command of the garrison in Santiago."**

—Vilma Espín

January 1, 1959, meeting at El Escandel, where Fidel Castro (left)
organized surrender of Moncada with Colonel José Rego Rubido
(right), the garrison's former commander. At center is Celia Sánchez;
Raúl Castro is partially hidden by Rego Rubido.

tacts, I used the name "Alicia." But the authorities captured Frank's address book with that name and my phone number.

Then either Frank or Taras Domitro gave me the name "Monica." That's what I was called until Frank's death. Frank was called "Salvador" at first, then "David." But at the end he was known as "Cristián." When he was captured, he had on him a little notebook of addresses and telephone numbers, in which the name "Monica" appeared. A couple of days later I left home, almost by intuition, and the next day they came looking for me and searched the house.

So I had to change my name again, and, since several of the pseudonyms began with "D," it was decided to call me "Débora." In the Second Front, they called me "Mariela," but "Débora" is the name that was best known.

QUESTION: What difficulties did you run into as a woman in the movement leadership?

ESPÍN: Nobody ever considered being a woman a problem. And I don't mean just in terms of organizing, because there were women who were heads of action, too. Besides, in Santiago de Cuba, for example, young men were in constant danger of being picked up and searched by the police if they went out at night, especially after November 30. But women didn't run as much risk.

So women acted as messengers, carried medicine and weapons, and even began to transport dynamite and carry out sabotage. The work was often done in couples, because a couple always aroused less suspicion than a group or a person alone. Women had a very important place and were very active during that stage of the struggle.

PART II

Birth of the Federation
of Cuban Women

★ MUJERES ★

"The first time in the history of the Cuban press that a poor woman, with black skin, brightened the cover of a magazine with her smile was the November 15, 1961, issue of *Mujeres*."

So explained Rolando Alfonso Borges, member of Communist Party's Central Committee, at November 2011 meeting in Havana, marking 50th anniversary of *Mujeres* (Women). **Above:** Cover of first issue of magazine, launched by Federation of Cuban Women after bourgeois women's publication *Vanidades* (Vanities) was taken over by workers.

Introduction to Part II

The defeat of the Batista dictatorship—sealed by a mass nation-wide armed insurrection and general strike in the opening days of January 1959—led to a deepening revolutionary mobilization of working people across Cuba. This momentous popular up-heaval was registered in countless ways. One of the most im-portant was the response of growing numbers of women who wanted to be part of the revolution. They began creating what became, in fact, their own organization—as yet without a name or structure—to participate in the social battles that were open-ing the first socialist revolution in the Americas.

Land reform was one of the first and most far-reaching so-cial measures of the revolution. Millions of acres of vast US- and Cuban-owned plantations were confiscated under the May 1959 decree, which set a thousand-acre limit on holdings and estab-lished that peasants working the land would now hold title to it. In an act expressing the profoundly popular character of the new government, the first of the hundred thousand deeds was issued to Engracia Blet, a peasant from Baracoa in eastern Cuba who was a woman. This transformation of social relations on the land struck a devastating blow to US imperialist families and corpo-rations and to the Cuban capitalist class, whose profits came largely from exploiting the backbreaking labor of Cuba's landless rural poor in the island's cane fields and sugar mills.

In early 1961, tens of thousands of young women, most still in their teens, joined the quarter million volunteers who, in one year's time, wiped out illiteracy. Having won their parents' consent, they spread out to the most isolated corners of the country to live, work, and study together with peasant families. In prerevolutionary Cuba, women accounted for fifty-five percent of adults who could neither read nor write, and a much higher portion in the countryside. Fifty-nine percent of literacy brigade volunteers were women. For most it was an experience that transformed them—as well as those they taught—for life.

As the revolution deepened, many women joined emergency medical brigades to learn to treat those wounded in combat defending Cuba against US-backed counterrevolutionary forces. Women organized public health brigades to carry out vaccination programs, broaden education on nutrition and hygiene, and improve basic sanitary conditions for all. They helped open public primary and secondary schools for children of all ages and led the campaign to start raising the adult educational level as well. They insisted on being organized into the Revolutionary National Militias, to be prepared to fight arms in hand.

With the support of the revolutionary government, women organized schools to acquire much needed skills and teach those skills to others. They learned how to sew and make clothes for their families. They trained for jobs as office workers, bank tellers, taxi drivers, mechanics, poultry farmers, tractor operators, and more. As women entered the work force in increasing numbers, they helped build child care centers and set up schools to train women to staff them. They organized to open a productive future for the some one hundred thousand prostitutes and their children entrapped in degrading conditions of brothels. They joined in the battle to eliminate race discrimination, to eradicate the institutions and "customs" that fostered racial prejudices and divisions, on which capitalist exploitation had depended for centuries. They shouldered leadership responsibilities in neighborhood committees, trade unions, the small farmers association, high school and university student organizations, and the consolidation of political forces out of which the Communist Party of Cuba was founded in 1965.

Washington and its Cuban capitalist and landlord allies used every means at their disposal to try to crush the new government and erase what to them was the unimaginable example being set by Cuba. Cane fields and sugar mills were firebombed. Neighborhoods, stores, and ships at dock in Havana harbor were targeted for terror attacks. Counterrevolutionary bands, supplied with armaments by Washington, carried out murderous raids. These attacks included the brutal slaying of young literacy brigade volunteers and members of the peasant families they were teaching to read and write.

The US rulers slashed sugar imports and opened an economic war against the Cuban people, a war—now in its sixth decade—whose goal remains to crush the toilers' revolution. Washington organized the April 1961 mercenary invasion at the Bay of Pigs, which was defeated at Playa Girón by Cuba's volunteer militias, armed forces, and police in fewer than seventy-two hours. And they threatened the people of Cuba with nuclear annihilation in retribution for their attempts to defend their country.

Millions of Cubans responded to these counterrevolutionary attacks by demonstrating their determination to defend their conquests, arms in hand. They responded by deepening the social and economic transformation of conditions they had inherited, winning ever-broadening support as they did so. Women joined in these class battles in massive numbers, transforming not only themselves but the men together with whom—shoulder to shoulder—they built, taught, and fought.

Asela de los Santos, Vilma Espín, Yolanda Ferrer (left to right), 2004.

What It Meant to Be Female Began to Change

INTERVIEW WITH YOLANDA FERRER

THIS INTERVIEW HAS BEEN some seventeen years in the making. It took shape during trips through the provinces, at meetings and discussions with local chapters of the Federation of Cuban Women, and in conversations while climbing up Buey Arriba or crossing the Zapata Swamp after Hurricane Lili.[1]

Preparations for events celebrating the FMC's fortieth anniversary in 2001 provided the spark to put it down in writing. Due to the daily press of events in a country in revolution—and the fact that necessary and just social transformations are seen as natural—the integration of women into every facet of society has not always been fully appreciated for its far-reaching, profoundly new, creative, and revolutionary scope. That integration led to rethinking and broadening what had traditionally been considered the role of women and that of men.

That's why we decided to pull together conversations—ones that had been scattered here and there—and put them in interview format.

Interview given to Isabel Moya, director of Editorial de la Mujer, published as "1961—A Tremendous Year" in *Mujeres*, magazine of the Federation of Cuban Women, issue no. 2 (April–June), 2001.

Interviewed here is Yolanda Ferrer, general secretary of the Federation of Cuban Women. She comes with her usual energy and with even more dreams than when she first showed up at the FMC offices in Casa de las Américas a little more than forty years ago, when she was barely in her teens.[2]

ISABEL MOYA: How did the FMC succeed, so soon after it began, in developing such ambitious and widely different projects as the Ana Betancourt School for peasant women, the child care centers, and the public health brigades?

YOLANDA FERRER: It was the power of the revolution itself. That's what made it possible. By that I mean the patriotic fervor, the sense of responsibility, the discipline, dedication, and enthusiasm of the leadership of the revolution at every level, as well as of the FMC membership, of women getting involved in massive numbers to take part in the work of the revolution.

It was the determination of revolutionary women who asked to be organized—that's how the federation was created. They wanted to participate, to contribute to that incredibly wonderful process that began January 1, 1959, opening the doors to a new life full of freedom, independence, sovereignty,

1. See map, pp. 50–51. Buey Arriba is a mountainous area in eastern Cuba; combatants under Ernesto Che Guevara fought several battles there in 1957 and 1958. The Zapata Swamp is a sparsely inhabited coastal region in southern Cuba. Both the Bay of Pigs, the site where the US-backed mercenary invasion of Cuba took place in 1961, and Playa Girón, where the counterrevolutionary forces were decisively defeated seventy-two hours later, are located there. Hurricane Lili pounded the area in October 1996.

2. Casa de las Américas houses the Latin American cultural organization of the same name established in 1959, under the leadership of Haydée Santamaría, who served as its president for more than two decades.

and social justice. For the first time in history, we could see the possibility of a promising and happy future for all.

When our organization was officially founded August 23, 1960, we were already building on more than a year of work. Thousands of women were organized in hundreds of local chapters across the country. We were already carrying out very important work, such as recruiting and training women who had the necessary minimum level of education to be elementary school teachers. We were drawing in the street children and making sure they were being cared for. We were working to motivate and convince parents to enroll their children in school and not miss classes. We were mobilizing women to build schools and hospitals. We organized participation in the first public health programs and initiated the first emergency medical courses. And more.

Organizing what became the FMC began with preparations for Cuban women to take part in the Congress for the Rights of Women and Children, held in Santiago, Chile, in November 1959. It had been convened by the Women's International Democratic Federation. We received the invitation in May and set up a national committee to sponsor participation. Then we set up provincial and citywide committees, drawing in compañeras who had distinguished themselves in the struggle, as well as mothers and wives of martyrs killed in combat.

These groups—which we initiated in the Sierra Maestra, in towns, rural areas, and cities—later became the organizational basis of the federation. They explained the aims of the congress in Chile and the questions it would take up, seeking to increase consciousness about the conditions and needs of women in the underdeveloped world.[3] Responding

3. For Vilma Espín's account of organizing participation in the Chile congress, see pp. 217–21.

"Organizing what became the FMC began with preparations to take part in a women's congress held in Chile in November 1959. We set up committees across the country involving compañeras who had distinguished themselves in the struggle, as well as mothers and wives of martyrs killed in combat."—Yolanda Ferrer

Part of the Cuban delegation of more than 80 at Havana airport, bound for Chile. Vilma Espín is just left of center, with beret.

to the thousands who were asking what they could do for the revolution, they mobilized women around a wide variety of tasks.

When we returned from Chile, we decided to continue laying the groundwork for a nationwide women's organization in Cuba. Local units elected their leaders. We worked to carry out the decisions of the congress and took on the most urgent tasks of the day.

Though it had yet to be officially constituted, the women's organization we were building grew stronger. It already had a small leadership group made up of representatives from every sector that had helped prepare the delegation to the event in Chile.

The FMC was created to bring together all revolutionary Cuban women to work and fight for their country. We wanted to prepare them to participate actively and effectively in the economic, political, cultural, and social life of the country. This required many different programs, all of them urgently needed.

In those days, women were greatly limited by social norms. They were expected to restrict their interests to the confines of the home and to subordinate themselves to the males in the family. But there was enormous political ferment, and women felt they had to support and defend the revolution. They wanted to volunteer to work wherever needed. These feelings were so strong they led women to break with traditions going back thousands of years.

Moreover, the examples of Vilma Espín, Celia Sánchez, Melba Hernández, and Haydée Santamaría—women who had fought in the underground struggle and then in the Rebel Army—were very important in this process.

Attacks by our enemy began immediately after the victory in January 1959. Women responded, making clear they weren't going to allow their revolution to be snatched away. They requested emergency medical training, and the federation organized courses across the country. They joined the Revolutionary National Militia, established in October 1959. Tens of thousands of housewives and working women, who had never before handled weapons or treated the wounded, decided to join in defending their country.

At the official founding August 23, 1960, our commander in chief Fidel Castro assigned the organization a number of very important tasks, including the ones you mention—the Ana Betancourt School for campesinas and the establishment of child care centers. Later many other tasks were added, including the historic literacy campaign of 1961 and, amid all that nonstop activity, there was the battle of Playa Girón (Bay of Pigs).

With all her talents, capable leadership, and inexhaustible capacity for work, Vilma shouldered central responsibility in successfully bringing to fruition all those projects. She led an accomplished team of compañeras who, in turn, took on the huge load of work we faced. They did it responsibly and with love.

To mention just one of the federation's tasks, consider the careful and persuasive work required to launch the Ana Betancourt School, something done at the same time the federation itself was being organized. There's no better assessment of that process than the one by our commander in chief. In July 1961, at the graduation of the first class of eight hundred women from the Ana Betancourt School, Fidel said:

> It was no simple task. First, to house and care for such a large number of students, we had to find facilities that were adequate. Then these had to be adapted, to provide them with whatever was necessary to turn them into

schools. Perhaps even more difficult was organizing the schools themselves, providing teachers and administrators. Another difficult task was the selection of the students. We wanted them to represent all areas of Cuba in the countryside, the mountains, and the plains.

Fidel added:

> One can easily talk of a figure of 10,000, 12,000, 14,000 students. But it's something quite different to organize them, care for them fully, see to each aspect of what they need, and prepare them in every way. That's an undertaking ambitious enough to overwhelm even the most determined person. But in fact, the same thing happened with the schools that happened with many other things in the revolution—what happened in real life surpassed the most ambitious aspirations.[4]

MOYA: Many of these programs involved new, qualitatively superior ways of approaching what today we call the "gender" question. What do you think about this?

FERRER: Vilma always explains that in the early years of the revolution, we didn't even use the term "equality." We spoke of the full participation of women.

The challenge was to change the way women—and the entire population—thought about women's role and place in society. It was necessary to raise women's sense of dignity. The federation began by focusing on simple tasks that motivated women to reach beyond the home, that made them

4. Speech in Havana, July 31, 1961, at first graduation ceremony of the Ana Betancourt School. In *Mujeres y Revolución* (Havana: Editorial de la Mujer, 2006, 2010), pp. 43–44.

It has been proven that not only men can fight, but in Cuba women also fight, too. The best evidence is the Mariana Grajales Platoon, which so distinguished itself in numerous battles. Women make excellent soldiers, as good as our best male soldiers. . . .

At the beginning, there was a lot of prejudice. There were men who asked how we could give a rifle to a woman when a man was available. Within our own ranks, women remain a layer that needs to be liberated, since they are still victims of discrimination on the job and in other aspects of life.

So we organized the women's unit. They demonstrated that women can fight. A people whose women fight alongside men—that people is invincible. . . .

We will organize female combatants, female militias; we will keep them trained—all of them, on a voluntary basis. And to all the young women I see here with their dresses draped in the red and black of the July 26 Movement, I ask you to learn how to handle weapons.[*]

FIDEL CASTRO
JANUARY 1, 1959

aware of their own possibilities, capacities, self worth, and rights.

As we said in the report to the FMC's second congress in November 1974, we had a dual goal from the beginning. Through political education we wanted to increase consciousness about the tasks that were necessary, while the tasks themselves be-

[*] Speech in Santiago de Cuba, January 1, 1959, in *Mujeres y Revolución*, pp. 31–32.

came vehicles to advance our political education.

This included sewing classes. Women were very interested in learning how to make clothes for themselves and their families. It included voluntary work to harvest crops before they spoiled, or to sell agricultural products. It included classes in emergency medical treatment, so women could participate in defense. It included the literacy campaign and initial steps to raise women's educational level.

Women learned they were capable of the most diverse kinds of activities. As they demonstrated what they could do, they increasingly won social respect. Prejudices began to lose ground.

From the first day of the revolution, what it meant to be female began to change. In his first address to the nation, from Santiago de Cuba, on January 1, 1959, our commander in chief said it had been proven that in Cuba not only men but women, too, could fight. The Mariana Grajales Women's Platoon, he said, had given eloquent proof that women soldiers were as good as the best of men.

Subsequently, in his speech at the closing of the FMC's first congress in October 1962, Fidel said, "In the world we are building, all vestiges of discrimination against women must disappear." And he added, "But even when all vestiges of discrimination—both legal and objective—disappear, there will still be a whole series of natural circumstances and customs that makes it important for women to be organized, to work and fight."[5]

In that speech, Fidel talked about advancing women to

5. The congress took place on October 1, two weeks before the US administration of John F. Kennedy launched what in the United States is called the "Cuban Missile Crisis" (see "October 1962 'Missile' Crisis" in glossary). The excerpt from Castro's speech at the FMC conference can be found in *Mujeres y Revolución*, p. 89.

In our country, women were denied access to many jobs. Only now are we beginning to open the road to women's participation in many job categories. In the past, for example, it wasn't easy to find a woman manager of a factory or sugar mill. This was the product of custom, above all of the prejudice and discrimination under which women lived in the previous society.

It's necessary that women keep advancing, not only in manual labor but also in intellectual work. It's significant, for example, that for a course that will begin within a week, preparing for medical school, young women make up more than five hundred of the twelve hundred applicants. Women's presence in science will be a much higher proportion than in the past.

Not only is it fair that women have the opportunity to develop their capacity to benefit society. For society to advance, it's also necessary that all possibilities be opened to women to develop their full potential.[*]

FIDEL CASTRO
OCTOBER 1, 1962

leadership responsibilities, eliminating barriers to integration in manual and intellectual labor, to women's presence in the sciences, in nontraditional jobs, and to their right to fully develop their capacities. He explained clearly how domestic work had enslaved women throughout history, how women had traditionally been relegated to domestic responsibilities such as cooking.

In his historic speech at the conclusion of the FMC's fifth national leadership meeting in December 1966, Fidel said

[*] In *Mujeres y Revolución*, pp. 89–90.

women were making a revolution within the revolution. He said that the most revolutionary thing happening was the revolution taking place among women. He explained that women in previous societies had been doubly discriminated against and degraded, both on account of their class and of their sex.

I want to remind you of a part of Fidel's speech that I consider very important. He spoke of compañera Osoria Herrera and her leadership in the Banao project.[6] The skilled personnel and administrative staff there were almost all women, he said, and they had shown a great sense of responsibility, discipline, and enthusiasm. Fidel added:

> This is one of the great lessons we spoke about before; one of the great lessons and perhaps one of the greatest victories over prejudices that have existed, not for decades or centuries but for millennia. Over the belief that all a woman was good for was to scrub, wash, iron, cook, keep house, and bear children—age-old prejudices that placed women in an inferior position in society. In effect, women did not have a productive place in society.
>
> Such prejudices are thousands of years old and have survived through various social systems. If we consider capitalism, women—that is, working women—were doubly exploited, doubly humiliated. A poor woman, whether a worker or belonging to a working-class family, was exploited simply because of her humbler status, because she was a worker.
>
> Moreover, within her own class, as a working woman, she was looked down on and underrated. Not only was

6. An agricultural development program in the Escambray Mountains of central Cuba, focused on producing fruit and vegetables.

she underestimated, exploited, and looked down on by the
exploiting classes, but even within her own class she was
the object of countless prejudices.[7]

In the program we approved at the FMC's First Congress, in
October 1962, we adopted the goal of forging a new woman. A
woman who could utilize all her rights, both within the family as well as in political life. A woman actively incorporated
into the workforce and social life. A woman freed from the
system of domestic slavery, in which housework absorbs all
her time and energy.

In the early 1960s in our country, we sought to highlight the
way society had traditionally imposed and perpetuated different responsibilities expected of women and men, and we
sought to change that situation. Since its founding, the federation has tried to bring about concrete changes in the way
women—and men, too—think and act.

We were motivated by women's determination to participate and the need to incorporate them into the colossal effort
that the entire people, led by Fidel, was making. We wanted
to turn each of the rights the revolution guaranteed to women
into a reality, so they could become fuller human beings.

Ideas regarding women's social role began to change in
Cuba as a result of the revolution and the work of the federation. Women started to burst into public life. They began to
confront and destroy stereotypes that were deeply rooted in
a culture of discrimination.

Women learned to read and write. They took classes, became workers, militia members, scientists, intellectuals, professionals in the most diverse specialties, leaders. The "des-

7. In *Women and the Cuban Revolution* (Pathfinder, 1981), pp. 67–68
[2011 printing]. Also in *Mujeres y Revolución*, p. 118.

tiny" of Cuban women ceased being solely wives, mothers, and housekeepers.

From the time we began them in April 1961, programs in child care centers have focused on what we today call gender education. In these important institutions, girls and boys receive a nonsexist education, sharing the same toys and responsibilities.

It was at the FMC's second congress in November of 1974 that we began to speak—to use the words of our commander in chief—of the battle for the full exercise of women's rights. We did a detailed study of what we had achieved and what remained to be won. We evaluated the factors—objective, subjective, material, and political—within which we were fighting to advance the scope and weight of women's participation and leadership.

By then the federation was working to educate around the Family Code.[8] That dealt another big blow to stereotypes. Among its many advanced ideas, the code stressed the responsibility of both spouses to care for the family they had created and to work together to educate and guide the children and run the household. The duty to share domestic chores and care for the children was made explicit. These laws were discussed and debated by the entire country.

The documents and results of our congress served as a basis for the theses and resolution on women's equality adopted by our party's first congress the following year, in December 1975. That document set a goal of eliminating every manifestation of discrimination. Among many other things, it explained the need for couples to share housework, noting

8. Adopted in February 1975, the Family Code replaced prerevolutionary laws on marriage, divorce, adoption, and alimony. For major excerpts, see *Women and the Cuban Revolution*, pp. 182–200.

the injustice of women's greater workload. Regarding the question of sexual relations, it was also affirmed that there cannot be one set of moral standards for women and another for men.[9]

In the early 1970s, all over the world, there began to be more talk about women's equality. When a United Nations Conference on Woman adopted initial goals for action, Cuban women had already been working for many years to accomplish such goals. And we had important gains to show for it.

No other head of state or world political leader had made such important statements on gender equality as Fidel (to use today's terminology). In 1974 he said the struggle to end discrimination against women, the struggle for equality and the integration of women, had to be waged by all of society. He emphasized that it was a task, above all, for our party, our educational institutions, and all our mass organizations. We should remember that historic declaration in his speech at our second congress in 1974:

> The day must come when we have a party of men and women, a leadership of men and women, a state of men and women, and a government of men and women. And I believe that all compañeros are aware that this is a necessity of the revolution, of society, and of history.[10]

It fills us with pride to say that, from the time of the battle to today, Fidel has been a true standard-bearer of the struggle for women's equality in all areas and on all levels of economic,

9. See "Theses on the Full Exercise of Women's Equality," in *Women and the Cuban Revolution*, pp. 97–137.

10. *Women and the Cuban Revolution*, pp. 94–95. *Mujeres y Revolución*, pp. 164–65.

"From the first day of the revolution, what it meant to be female began to change. Prejudice started to lose ground."

YOLANDA FERRER

GRANMA

COURTESY TETÉ PUEBLA

Above: Santiago de Cuba, January 1, 1959: Fidel Castro, Raúl Castro, and Luis Orlando Rodríguez (right to left) on balcony of city hall. "Women make excellent soldiers, as good as our best men," said Fidel Castro in victorious Rebel Army's first address to Cuban people. "The best evidence is the Mariana Grajales Platoon."

Inset: Members of Mariana Grajales Platoon in Freedom Caravan, January 1959. The caravan traveled from Santiago to Havana, greeted by outpourings of popular support in every town along the way.

"After the victory of the revolution, many women felt their place was no longer limited to the home. There was a whole field of action, of work, of struggle, they intended to be part of."

ASELA DE LOS SANTOS

VERDE OLIVO

BOHEMIA

Above: Women training as emergency medical aides learn how to tape broken arm, late 1960. "The federation organized Emergency Response Brigades for women who wanted to take an active part in defense against US-backed mercenaries," said Vilma Espín. The brigades were organized "through the armed forces to be ready to act in time of war." **Inset:** Workers at La Filosofía department store in Havana support nationalization of imperialist-owned enterprises, August 1960, in response to Washington's stepped-up assault on revolution.

La presidencia, integrada por las delegadas de cada provincia y de las organizaciones femeninas nacionales, declara la unidad de la mujer cubana,

Fuerza indestructible es la unidad de mujeres cubanas

ORGANO DEL MOVI-
MIENTO 26 DE JULIO

"A women's organization was created because women themselves demanded it," said Vilma Espín.

Above: Presiding committee at founding of FMC, August 23, 1960; Espín at center. Delegates came from each province and several national women's organizations. "Unity of Cuban women is an inde-structible force," says headline of daily *Revolución*.

Below: Fidel Castro, Celia Sánchez (center), and Espín at FMC founding. At the time, Espín said, Fidel "had a much clearer idea than we did of the degree of inequality that existed in our society and what we needed to do."

"Who will take the revolution into the homes of the peasants? Their own daughters."

FIDEL CASTRO, 1960

BOHEMIA

FEDERATION OF CUBAN WOMEN

During first four years of revolution, more than 21,000 young women from rural Cuba came to Havana to attend the Ana Betancourt School. "The first political cadres to emerge in the mountain areas were women," said Espín—among them many "Anitas," as graduates of the school were called.

Above: Learning to measure and cut fabric. **Inset:** Graduation ceremony of 8,000 "Anitas," December 1961. Each graduate received a sewing machine and pledged to teach ten others how to sew. "The graduates hadn't just learned to read and write; they hadn't just learned to sew," Espín said. "They had also learned about the revolution."

GRANMA

"Schools were created for women who used to work as maids in houses abandoned by the bourgeoisie," said Vilma Espín. "When the owners left Cuba, they left their servants with nothing. So we created schools to teach them skills." **Above:** Part of graduating class of former domestic workers trained as taxi drivers, 1961. **Inset:** Cartoon on cover of 1961 Cuban humor magazine parodies bourgeois woman's shock at encountering her former maid, now a bank worker.

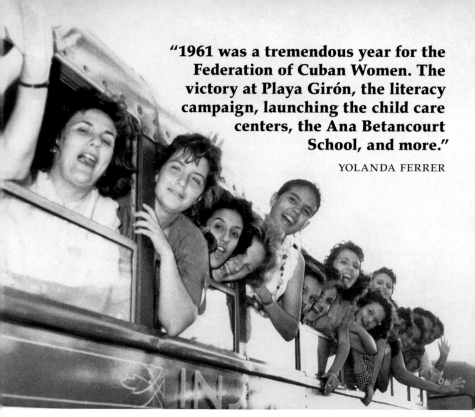

> **"1961 was a tremendous year for the Federation of Cuban Women. The victory at Playa Girón, the literacy campaign, launching the child care centers, the Ana Betancourt School, and more."**
>
> YOLANDA FERRER

ABOVE: GRANMA

RAÚL CORRALES

GRANMA

JUVENTUD REBELDE

Above: Cuban teacher in Nicaragua's Atlantic Coast region, 1981. "In 1979, when Nicaragua asked for 2,000 teachers, 30,000 Cubans volunteered," said Fidel Castro in 1998. "When some were murdered by US-organized counterrevolutionary bands, another 100,000 volunteered!"

Below: Lieutenant Milagros Katrina Soto (center) and other members of Women's Antiaircraft Artillery Regiment, serving in Angola, 1988, defending country against invasions by US-backed apartheid regime of South Africa. Giving women the opportunity to fight as part of Cuba's 16-year internationalist mission in Angola was "a moral necessity, a revolutionary necessity," said Fidel Castro.

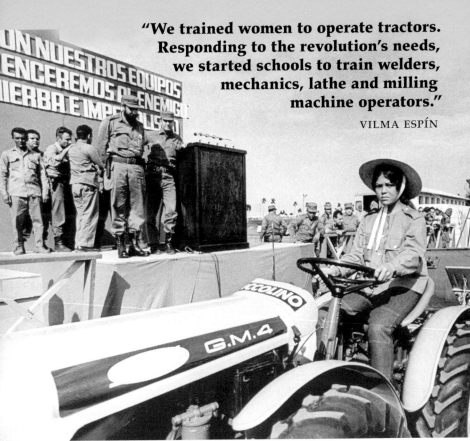

> "We trained women to operate tractors. Responding to the revolution's needs, we started schools to train welders, mechanics, lathe and milling machine operators."

VILMA ESPÍN

GRANMA

JOSÉ RICARDO LÓPEZ HEVIA/GRANMA

Above: Havana, September 1968, Fidel Castro reviews graduates of first class of 196 women tractor drivers, known as "Las Piccolinas" after nickname for small Italian tractors they operated. **Below:** Students in laboratory at Havana School of Chemistry, March 2011. In 2009, 64 percent of Cuba's doctors and 52 percent of university graduates were women.

MUJERES

RAÚL GONZÁLEZ/BOHEMIA

Above: Workers at Comandante Ernesto Che Guevara nickel processing plant at Moa Bay in eastern Cuba. "At Moa Bay, nontraditional has become traditional," said FMC magazine *Mujeres* in 1997. Women comprised one quarter of 2,000 engineers, electricians, chemists, geologists, warehouse workers, and quality-control inspectors there.

Below: Learning to use torch at technical school, 1971. "Women's participation in the labor force has increased enormously," said Espín. "In the process, women have become more conscious of their contributions to society."

"The 54 child care centers we built in less than a year are a symbol of the rectification process, a symbol of the people's strength, of our ability to transform Cuba if we take the right direction."

FIDEL CASTRO, DECEMBER 30, 1987

PHOTOS: BOHEMIA

Above: Newly built child care center, 1990. **Inset:** Workers in volunteer construction brigade, many of them women, build child care center, late 1980s. Construction minibrigades launched in 1986 grew to more than 30,000 volunteer workers. Beforehand only one child care center a year was being built in Havana. "Those who advocated reactionary ideas within the revolution argued that building child care centers was an unnecessary social expense," said Fidel Castro.

Above: Minibrigade members construct apartment building in Havana, January 1988. "We revived voluntary work," said Espín. "We renewed its role in training new generations, in harnessing the creative activity of people in solving their own problems."

Below: Members of Communist Youth and other volunteers pack plantains in Holguín province, September 1994, during worst months of 1990s economic contraction precipitated by cutoff of Soviet Union's trade and aid. Crisis ended new construction plans and expansion of production, but Federation of Cuban Women waged successful fight to halt decline in women's rate of participation in workforce.

> "One of the ways our revolution will be judged in years to come is how we have resolved the problems facing women in our society and our country."
>
> FIDEL CASTRO, 1974

PHOTOS: EDGAR BATISTA/AHORA

Above: FMC-organized march and rally of 5,000 women in Holguín, Cuba, November 19, 2011, demands freedom for Gerardo Hernández, Ramón Labañino, Antonio Guerrero, Fernando González, and René González—five Cuban revolutionaries framed and imprisoned by Washington since 1998. **Inset:** Among those on front line were (from right) Rosa Aurora Freijanes and Elizabeth Palmeiro, wives of Fernando and Ramón; Magali Llort (fourth from right) and Mirta Rodríguez (foreground), mothers of Fernando and Antonio; and Roselia Taño (behind Mirta, clapping), FMC general secretary in Holguín province.

True equality between men and women can become a reality only when the exploitation of both by capital has been abolished, and private work in the home has been transformed into a public industry.[*]

FREDERICK ENGELS
JULY 5, 1885

Women cannot complain about the *"International,"* as it has just appointed a lady, Madame Law, as a member of the *General Council*. . . . [V]ery great progress was registered at the last congress of the American *"Labor Union,"* which among other things treats the women workers with full equality, whereas a very narrow-minded spirit burdens the British and even more so the gallant French on this matter.

Anyone who knows anything about history knows too that great social revolutions are impossible without female ferment. Social progress can be precisely measured by the social position of the [female sex].[†]

KARL MARX
DECEMBER 5, 1868

---

[*] Letter to Gertrud Guillaume-Shack, in *Karl Marx, Frederick Engels, Collected Works* (New York: International Publishers, 1975–2004), vol. 47, p. 312.

[†] Letter to Ludwig Kugelmann, in *Collected Works*, vol. 43, p. 185 (translation above by Pathfinder). Harriet Law, a campaigner for atheism in Britain and—almost unheard of for the time—a champion of women's right to vote, served on the General Council of the International Working Men's Association from 1867 until the IWMA's final congress in 1872.

political, cultural, and social life in our country.

MOYA: Integrating women into public life, into nontraditional jobs, into the literacy campaign, into tasks that challenged what was viewed as appropriate for women—what was the reaction to all this? How did this process unfold?

FERRER: It was an intense process. Tens of thousands of women became actively involved, propelled by their desire and determination to help convince and motivate all revolutionary Cuban women to study, to work, to integrate themselves into the country's political, economic, cultural, and social life.

In voluntary work women discovered their capacities, skills, and potential. In the fields and factories, they demonstrated their sense of responsibility and discipline; in the trenches, their determination to defend the future conquered with so much blood; in the classrooms, their eagerness to raise their educational and cultural level in order to contribute to building a new life. In the communities, they showed their aptitude and alertness to spotting neighbors who needed help and taking preventive action, for advancing education and public health programs. In confronting the enemy, they proved their combativity and revolutionary fervor.

Participating in this way, women discovered themselves as they won the respect and admiration of their compañeros, husbands, fathers, and children. Because shoulder to shoulder with them, they shared the work and struggle to fulfill the aims of the revolution. Women gained in stature—in their own eyes and throughout society. They entered into public life as farmers, raisers of poultry and rabbits, tractor operators, taxi drivers, bank workers, watch repairers, soldiers, militia members, factory workers, directors and assistants in child care centers, teachers, social workers, participants in emergency medical brigades, health care workers, and leaders of the FMC and other mass organizations.

They enriched the work of all with their talent, optimism, and certainty of victory. It was a historic transformation of women's place in the family and society.

MOYA: Was 1961 a tremendous year for the FMC?

FERRER: Without a doubt, it was tremendous. When the mercenaries attacked at Playa Girón in April 1961, the FMC threw all its forces into action. The emergency medical brigades were mobilized, and at Ciudad Libertad[11] they formed the Medical Services Auxiliary Corps of the Revolutionary Armed Forces. They left for Matanzas province to carry out their mission, and provided medical care on an equal basis both for the cowardly mercenaries and for our heroic combatants.

Members of the federation helped supply food for emergency medical stations near the combat zones, as well as serving in a hundred kitchens and three hospitals. We mobilized women to fill in on the job for combatants who had been called to the front. We collected donations of clothes, medicine, and food.

At the same time, the federation had responsibility in 1961 for the young peasant women at the Ana Betancourt School. More than 12,000 young women graduated from the school that year.

The federation was also responsible for maintaining the first school for directors, assistants, and health counselors of the children's circles, the child care centers we were creating. We raised funds to convert houses into child care centers and to build new ones.

We also set up night schools for the advancement of domestic workers in 1961, as well as classes to teach driving, typing,

11. See footnote 22.

stenography, and other office skills.

And thousands of federation members were engaged in the great literacy campaign, as well. That was the year our country was able to declare itself free of illiteracy. The federation took part in the literacy councils at all levels, participated in the literacy census, and mobilized women as literacy brigade teachers. The federation worked to encourage women who couldn't read or write to begin taking classes. In more than a few cases, federation members took care of other women's children and housework, so those women could study.

Federation members served as literacy brigade leaders, organized hostels to house young literacy teachers, traveled with them, and stayed with them until the task was accomplished. Others took care of literacy volunteers requiring hospital care, or distributed mail to them.

Thousands of compañeras opened their homes to brigade members in transit, or who needed a place to live, taking care of them as if they were their own children.

To allow teachers to continue as literacy volunteers until the end of the campaign, federation members took teachers' places in classrooms. They organized recreational and educational activities, choruses, bands, and excursions for the children, teaching them arts, crafts, and gardening.

FMC members mobilized for volunteer work in construction and in making clothes for children in the child care centers. After the nationalization of the [bourgeois women's] magazine *Vanidades* [Vanities], the federation launched and assumed editorial responsibility for our own magazine, *Mujeres* [Women]. We inaugurated our national school for leadership development.

In 1961 we were also the driving force behind major public health campaigns in rural areas and poorer communities. We taught women various aspects of health and home hygiene,

Yolanda Ferrer, general secretary of Federation of Cuban Women, presents President Raúl Castro with Pledge of Cuban Women on 50th anniversary of FMC's founding, August 23, 2010.

"Today's society bears little resemblance to the capitalist past," the document affirms. "Old forms of thinking and acting have been transformed, but we know a long road still lies ahead."

such as how to boil milk and water and how to prepare different foods. We educated women and their families about the importance of giving birth in a medical center.

And I forgot to mention that the federation also took on important responsibilities in the drive to expand poultry farming, since the country needed to increase egg production.

Our organization lived up to the confidence placed in it by women and by our commander in chief. In 1961 we rose to the demands of that historic, unforgettable moment of the revolution.

With No Preconceived Structure or Agenda

INTERVIEW WITH VILMA ESPÍN

THE FEDERATION OF CUBAN WOMEN was launched on August 23, 1960. In reality, however, we had been laying the foundations for more than a year.

In 1959, the first year after the triumph, women wanted to organize to participate more effectively in the tasks of the revolution, and we responded to this pressure. I remember being struck, in the first months after the January 1 victory, by the large number of women, some carrying babies, who took part in demonstrations and street actions. There was strong support for the revolution, even before it had demonstrated its full meaning.

Women who were already organized in various small groups approached me. They wrote letters; they asked to meet. These included people from the women's sections of the political parties that supported the revolution. Others came from religious organizations, such as groups of Catholic and Baptist women. There were trade union members—from the garment union, for example. There were peasant women. And, of course, there were women who had taken part in the war.

Excerpted from October 1987 account given to José Estrada Menéndez of the Film Studios of the Revolutionary Armed Forces. In Vilma Espín, *La mujer en Cuba* [Women in Cuba] (Havana: Editora Política, 1990).

As you might expect, those of us who had participated in the war—whether in the urban underground or in the mountains—were approached by women who wanted to do precisely what we had done, to take part in the revolution. They looked to us for leadership.

"What can we do?" they asked.

"How can we show our support for the revolution?"

"What's needed most?"

They asked to be trained in emergency medical care, because of the threats and attacks from imperialism. So that became one of our first tasks, even before we organized the Federation of Cuban Women. It was these classes, in fact, along with the sewing classes we organized, that gave birth to the federation—not the other way around.

The classes weren't just a way of responding to women who had asked for emergency medical training. They were a way of bringing women together, so we could discuss things they wanted to know about the revolution.

Then the first revolutionary laws started to be issued by the new government.[1]

From the very beginning we decided that all children would go to school. Parents were required by law to make sure they did so. So the first big job was to find enough teachers. Women responded to this need, both those who were already teachers and those who had finished sixth grade and were taking review courses to prepare for teaching.

1.   Beginning in early 1959, revolutionary measures began to be implemented. Tribunals tried and sentenced the murderers and torturers of the Batista regime. Rents were slashed. Electricity and telephone rates were cut. Racial discrimination was made illegal and the law enforced. An agrarian reform law expropriated landholdings over 1,000 acres, and 100,000 peasant families were given title to the land they worked.

Many women who were housewives, who didn't work outside the home, who had devoted themselves only to their children and their families, reached out to us. They, too, asked us what they could do.

We began to organize women who were already in trade unions, women who were workers, and women who had some kind of political experience, either in the past or more recently. We helped them set up classes in emergency medical treatment and sewing. The medical care classes were taught with the help of the Armed Forces and the Red Cross. The sewing classes were taught by women who had completed the initial courses. This was a way of organizing women who were housewives. They were very eager to learn how to make clothes for themselves and their children.

Women in the classes who had some political experience explained the new laws to others. When the Agrarian Reform Law [2] was adopted, women asked a lot of questions about it. Peasant women, of course, had a better understanding of what the law meant. But many women approached others known for their activity during the revolutionary struggle to learn about it and how they could support the revolution.

So the federation arose not so much as a decision of the revolutionary leadership but as a response to the demand from masses of women from different layers of society who were already in action.

Women's congress in Chile

In May 1959 we received an invitation from the Women's International Democratic Federation to participate in the Congress for the Rights of Women and Children, scheduled to take place in Santiago, Chile, in late November. This gave

2. See glossary, Agrarian Reform Law.

We have always stressed that the idea of creating an organization came from the women themselves. There was no preconceived structure or agenda, just a desire by women to defend the revolution. They wanted to participate in a revolutionary process, whose aim was to transform the lives of those who had been exploited and discriminated against, and create a better society for all.

When we told Fidel that women wanted to unite, to organize, to participate actively in the revolution—that they didn't want to just receive benefits but to give something back as well, to change themselves into socially useful human beings—we received a very positive response. He understood how important this step was and strongly supported it.[*]

VILMA ESPÍN
1997

us an opportunity to begin to create an organization—that is, to set up an organizational structure. We formed a committee to promote the conference and began publicizing its themes. It was a way of raising consciousness about women's needs around the world, especially in underdeveloped countries. This in turn helped us begin the process of organizing the federation.

The committees to promote the Chile congress got moving quickly. We worked with women in the provinces respected

---

[*] "Architects of Their Own Destiny," interview with Vilma Espín by Trine Lynggard in issue no. 1 (1997) of the Norwegian magazine *Kvinner Sammen* [Women together]. Reprinted in the FMC magazine *Mujeres*, Special Issue, August 1997.

for their participation in the struggle. We worked with wives and mothers of men and women who had been killed in combat. With their help, we organized support committees in every province, then in the municipalities. We set up committees everywhere—from the cities, to the Sierra Maestra and other mountainous and rural areas. In time these committees would become the foundation of the federation.

We went to the congress in Chile with a delegation of more than eighty women from all sections of Cuban society. And we financed the trip with contributions by women across Cuba, in fact by the whole population. Many businesses— at the time they were privately owned—contributed to the trip. That helped defray the expenses of such a large delegation. Delegates included women workers from many sectors; housewives; women who belonged to political parties, such as the Orthodox Party and Popular Socialist Party; peasant women; and women who had fought in the mountains and in the urban underground in the July 26 Movement.

After the January 1 victory, other women's organizations had been formed as well. These included an organization of peasant women, groups that formerly had been social clubs, and a religious organization called With Cross and Country.[3] All of them supported the revolution.

Representatives of all these women went to the congress in Chile. This was how the federation started. It wasn't yet called the federation, but the idea of creating a women's organization to participate in the urgent tasks of the revolution was already there. The women who started by organizing support committees for the Chile congress knew this was only the beginning. They knew that a women's organization was being created because women themselves demanded it.

3. See glossary, With Cross and Country.

"World War II culminated in the struggle of colonial
peoples for their sovereignty. Between 1945 and 1957
more than 1.2 billion human beings had conquered
their political independence in Asia and Africa. The
blood shed by the peoples was not in vain. The movement of the colonial peoples, universal in character,
agitates the world and places its mark on the final crisis of imperialism."[*]

SECOND DECLARATION OF HAVANA
FEBRUARY 1962

By this time the sewing and emergency medical training
classes were under way, and we began to give diplomas to
the medical care graduates. We also began to take on other
responsibilities that flowed from current public health needs.
All this happened without there being anything called the
Federation of Cuban Women. In other words, the federation
existed, but without a name.

At the Chile congress in November 1959, we were able to tell
others about what was going on in Cuba, the meaning of this
stage of the struggle against the dictatorship, the new laws,
the revolution that was unfolding. It helped us establish relations with many women and revolutionary organizations
across Latin America and even from countries in Europe and
Asia. Although the conference focused on the Americas, representatives of women's groups came from every continent.
There were women from North America, and there were representatives of the leadership of the Women's International
Democratic Federation. Women also came from the Soviet

[*] In *First and Second Declarations of Havana* (Pathfinder, 1962, 1994,
2007), p. 44 [2007 printing].

Union. We made our first contact there with women from the socialist countries.

Starting from the work we had done to go to Chile, we decided to continue laying the groundwork for an organization in Cuba. We already had a small group of leaders, made up of representatives of all the groups that had been working together. We went to the ranks and held elections for each local unit, even though the organization was still without a name.

We sent out a call for a meeting to implement the decisions of the Chile congress, adding some of our own priorities. We included a point on making the emergency medical classes more of an institution, extending them to the whole country. We set up a new and simple method to teach sewing, which we named after Ana Betancourt.[4]

By then there were people starting to turn against the revolution, and we began to see women responding to them, speaking their minds. They sought out women who had participated in the war, in the underground struggle, and asked for help in answering those who were beginning to speak out against the revolution. By early 1960, small demonstrations were being organized out of churches by reactionary priests who sought to stir people up, and women began confronting them in the streets.

The nascent women's organization was growing. Every newly organized unit chose a president and assigned women to the public health campaigns and other responsibilities. Street demonstrations were being organized, and women went to the rallies to support the revolution. They were active across the country, and not simply in spontaneous, undirected ways. When something happened, women would not

4. See glossary, Ana Betancourt, and p. 281.

It's a happy coincidence that at the very moment the
mighty empire is mobilizing its wealth and influence
against our country, encircling it, and trying to justify
further aggression in the Organization of American
States[*]—today, this very day!—the Federation of Cuban Women has been founded as a worthy response.
. . . This is the living expression of what a revolutionary people, a people who are truly free and sovereign,
can do! . . .

The task of the Federation of Cuban Women is to organize Cuban women, help them gain access to education and culture, help them advance in every conceiv-
able way. . . . This will give the revolution another point
of strength, a new organized force, a tremendous social and revolutionary force.[†]

FIDEL CASTRO
AUGUST 23, 1960

Today we are beginning a new struggle. On January 1,
when everyone thought we had attained victory, it was
really only the beginning. . . .

We women will take our place in this great battle. It
is the struggle of a new country, one that is building

---

[*] The Organization of American States—the "Yankee Ministry of
Colonies," as Che Guevara described it—met in San José, Costa
Rica, August 22–29, 1960, where the US government lined up most
member states against Cuba. Cuba's response in defense of its sovereignty was presented in the "First Declaration of Havana," which
was adopted by a September 2, 1960, assembly of more than one
million. See *The First and Second Declarations of Havana*, pp. 25–33.

[†] Speech at founding of Federation of Cuban Women. In Fidel Castro,
Mujeres y Revolución, pp. 34–40.

schools, one that is creating cooperatives to benefit peasant families, a struggle, finally, for the dignity of the citizens.

This victory is rousing hatred by our enemies. But Cuban women understand the historical moment through which we are living and have decided to remain loyal to the revolution, to defend it alongside the peasants, workers, and people of Cuba, for the happiness and future of our children.[‡]

VILMA ESPÍN
AUGUST 23, 1960

only leave their homes and take to the streets, they would go to the emerging national leadership for guidance.

When the federation was formally constituted August 23, 1960, it had in reality already existed for some time. Its structures were in place, and it had held elections right up to the national level. We held off for a bit in taking the formal step, however, because of the enormous responsibilities we faced in 1960. And, of course, because we wanted Fidel to preside at the founding conference.

By June and July 1960 we began to ask: "OK Fidel, when?"

"As soon as I have a little time, we're going to set up the organization," he'd reply.

It was at the founding meeting that the organization was given the name Federation of Cuban Women. It was Fidel himself who decided. There were several different proposals, and Fidel said: "OK, let's call it the Federation of Cuban Women."

‡ Speech at founding of Federation of Cuban Women. Excerpts in Havana daily *Revolución*, August 24, 1960.

The Government of the proletarian dictatorship, together with the Communist Party and trade unions, is leaving no stone unturned in the effort to overcome the backward ideas of men and women, to destroy the old uncommunist psychology. In law there is naturally complete equality of rights for men and women. And everywhere there is evidence of a sincere wish to put this equality into practice.

We are bringing women into the social economy, into legislation, and government. All educational institutions are open to them. We are establishing communal kitchens and public restaurants, laundries and repair shops, nurseries, kindergartens, children's homes, and educational institutions of all kinds.

In short, we are seriously carrying out the demand in our program to transfer the economic and educational functions of the separate household to society. That will mean freedom for the woman from the old household drudgery and dependence on a man. That will enable her to exercise to the full her talents and her inclinations. The children will be brought up under more favorable conditions than at home.

We have the most advanced protective laws for women workers in the world, and the officials of the organized workers movement carry them out. We are establishing maternity hospitals, homes for mothers and children, organizing courses on child care and exhibitions teaching mothers how to look after themselves and their children. We are making serious efforts to support women who are unemployed and not provided for.

> We realize that this is not very much in comparison
> with the needs of working women, that it is far from be-
> ing all that is required for their real freedom. But still it is
> tremendous progress, as against conditions in tsarist-
> capitalist Russia. It is even a great deal compared with
> conditions in countries where capitalism still has a free
> hand. It is a good beginning in the right direction, and
> we shall develop it further. With all our energy, you may
> believe that. For every day of the existence of the So-
> viet state proves more clearly that we cannot go for-
> ward without the women.[*]
>
> V.I. LENIN
> 1920

Participation: essence of the revolution

When I talk about how the federation was created, I always emphasize that at the time we didn't talk about women's liberation. We didn't talk about women's emancipation, or the struggle for equality. We didn't use those terms then. What we did talk about was participation. Women wanted to participate. This included women who had taken an active part in the struggle, who had been in the mountains. They, like other women across the country, wanted to help in this new stage that was dawning, which was a genuine revolution.

From the very beginning, the new laws made it clear to the mother, the housewife, the woman who had lost her children in the struggle, that this revolution was in her interests. It was

[*] In Clara Zetkin, *Reminiscences of Lenin* (London: Modern Books, 1929), pp. 69-70. Another translation appears in V.I. Lenin, *The Emancipation of Women* (New York: International Publishers, 1934, 1938, 1951, 1966), pp. 115–16.

in the interests of her children and her family.

Women had confidence in the revolution—because there was real proof, every day, that the revolution wasn't just hot air, it wasn't empty phrases of the kind people were used to hearing from politicians in the past. This was the genuine thing. And women wanted to be part of it, to *do* something. The more the revolutionary laws strengthened this conviction, the more women demanded a chance to contribute—and the more they saw how necessary their contribution was.

Sometimes I'm asked to give a one-word definition of the Cuban Revolution. I reply that it's about participation—the participation of the entire people in everything. Together, the population went through difficult years. For women, this had an impact right from the beginning. They began to understand the point Lenin emphasized over and over—that for a revolution to move forward, to develop, women had to participate.

This was the beginning of political consciousness for women. When Fidel on August 23, 1960, officially gave a name to this organization—an organization that was already functioning and carrying out work related to public health, education, sewing, teaching jobs skills, and emergency medical training—and when he gave it new responsibilities such as setting up child care centers, women were already convinced they had a growing opportunity to help push forward the revolution.

As we organized the local units, especially in 1960, we focused on the most urgent responsibilities, those that emerged with the revolution. As I mentioned earlier, one of the federation's first tasks was to provide crash courses to women who had more than a sixth grade education so they could become teachers. Before the revolution there were ten thousand unemployed teachers. They weren't working in any school. But

We had to change women's mentality—accustomed as they were to playing a secondary role in our society. Our women had endured years of discrimination. We had to show women their own possibilities, their ability to do all kinds of work. We had to make women feel the urgent needs of our revolution in the construction of a new life. We had to change both women's image of themselves and society's image of women.

We started our work by simple tasks that allowed us to reach out to women, to raise them beyond the narrow, limited horizons of their existence. To explain the revolution's purpose and the part they would have to play in the process.

From the very beginning, we pursued a double goal:

To raise consciousness through political education, so that new tasks could be performed.

To raise the political level through the tasks themselves.[*]

VILMA ESPÍN
NOVEMBER 1974

immediately after January 1, these ten thousand teachers weren't nearly enough to meet our needs.

As we organized medical aid and sewing classes and began establishing more local units, it became clear that we had to take on more responsibilities in education and public health programs as well. We organized campaigns to eliminate

---

[*] Main report, in *Memories: Second Congress, Cuban Women's Federation* (Havana: Editorial Orbe, 1975), pp. 94–95. Also in *Women and the Cuban Revolution*, p. 56.

unhealthy neighborhoods, *"barrios insalubres,"* as they were known, where people lived in crowded shacks without water, electricity, or sewage disposal.[5] We organized to wipe out malaria and gastroenteritis, to get rid of flies and mosquitoes, and to raise sanitation standards in general. For example, we needed to teach women how to boil milk and water—not just tell them to do it, but explain how, in detail.

Toward the end of 1959, planes from Miami started to bomb cane fields and sugar mills.[6] Counterrevolutionaries began to sabotage factories. So in 1960, we instituted the Emergency Medical Response Brigades. These were more than just classes on a massive scale. They were intended for women who wanted to take an active part in defense. We organized the Emergency Medical Response Brigades through the armed forces, to be ready to act in time of war. That included tasks like clearing rubble and making stretchers. Our concept of what these brigades should be came out of the reality of those attacks.

In coordination with the Ministry of Health, the Emergency Medical Response Brigades took on other tasks related to public health. We carried out the first vaccination campaign

5. In capitalist countries throughout Latin America, "eliminating unhealthy neighborhoods" is a euphemism for bulldozing shantytowns and driving out working people. In Cuba after January 1959, this term referred to broad efforts by the revolutionary government to improve conditions in impoverished residential areas—with the involvement of the local population—by repairing or rebuilding dilapidated housing and introducing sewage, water, and electrical services, clinics, and schools.

6. The fire-bombing of Cuban crops began in October 1959 and continued throughout 1960. These attacks were stepped up after the defeat of the US-organized invasion at Playa Girón (Bay of Pigs) in April 1961.

"Toward the end of 1959, planes from Miami started to bomb cane fields and sugar mills. Counterrevolutionaries began to sabotage factories."—Vilma Espín

Above: Workers and militia members fight fire at El Encanto department store in central Havana after counterrevolutionary attack, April 13, 1961. Four days later US-organized mercenary invasion at Bay of Pigs began. In 1960–61 there were nine attacks on Havana department stores, with explosives or other incendiary devices along with many such assaults on supermarkets, movie theaters, hotels, factories, warehouses, and other public facilities. **Inset:** Fe del Valle, militia member and worker at El Encanto who was guarding store the night of attack. She died trying to rescue funds collected by workers to build child care center there.

against polio, for example.[7]

We were also responsible for the mother-and-child program, which grew beyond the goal of winning women to give birth in hospitals. That was our initial objective in the mountain regions, where there had never before been hospitals. We built hospitals there for the first time. The federation had been established in these areas, and its members helped in everything from laying bricks for hospitals and schools to organizing the population. Women in those areas, many of them illiterate at the beginning, took on major political responsibilities.

What did we find in 1960–61, when we'd go to one of those remote areas—say the Sierra Maestra—or other mountainous areas where previously nothing reached the population, and we were taken to meet the political leadership? There were four components. There were doctors, the first doctors to arrive in the mountains and rural areas. There were teachers, usually women who were members of the very first voluntary literacy contingents, named after Frank País.[8] Members of the Federation of Cuban Women in the area were also an important political component—because, remember, the party hadn't been formed yet. And, in terms of defense, there were the leaders of the Sierra Militias. Those were the four elements of leadership in those communities.

In a real sense, the first to carry out political work in the countryside were the women. And this gave them confidence

---

7. The first vaccination campaign against polio was carried out in February 1962. More than two million children were vaccinated by 70,000 volunteers from the Committees for Defense of the Revolution, National Association of Small Farmers, and Federation of Cuban Women.

8. See pp. 255–59.

Arriving here this evening, I commented to a compañero that the phenomenon of women's participation in the revolution is a revolution within another revolution. If I were asked what is the most revolutionary thing the revolution is doing, I would answer that it is precisely this—the revolution that is occurring among the women of our country. . . .

If women in our country were doubly exploited, doubly humiliated in the past, then this simply means that women in a socialist revolution should be doubly revolutionary.

And perhaps this is the explanation, or at least the social basis, for the resolute, enthusiastic, firm, and loyal support given by Cuban women to this revolution.[*]

FIDEL CASTRO
DECEMBER 9, 1966

and prestige. The ANAP, the National Association of Small Farmers, was also set up around this time.[9]

The federation also helped build the Committees for the Defense of the Revolution on a block-by-block basis, taking advantage of more than a year's experience working in local areas.[10] Organizing the CDRs began September 28, 1960, just a month after the federation was founded. Many compañeras

9. See glossary, National Association of Small Farmers, founded in May 1961.

10. See glossary, Committees for the Defense of the Revolution.

[*] Speech at fifth national meeting of the Federation of Cuban Women, in *Women and the Cuban Revolution*, pp. 64–68. Also in *Mujeres y Revolución*, pp. 115–19.

were in fact leaders of both organizations. So another early responsibility given to the federation was to find additional cadres for the CDRs.

All this work helped women believe even more in their capabilities, because they had to take on new responsibilities, without having any idea beforehand what their particular tasks would be. This willingness to take on whatever had to be done was what drove all the campaigns, including health and education. Those were truly heroic years, beautiful years, in which women grew tremendously.

The prestige women have achieved in our country—the understanding in society as a whole of their capacity to take on any kind of work—has its roots in how they responded so quickly to new responsibilities all over the country. And it was through the creation of the federation, through the organization of its local units, that women took on these new tasks.

Public health: new challenges

Work in the area of public health was very important in those years. Health care is fundamentally a political question. You can see that when our doctors go anywhere, including to countries in a state of war, as was the case with the medical brigade that went to Nicaragua during the Somoza era.[11] The

11. Following the devastating 1972 earthquake that leveled Managua, Nicaragua, the Cuban government sent a brigade of volunteer doctors and other medical personnel there, as well as a hundred tons of medicine and food. Cuban revolutionists considered this an elementary act of working-class internationalism, despite their intransigent opposition to the Somoza family dictatorship and active support and solidarity with the fight to overturn that tyranny, led by the Sandinista National Liberation Front. Some seven years later, in July 1979, Nicaragua's workers and peasants overturned the Somoza regime.

medical brigades that went to Honduras, or to various African countries over the years, were welcomed by the people there. Someone was coming to cure their children, to give them medicine, to care for their wounded—this has had an enormous political impact!

Today the family doctor, too, is a formidable political institution.[12] He or she is the human face of the revolution, the person in most direct contact with the entire family. The federation has worked from the very beginning with all these institutions. There are brigades working in every aspect of public health. Participation of the population as a whole in health campaigns has been an important factor in our ability to reduce infant mortality. Simple measures we initiated, such as boiling milk and water, were decisive. Gastroenteritis was reduced, polio was wiped out, and malaria was almost eliminated in the first few years. This was accomplished through mass work. This even included cleaning houses!

Many women were still illiterate. Nonetheless, they understood very well that the health of their children depended on cleanliness and on the type of food they were given. Nutrition, we learned, was sometimes determined by more than just a family's income level. Some families knew little about how to prepare food, or what foods were more nutritious. There were places, for example, where milk had never been available, and mothers did not know how much children's development could be affected by making milk part of their daily diet.

The federation put great emphasis on issues of cleanliness and hygiene in the home and in food preparation. It taught

12. The family doctor program in Cuba, established in January 1984, set a goal of making a neighborhood doctor-nurse team available to every 120 families.

people how to prepare food to avoid contamination, how to prepare a baby's bottle. As we built hospitals, we had to convince peasants that it was better for women to give birth there. At first this took a little work. Then the peasants began to see that this meant their children didn't die, didn't get infections. Mothers didn't get sepsis—the blood poisoning that had previously been very common after giving birth. Those were our first tasks in health care.

Today there is a close link between the family doctor, the health brigade, and the federation's local unit, both in general and in terms of ongoing campaigns such as sex education. In the early years, ignorance was responsible for a high rate of pregnancy in many areas of the country. So in 1964 we began to educate families on issues related to procreation and its scientific basis. We began to publish discussions about this in the federation's magazine, *Mujeres*.

We used the magazine to educate on issues of women's health and in that context took up different aspects of sex education. We explained how to avoid venereal diseases. How to avoid pregnancies through the use of contraceptives, which we had begun providing. And we campaigned energetically for all women to see gynecologists and obstetricians.

Later we stressed the importance of pap smears, which are important in avoiding deaths from cervical and uterine cancer, and of tests for early detection of breast cancer. These are all things we have worked on consistently and are now the norm.

Among the institutions the federation established in the early years were homes for expectant mothers. Often the problem wasn't that women resisted going to hospitals to give birth, but that they lived too far away. Roads were poor, and transportation was inadequate. The Ministry of Health established maternity homes for these women, so they were

Since the earliest years of the revolution, the FMC has confronted serious problems arising from women's lack of knowledge about their own bodies, their reproductive system, their sexual health, and the possibility of planning both the number of children and the time between births.

We soon won the right to have abortions included as a service of the health system, legalized under condition that they be performed by specialists and in hospitals, assuring all necessary sanitary conditions. The federation then called on the country's health and education institutions to carry out massive educational efforts and to organize a genuine program of sexual education, open to all and based solidly on advanced scientific concepts.[*][†]

VILMA ESPÍN
1997

[*] "Architects of Their Own Destiny," in *Mujeres*, Special Issue, August 1997.

[†] Abortion became illegal in Cuba in 1879 under the penal code imposed by the Spanish colonial rulers. A 1938 revision of the law allowed the procedure in case of rape, certain birth defects, or to save the life of the woman. In the opening years of the revolution, social attitudes still broadly accepted in Cuba, especially in the countryside, opposed a woman's right to abort a pregnancy and the 1938 law was enforced. The availability of medically safe abortions was also limited by the fact that half of Cuba's 6,000 physicians—including the majority of specialists such as gynecologists and obstetricians—left the country for the United States.

In 1965, a regulation issued by the Health Ministry interpreted the 1938 law as permitting all early term abortions. Like other medical procedures, abortions were provided free of charge. With the adoption of a new penal code in 1979, the old law was wiped off the closer to hospitals. In some cases, women came forty-five days before their delivery date. If they were having difficult pregnancies and the doctor didn't want to leave them so far away, some young women came even earlier.

Public health brigades

Our public health brigades, our social workers, our Militant Mothers for Education,[13] are a real force in massively organizing and involving people in the eradication of serious medical problems. The brigades began with basic tasks of sanitation but are now part of a coherent, well-planned program reviewed every year by the Ministry of Health.

Each year new tasks are added. Follow-up for pregnant women, for example, is much more developed. Today we have programs in place to assure pregnant women get monthly checkups. Once the baby is born, we follow whether the mother is keeping to the regular vaccination schedule and is taking her children for regular check-ups.

Our health brigade volunteers have a program in place in case of war. They are prepared for it. Our first health brigades, which were linked directly to the Revolutionary Armed Forces, were part of defending the revolution at Playa Girón, caring for the wounded there.[14]

13. See pp. 264–65.

14. See glossary, Playa Girón (Bay of Pigs).

---

books, and abortion—performed according to established medical procedures—was decriminalized. Under current law there is no restriction on abortion in the first trimester of pregnancy. No one but the woman has to give consent. In the second and third trimester, medical approval of the hospital director is required.

Abortion as a routine means of contraception is strongly discouraged through the broad availability of safe birth control methods and educational campaigns.

Historically, more women than men have tended to work in the areas of education and health. After the triumph of the revolution, however, the participation of women became even more pronounced. Now there are a large number of women doctors, as well as women directors of hospitals and medical research institutions.

Many of the efforts to "humanize" health care—as Fidel puts it—came from demands women put forward through the federation. Mothers asked to be allowed to stay with their children in the hospital, for example. The Ministry of Health at first resisted, citing the danger of infection and other problems. But we discussed it more, and several years ago a decision was made to institutionalize the practice of mothers staying with their children in hospitals. And in the last few years, since the federation's fourth congress in 1985, the idea that it can be also useful for fathers to be at the hospital has gained broad acceptance.

In 1961 the launching of the great literacy campaign brought new responsibilities. The federation not only helped make sure parents sent their children to school. We also got directly involved in creating conditions so women could study, could go to school, could learn to read and write. That's something Fidel stressed at the federation's founding congress.

During the literacy campaign, the majority of literacy brigade members were female. That's because, at the time, most teachers were women. But it's also true that the majority of people who couldn't read—55 percent—were female. So this was a campaign that required a lot of work by women, both teaching others and learning to read and write themselves.

Ana Betancourt School for peasant women

In January 1961 the first of what would eventually be more than twenty-one thousand peasant women enrolled in the

Ana Betancourt School, established at Fidel's initiative.[15] Both
the federation and the revolutionary leadership understood
the importance of women becoming fully conscious of what
the revolution was, of what women could become as a political force. By the time counterrevolutionary actions began in
some mountainous areas, it was evident that many campesinas had already begun to see what the revolution could do
to benefit their families and children.

The leaders of the counterrevolutionaries in the mountains
were generally landlords. They counted on ignorance to get
people to follow their orders or accept their arguments. So it's
no accident the counterrevolutionary bands chose to focus on
areas with a higher rate of illiteracy, and where people had
the least knowledge about what the revolution meant.

When Fidel saw what was happening in some of the most
undeveloped mountain areas, we began the work to recruit
young women from there to come to the campesina schools.
As Fidel suggested, the federation worked together with the
National Association of Small Farmers, which was preparing its founding meeting. We began to encourage peasant
families to bring their daughters to Havana to learn how
to sew.

Women all over the country were interested in taking these
classes. Most families were poor, and there was little financial
leeway to buy clothes of any quality in a store. Even before
the victory of the revolution, Cuban women wanted to learn
how to sew, how to cut material for an attractive dress. It was
something they were excited about and could learn quickly.

The offer of the classes met an enthusiastic response. By
January 1961, the first of thousands of young women from

---

15. More than 12,000 graduated in three different classes in 1961. An-
     other 9,200 graduated in December 1963.

the countryside had arrived in Havana by train. Most were housed in the Hotel Nacional.[16] Others stayed in abandoned homes of bourgeois families who had left the country.

These young peasant women often arrived with health problems. Many had intestinal parasites and little knowledge of nutrition. The first thing we did was take them to dentists and doctors. They received medical examinations and treatment to eliminate parasites. Many had lost teeth due to cavities, so they got dental restoration work. After the first month of their stay in Havana, they had begun to change. Their physical condition improved. They learned new habits of hygiene. And they overcame a series of taboos previously accepted through ignorance.

The counterrevolutionaries saw how dangerous it was for these daughters of peasants to learn the truth about the revolution. So they organized campaigns to scare the parents. The girls were going to be turned into prostitutes, the counterrevolutionaries said. Or they were going to be sent to Russia and returned to their families as canned meat!

These were horror stories, but many peasants were frightened by them and came to Havana to take their daughters back. When they got there, they found their daughters in school. They saw young women who had changed. They looked healthier. They were happy. They were all learning to sew. Those who had been illiterate were beginning to read and write.

So when parents came to find their daughters who had spent two or three months in Havana and take them home, the young women started to cry. Nothing in the world could make them leave before they finished their courses, they

16. Built in 1930, and refurbished before the victory of the revolution, the Nacional was one of the most luxurious hotels in Havana.

said. They were going to fulfill their promise to Fidel. And, they added, Fidel was going to give every one of them a sewing machine, so each of them could give classes to ten more campesinas when they went home.

That was the plan, and it was carried out very quickly. It was another reason the first political cadres who emerged in these mountain areas were women. I remember the comments of many of the parents when, later, we'd run into them in the mountains.

"Just imagine," they'd say. "It used to be that when visitors came, my daughter would hide behind the door. Nobody could get her to come out. But after she returned from those courses, she'd grab a table, put it in the middle of the *batey*,[17] and begin to call all the campesinos together to explain what the revolution was."

The young women hadn't just learned to read and write. They hadn't just learned to sew. They had also learned about the revolution. They had come to Havana and seen all the possibilities that existed here, things that were eventually going to be brought to their own communities. They'd learned about the programs for health care, for education, how schools were being built in areas that never had them before. They'd become aware of what the revolution meant.

So no one was going to "pull the wool over their eyes," as the saying goes.

"No one can fool *my* daughter," parents would say. "When she came back, she was very clear about everything. And the very first thing she did was to begin to convert me!"

These young women took on important tasks in places

---

17. In Cuba prior to the revolution, the sugar mill complex included the company-owned *batey*: the shacks where workers lived, the company store, and other facilities.

The graduates of the Ana Betancourt School are going to repay what they have received from the country by teaching other campesinas, by each one teaching ten other peasant women to sew.

Afterward many will be able to earn a living with the knowledge they've acquired, teaching in the cooperatives, the people's farms, the peasant associations.

As soon as these eight hundred young women who are today graduating return to their cooperatives we'll have eight hundred more working for the revolution.

They will take back a more complete idea of what the revolution is, they will take back a clear idea that the effort that is being carried out is the effort of the entire people.

They will be returning with their revolutionary spirit more developed, returning to help the revolution, to organize women in the federation, to organize the youth, to organize the children, to organize and be part of the Committees for the Defense of the Revolution, and to continue awakening the revolutionary consciousness of the peasants where they live.[*]

FIDEL CASTRO
JULY 31, 1961

where their parents had been influenced by, or had come under pressure from, the first counterrevolutionary bands and the landlords who organized them. The landlords used these impoverished peasants, those who were most backward, as cannon fodder, telling them horror stories about how the

[*] Speech in Havana at first graduation ceremony of the Ana Betancourt School. In *Mujeres y Revolución*, pp. 46–52.

"The leaders of the counterrevolutionary bands in the mountains focused on areas with a higher rate of illiteracy, where people had the least knowledge about the revolution. So we began to recruit young women from the mountains to come to the campesina schools in Havana."—Vilma Espín

The Ana Betancourt School brought young peasant women to Havana to learn how to read and write, sew, and gain other skills.
Top: School administrator Alicia Imperatori, standing, at celebration with some of school's instructors. **Bottom:** Scene from graduation of first class, July 1961.

revolution was going to take away their pigs, their chickens, and their children.

I remember when we captured some of the first bands operating in the area of Baracoa, on the eastern tip of Oriente province. Raúl Castro went to talk with the peasants. Why are these peasants fighting us? he wanted to know.

Raúl joked with them. "And what would I want with those potbellied little kids you've got here, *chico?*"

He kidded them, and they realized the stories were absurd. But they'd been terrified. And, of course, there had never been a real revolution before. They didn't yet understand what the revolution meant. It was their own daughters who helped them understand.

The Ana Betancourt School sessions lasted until secondary schools reached the mountains, when they were no longer needed.[18] They made it possible for these young women to receive an education and become politically active. Many of those first "Anitas," as people called them, are today doctors, teachers, technicians, and political leaders. They had all the opportunities the sons and daughters of our people can have.

Alicia Imperatori organized the school and spent a great deal of time at the Hotel Nacional with the Ana Betancourt students there.[19] Her stories are wonderful, including about all the childhood diseases they came down with—measles, mumps, chicken pox—you can imagine what it was like. Former students still write Alicia and send her news.

The Ana Betancourt School was really one of the great things Fidel initiated. It began the moment he said, "We have

18. The last class of the large school in Havana graduated in December 1963.

19. See glossary, Alicia Imperatori.

"Night schools were created for young women left behind in houses abandoned by the bourgeoisie. When the owners left the country, they left their servants with nothing. So we created schools to teach them office skills and management and other trades."—Vilma Espín

First graduating class of taxi drivers, 1961. They were popularly known as the *Violeteras* because the taxis they drove were painted violet.

to take the revolution to the homes of the peasants. And who will do it? The young women, their own daughters." It was marvelous.

Night schools for domestic workers

Nineteen sixty-one was a year of intense work. The federation participated actively in the literacy campaign, which we'll get to later.

The Ana Betancourt School was going on at the same time as the night schools for domestic workers.

And of course there was Playa Girón.

The night schools were created for young women who used to work as maids and were left behind in houses abandoned by the bourgeoisie in Cubanacán, Miramar, and other wealthy Havana neighborhoods. Before the revolution, tens of thousands of women worked these kinds of jobs. It's estimated that more than seventy thousand women worked in domestic service, with exhausting days, very poor pay, and no legal protections of any kind.

When the owners left the country, they left their servants with nothing. These young women started coming to us, asking, "What do we do? We have no wages, nothing." So we created schools to teach them skills.

There was one school training taxi drivers, and another one teaching office skills. Many bank workers, who had been part of the so-called labor aristocracy in Cuba, had left the country along with their bosses. So these former domestic workers took their place.[20]

20. By the end of 1961, seventeen schools were established to provide former domestic workers with job skills. A few years later there were seventy schools in Havana alone. In 1968, when the program ended, virtually all former domestic workers had received training for other work.

Creation of child care centers

In January 1961 we also initiated courses to train aides, directors, and health personnel for the children's circles. On April 10, just before the battle of Playa Girón, the first centers had been opened. All throughout 1960 and 1961, the federation had been working to collect money for them. Many people remember the "little cup of coffee" campaign, where we asked people to pay three cents more for each cup of coffee. The extra money was a donation for the children's circles.

Establishing child care centers was one of the responsibilities Fidel gave us the very day the federation was founded. We had to solve the problem of child care for women who worked.

We heard terrible stories from before the revolution about women who had no alternative but to go to work as domestic servants and leave their own children locked up at home. There were cases of oil lamps falling over in the house and children being burned. Children drowned. Some really terrible things happened.

Fidel spoke about these miserable conditions at the founding of the federation and said we had to find a solution. So in the whirlwind of those early years, we had already begun to talk about setting up child care centers.

Little by little the idea became more defined. At the time we were setting up "workers' circles," as they were called, in what had been clubs of the bourgeoisie. Fidel said, let's call these new centers "children's circles" (*círculos infantiles*)—a society of children who are going to be sharing a collective life there.

We thought from the start that the concept of child care centers was very good. Fidel said they weren't going to be just a

We have to bring together all Cuban women who want to fight, struggle, and work to carry out the tasks the revolution has put before us. There are hundreds of thousands of women who want to do this. We've already begun to organize the initial institutions through which we'll reach out to young women who are neither working nor going to school.

There are women working who have no place to leave their children. There aren't enough children's circles. The state and the municipality can't change this themselves. Their resources are limited.

What we can do is organize these tens of thousands of young women who are neither working nor in school. They are human material that can be trained. They are the human beings who can organize all the children's circles the working women of Cuba need. . . .

The revolution is counting on the women of Cuba to do this, and on the Federation of Cuban Women to organize and train them to do it.[*]

FIDEL CASTRO
AUGUST 23, 1960

guardería, just a place to keep an eye on children. They should be "a place where children are educated, taken care of," Fidel said, "where they are treated with love, where they learn."

We had very little experience when we took those first steps. There were no trained personnel, very few preschool teachers at all. Those there were hadn't been trained to take care of a child all day long in a child care center. Nor had they been

[*] Speech at founding meeting of Federation of Cuban Women. In *Mujeres y Revolución*, pp. 40–41.

trained to take care of children of all ages, from forty-five days to six years.

A year after the first centers were founded in April 1961—after we had established relations with the Soviet Union and other socialist countries—we began to send people to those countries to be trained as teachers. These countries already had experience with this type of institution and, later, we were able to ask them to send us advisers too. We also took advantage of opportunities to learn from the experiences of capitalist countries in caring for children.

Little by little, our organization of the centers improved. But from the beginning we had a clear concept of how important it was to take good care of children—to look after their health and nutrition, to help keep them from getting sick, and to give them love. As we were able to raise the skill level of the teachers and women who worked in the child care centers, as we trained them better, they learned to help children develop their talents, their ability to think.

We might not have had all the resources necessary. But we asked for suggestions from the best-trained teachers we had, the best psychologists—especially those who knew how to take care of very young children—and they worked hard on this. The very first plans for the child care centers included activities designed to develop children's abilities and intelligence.

When we began the child care centers, we set up schools to train many of the young women who'd been domestic workers, especially those who really liked children. We brought in young women from all over the country for training, because every place we went to open a center, we needed workers from that region. Many peasant women came to be trained.

At that time, we could only require that trainees have a fourth-grade education, more or less. We tried to make sure that directors were either teachers or had finished the eighth grade at least.[21] We trained three hundred directors and another three hundred health workers—nurses who specialized in children's hygiene and nutrition.

Another 1,200 young women took training courses to become aides. Under the circumstances, we couldn't set the requirements very high. The aides did, however, receive some instruction in teaching, in psychology, and in using games with children. Most important, they received training in hygiene and in what to expect from each age group, from newborn babies on up. Today many of these women are directors of child care centers. Little by little they improved their skills, until they became the educators they are today.

We also had to train cooks. Many cooks who have worked a long time in the centers couldn't read or write when they started. But they worked very carefully, since they knew children's lives were in their hands. The women who worked in the kitchen, cleaned the centers, and did the laundry carried out these responsibilities with great care and dedication. Their desire to do the best job possible made up for any technical shortcomings they might have had.

Affection for children was important, too. The most important requirement for a person who works with children, we said, was that she love children. A child needs a lot of affection—and this is something we always emphasized.

In 1961 these women were being trained at a school that had been set up in Ciudad Libertad,[22] which was bombed and

21. At the time of the revolution, most of Cuba's teachers had completed no more than the eighth grade prior to receiving training for the classroom.

22. Ciudad Libertad—previously Camp Columbia, Batista's military base on the edge of Havana—was being converted into a school. On April 15, 1961, two days before the Bay of Pigs invasion, three US-supplied B-26s, painted to look like Cuban air force planes, at-

strafed prior to the attack on Playa Girón. These compañeras were trained under fire. They didn't leave the school, not a single one asked to go home because of Playa Girón. Everyone stayed.

Child care centers and the rectification process

Work with the child care centers has always been one of the federation's favorite tasks. Both as mothers, and as federation members, we have always been alert to shortcomings and problems.

Construction of the child care centers is one example. The construction sector fell far behind on meeting goals. What's more, centers were sometimes turned over to us without the quality of work we expected. This was a source of constant complaint at our congresses and yearly meetings. We took it directly to our revolutionary government at the highest level.

Our organization, through its local units, has also always spoken out strongly on providing clothing to children in the circles, especially to nursing babies. Since the state is now providing the necessary clothing and utensils, we haven't had to organize the kind of direct help from people that was necessary in the early years.

We've always had ambitious goals for creating child care centers, for trying to make them available for all working women with small children. But the truth is child care centers are expensive—beautiful but expensive. And we can't open one if the necessary conditions don't exist. Hygiene has to be adequate. The building has to be safe for a child. There has to be food suitable for the different ages of children attending the center. Requirements like these have to be met before

---

tacked the facility, killing seven and wounding fifty-three. The operation was authorized by President John F. Kennedy.

children can be brought to a center.

In the early years and in rural areas, we did open some centers—"little guerrilla centers," we used to call them—that weren't child care centers as we know them today. They were set up so that one woman, or two or three women, looked after a small group of children. It was simply an effort by the federation to provide a solution in areas where we couldn't establish a center because there were very few children but there were women workers who needed child care.

We still have institutions like that at some farm cooperatives, in certain sparsely populated areas. We work with the Ministry of Health and Ministry of Education to make sure standards are maintained. But in situations like that we can't have a full-fledged child care center with all its programs for child development and courses for training staff.

From 1970 until a year ago—1986—one of our biggest concerns was that child care centers weren't being built in the numbers necessary. More women were involved in production, more young women had reached working age and wanted to work, and more women were graduating from universities. They had problems finding care for their children.

For many years we were unable to respond to this need. No new child care centers were built. So last year, in 1986, Fidel initiated a big effort to construct child care centers, starting first in Havana and then across the island. This was a source of great joy for the federation, an enormous satisfaction. We had been fighting for this. [23]

When construction of the new child care centers began in the

23. In 1986, more than one million women were in Cuba's workforce. Child care centers that year, however, could accommodate only 96,000 children. By 1992, due to the efforts of volunteer construction minibrigades in which large numbers of women participated, the figure had risen to 149,000.

Today we no longer build only one day care center a year. Now one child care center seems ridiculous to us—we say fifty. It was going to take us fifty years to build fifty centers. Not only because there was no manpower but because there was no brainpower either. There was no power of imagination.

Those who advocated reactionary ideas within the revolution argued that building child care centers was a social expense. Social expenses were no good; investing in production was good. As if those who work in factories were bulls and cows, horses and mares, and not human beings, not men and women with their problems, especially women with their problems.

Whenever someone says no child care center, you can be sure there is a technocratic, bureaucratic, reactionary concept at work.

It never entered the technocrat's head that child care centers are essential to production.

Without child care centers, how can we have women join the workforce?[*]

FIDEL CASTRO
NOVEMBER 29, 1987

1970s, the federation joined in voluntary work to build them. Then a decision was made that this work needed more highly skilled labor and that the construction brigades working on them had to be specialized. In reality, this approach led to longer and longer delays in construction, and lower quality as well. This, too, has been a source of constant criticism at every

[*] Speech at close of Havana provincial party meeting, in *Granma Weekly Review*, December 13, 1987, and the *Militant*, January 29, 1988.

> The fifty-four child care centers we built in less than a year are a symbol of the rectification process, of the people's strength; of the minibrigade movement's ability to transform the capital and all the cities of the country.[*]
>
> FIDEL CASTRO
> DECEMBER 30, 1987

federation congress and meeting for many years.

Fidel decided this question had to be addressed. You can see in Havana how there's been a huge increase in the number of child care centers, more than fifty in the last year. Women can now work without worrying about whether their children are being well taken care of.

It has taken an extraordinary political, revolutionary effort[24] to build child care centers by mobilizing minibrigades based on workplaces, by organizing the participation of the population as a whole.[25] Housewives, even children, helped

24. This effort was part of what is known in Cuba as the rectification process. This course, implemented between 1986 and 1991, marked a turn away from the tendency in Cuba for more than a decade to copy political and economic policies long dominant in the Soviet Union and Eastern Europe. An aspect of that political retreat of the 1970s and early '80s had been less and less use of voluntary labor, which had been promoted by the Cuban leadership from the beginning as a proletarian lever enabling working people to take steps forward, through collective action, to address pressing social needs such as child care centers, schools, clinics, and housing.

25. The minibrigades, a central component of the rectification process, were composed of workers who volunteered to be relieved of their normal jobs for a period of time in order to build homes, schools,

[*] Speech on opening child care center no. 54 in 1987, in *Granma Weekly Review*, January 10, 1988.

build them. Moreover, they've been built with better quality. At times in the past we'd get child care centers with leaky roofs. The centers we're getting now—like the last fifty-four that were built—are of the quality they should be.[26]

It's true that the designs of the centers were different, and some looked better than others. But all have been built with quality, with commitment from the members of the minibrigade movement who helped build them, and with the help of voluntary labor from the neighborhood, from students. This pleases us greatly.

We achieved two things. First, construction of the child care centers themselves. But we also revived the spirit Fidel spoke of, that Che emphasized so much. We revived voluntary work. We renewed its role in training new generations, in harnessing the creative activity of people in solving their own problems.

Voluntary labor is a school

There's a broader point here as well. All the federation's work is done through the voluntary labor its members contribute to society. Today many members work outside the home, and on top of that they organize their time to carry out the federation's work.

Voluntary labor in those first years kept evolving and creating new forms—in production, for example. Through the

---

child care centers, clinics, supermarkets, and other high-priority social needs. Their co-workers took on their previous responsibilities. The minibrigade volunteers continued to receive the wages they earned at their regular jobs.

26. By January 1989, 111 new child care centers had been built in Havana, with room for 24,000 additional children. This was an increase of more than 60 percent above the previous 39,000 children, cared for in 300 mostly smaller centers, built or adapted in Havana earlier in the revolution.

federation, women asked to be assigned to voluntary labor in the fields and in the factories in order to replace men who were going to fight the counterrevolutionary bands in the mountains.[27] At the time of the Playa Girón (Bay of Pigs) invasion, Che made a strong point that factory production had increased, not fallen. The women who replaced men in those jobs had never worked in a factory before. It was their determination, their revolutionary drive, that made it possible for them to meet quotas every day that were higher than the previous regular goals. That happened in the fields, too.

Voluntary labor was a school for the federation. It was a way to politically strengthen women—in fact, all our people. Today, a new call has been made for voluntary labor in construction. I think that's very important for the revolution.

Voluntary labor has to be well organized: we have to make sure no time is wasted, that things are prepared, so there's work for all when they show up. Because an immense number of workers temporarily join those performing certain jobs on a daily basis. But at the same time, it's an important part of educating revolutionaries themselves, of educating new generations who perhaps have never been asked to carry out missions demanding a high level of sacrifice. It's always important to have a certain number of voluntary tasks through which people can learn what agricultural labor is, what construction work is—labor done directly with your hands.

The literacy campaign

Nineteen sixty-one was also the Year of the Literacy Campaign.[28] It was an enormous victory for our country, for our revolution, when Fidel's pledge before the United Nations

27. See footnote 32.

28. See p. 192.

If Che were sitting in this chair, he would feel jubilant. He would be happy about what we are doing these days, just as he would have felt very unhappy during that disgraceful period of building socialism in which there began to prevail a series of mechanisms, of bad habits.

For example, voluntary work, the brainchild of Che and one of the best things he left us during his stay in our country, was steadily on the decline. It became a formality almost. It would be done on the occasion of a special date, a Sunday. People would sometimes run around and do things in a disorganized way.

The bureaucrat's view, the technocrat's view that voluntary work was neither basic nor essential gained more and more ground. The idea was that voluntary work was kind of silly, a waste of time. . . .

The minibrigades, which were destroyed for the sake of such mechanisms, are now rising again from their ashes like a phoenix and demonstrating the significance of that mass movement, the significance of that revolutionary path of solving the problems that the theoreticians, technocrats, those who do not believe in man, and those who believe in two-bit capitalism had stopped and dismantled.

Now the minibrigades have been reborn and there are more than 20,000 minibrigade members in the capital. . . .

We could ask the two-bit capitalists and profiteers who have blind faith in the mechanisms and categories of capitalism: Could you achieve such a miracle? Could you manage to build 20,000 housing units in the capital without spending a cent more on wages? Could you build fifty child care centers in a year, when only five had been included in the five-year plan and they weren't even built, and 19,500 mothers were waiting to get their children a place, which never materialized?

At that rate it would take 100 years! By then they would be dead, and fortunately so would all the technocrats, two-bit capitalists, and bureaucrats who obstruct the building of socialism. [Applause] They would have died without ever seeing child care center number 100. Workers in the capital will have their 100 child care centers in two years, and workers all over the country will have the 300 or so they need in three years.[*]

FIDEL CASTRO
OCTOBER 8, 1987

was carried out to the letter.[29]

The celebration of that victory took place on December 22, 1961—the Day of the Educator, as it is known today. Nothing is gained, of course, if we teach people to read and write and leave it at that; later came the follow-up. The federation

---

29. "In the coming year," Castro told the UN September 26, 1960, "our country intends to wage its great battle against illiteracy. . . . Organizations of teachers, students, and workers—that is, the entire people—are preparing themselves for an intensive campaign. Cuba will be the first country of Latin America that, within the course of a few months, will be able to say it does not have one single illiterate person!" In Fidel Castro, Che Guevara, *To Speak the Truth* (Pathfinder, 1992), pp. 61–62.

[*] Speech at ceremony marking twentieth anniversary of death of Ernesto Che Guevara. In Che Guevara, Fidel Castro, *Socialism and Man in Cuba* (Pathfinder, 1968, 1989, 2009), pp. 41–49.

> When we said Cuba was going to eradicate illiteracy
> in just one year, it seemed like a bold statement, it
> seemed impossible.
>
> Our enemies may have mocked that promise, may
> have laughed at that goal that our people set for them-
> selves. . . .
>
> And it's true, it would have been an impossible task
> for a people who live under oppression! It would have
> been an impossible task for any people in the world,
> except a people in revolution.
>
> Only a revolutionary people could marshal the ef-
> fort and energy necessary to carry out such a huge
> campaign.*
>
> FIDEL CASTRO
> DECEMBER 22, 1961

was active in that as well. We were given a whole series of
tasks in literacy, more than just finding women who could
teach others to read and write. There were women, for example, who couldn't go to the mountains but who nonetheless had completed the sixth grade or more and were
capable of teaching other women to read and write. So we
looked for people these women could teach in their own
neighborhoods.

Groups of our members went to rural areas to help the
literacy teachers, who were often young people in the sev-
enth or eight grades, twelve or thirteen years old. Federation
members from the area itself—peasant women, as well as our
compañeras from the province and municipality—organized

---

* Speech in Havana celebrating victory of literacy campaign. In
Revolución, December 23, 1961.

to make sure the literacy workers were taken care of. This type of help was essential, above all in the mountain areas. Women from the federation brought the literacy workers mail from their families. They helped families of volunteers prepare for visits to their children.

Later, during the follow-up to the campaign, we proposed that women who had reached a certain level of literacy continue participating. It was part of our commitment to help women keep raising their educational level. That was the origin of the battle for the sixth grade—and later for the ninth grade, which we haven't yet won. The battle for the sixth grade was a resounding success.[30] For that campaign, the Federation of Cuban Women was awarded UNESCO's special "Nadezhda Krupskaya" prize four years ago.[31]

During the literacy campaign, the federation focused on women who, up until the triumph of the revolution, had had no access to learning, who could neither read nor write, and who needed our help to begin realizing their potential. But we also worked with women who already had some education, women who were preparing to work in factories where they were needed.

30. The campaign to raise all Cuban adults to the level of sixth-grade education was achieved in 1980.

31. The award is named after Nadezhda Krupskaya (1869–1939), a cadre of the Bolshevik party who had worked as a school teacher when she was in her early twenties. Following the October 1917 revolution, Krupskaya served as deputy people's commissar of education and enlightenment in the Bolshevik-led workers and peasants republic led by V.I. Lenin and helped guide the development of preschool education. Krupskaya was the wife and lifelong collaborator of Lenin.

First training courses, poultry program

In the early 1960s, during the struggle against the counterrevolutionary bands, women had volunteered to work in the factories and fields, filling in for men whose militia units were mobilized.[32] New workplaces were opening during those years, as well. And we were organizing classes to train women to operate tractors, plant crops, breed rabbits, and work in the big new poultry farms we were building.

One of the revolution's goals back in 1961 had been to lay the groundwork for large-scale poultry production. We needed more protein. The purchasing power of the population was increasing, but the growing demand for protein couldn't be met. One solution was egg production.

The federation was asked to select women to work in this program and to help train technicians for it. We began with a small team assigned to set up schools for the poultry program. We then organized the schools, recruited young women to attend them, and trained the students. Many took crash courses and then trained others. That's how the poultry program was launched.

In 1961 we also trained women to operate tractors and started schools for women welders, mechanics, lathe operators, and milling machine operators. We organized those

32. During the opening years of the Cuban Revolution, nearly four thousand counterrevolutionaries inside Cuba, organized in three hundred armed groups, were trained, financed, and supported by the US government. In December 1960 during Operation Cage (*Operación Jaula*) sixty thousand militia volunteers were mobilized to surround and capture them. For an account by a commander of the volunteer battalions in the Escambray mountains of central Cuba, where more than half of these counterrevolutionary forces operated, see Víctor Dreke, *From the Escambray to the Congo: In the Whirlwind of the Cuban Revolution* (Pathfinder, 2002). By 1965 the counterrevolutionary bands had been eliminated.

classes to respond to the demand for women workers in certain factories. At the same time, we continued organizing classes for the great mass of women, above all housewives, who had very little education, and for women working in agriculture, mostly growing fruit and vegetables.

When the revolutionary government opened the worker-peasant schools in 1962,[33] the federation helped select the women students for them. Through our local units, we began a campaign in each neighborhood to reach women who hadn't finished elementary school and encourage them to enter the worker-peasant schools.

Today we have a new generation of women technicians, engineers, and doctors who are also young mothers. Our concern is to solve the problem of child care, as well as to create conditions for solving problems in the home, above all the sharing of housework, so women can fully integrate themselves in their jobs. This takes political work. We don't want women to be held back by problems at home. We work to create understanding among the population of the need to share household tasks.

At present, more than 56 percent of the country's technical workforce[34] are women. That's an important indicator, an enormous difference from the past, when there were no women technical workers in industry. It's true this figure includes teachers, who are classified as mid-level technical

33. Part of the extensive adult education program established in Cuba after the revolution, the worker-peasant schools provide several semesters of accelerated primary education.

34. In Cuba, the term "technician" covers a broad range of occupations requiring specialized training. Examples include teachers, health-care workers, engineers, scientific researchers, secretaries, accountants, mechanics, and other skilled workers. In 2010, 65 percent of the technical workforce were women.

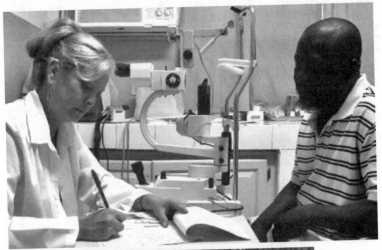

"In Cuba, every woman has the chance to aspire to any career she chooses."—Vilma Espín

Above: Surgeon and medical volunteer Gladys Montero Roca interviews patient prior to cataract operation, Port au Prince, Haiti, March 2011. **Below:** Arminda Meneses Unzué, shift manager, Ciro Redondo sugar mill, Ciego de Ávila, March 2011.

This graduation not only marks an enormous advance in our agriculture but something else equally important for the revolution: the incorporation of women into productive labor. It marks the real beginning of equality of opportunity for women—their access to activities they can carry out perfectly well, with the highest quality of work.

It also registers that we are creating the conditions for establishing a genuinely just system in our country. Because in the past we not only suffered the exploitation of man by man but also its by-product—a situation in which there was genuine discrimination against women in work and in many other aspects of life as well.[*]

FIDEL CASTRO
SEPTEMBER 30, 1968

employees, as well as nurses and other mid-level health technicians. But it's still an important reflection of how the revolution has changed women's roles.

We should also note that Cuba now has a large number of women engineers in all fields.

The revolution has given priority to training physicians for work both in Cuba and in internationalist missions, and in response women's interest in becoming doctors has grown. The academic levels women have reached, moreover, allow them to qualify for medical careers in much higher numbers than men. A very large number of university students are women. A woman's right to train for any profession is broadly

[*] Fidel Castro, speech at graduation of first class of women tractor drivers, known as *piccolinas* after the nickname for the Italian tractors they drove. In *Mujeres y Revolución*, p. 127.

guaranteed. Every woman in the country has the chance to aspire to any career she chooses.

Militant Mothers for Education

At the federation's founding, Fidel gave us the immediate and urgent task of helping women gain a higher educational level, to encourage them to go to school. But this wasn't our only priority in the struggle for education. We also dealt with women's place as mothers of schoolchildren, as members of society supporting the schools.

We often had to be creative in finding teachers, and federation members had to help in many other tasks involved in keeping the schools running. Since then women, organized by the federation, have become a great source of support for the schools.

Over those first years we learned, little by little, that we had to approach this effort in a more organized way. Rank-and-file members of the federation pointed this out to us. So we created a national program called the Militant Mothers for Education.[35]

What did federation members see when they visited schools? They found that teachers sometimes felt a little abandoned in the classrooms, which often had more than the recommended number of students. Federation members stepped in to help. School dining rooms were started, so working mothers with children in elementary school wouldn't have to go home to feed them lunch. Housewives who could do so came to the schools to help out.

This is how the movement of Militant Mothers for Education emerged. To help make schools more attractive, the mothers organized campaigns to clean bathrooms and din-

---

35. Founded in 1969 as a pilot project in the provinces of Camagüey and Matanzas, Militant Mothers for Education expanded across Cuba, incorporating more than forty thousand members in its first year.

ing rooms. Federation members started study groups in their own homes.

They campaigned against absenteeism, carrying out an important social task. When a student began to miss school, they would find out what was happening. At times they discovered the problem was of a social nature. When a child began having problems at school, that often indicated something else was going on. Sometimes parents had just divorced. Other times divorced parents weren't caring for their children well.

In some cases, the parents were simply antisocial elements—individuals who had lived by theft and violence—and the children had been raised in that environment. There were neighborhoods where serious social problems were still evident. A revolution doesn't solve the problem of crime overnight. A social worker had to go to those homes, and that's how the federation's social work began.

When we had projects to eliminate unhealthy neighborhoods, members of the mothers movement began to participate in social work and help build new housing. Sometimes this involved organizing residents of rural zones to move to more urbanized areas, where new campesino communities were built, with electricity and running water. We offered help in teaching the families to use household appliances. The federation was responsible for this work as well.

Eradication of prostitution

In the first years of the revolution, back in 1960, 1961, and 1962, we gave high priority to the social task of ending organized prostitution. Tens of thousands of women had been caught up in this terrible situation, driven by economic conditions before the revolution. We thought it would be a long and difficult job to get rid of this social evil. So we were surprised when it disappeared in less than two years.

The federation worked together with the Interior Ministry. The approach differed according to the situation in a given area, such as the number of brothels and pimps there.

We took advantage of the literacy campaign to begin the work. As we conducted the census of women who couldn't read or write in early 1961, we included the women and others in houses of prostitution. I was in Santiago de Cuba when the campaign began, and I visited several brothels to see what conditions were like.

Some were horrifying, with dirt floors even in the middle of the city. You encountered a scene out of Dante's *Inferno*—young women who were mentally retarded, children left naked. An appalling spectacle! Many of those young women had been born and raised under these conditions—it was all they knew. Others had ended up in that life because of economic pressure, in some cases because their children were starving.

By 1961 many women—perhaps hundreds—who had worked as prostitutes had already begun looking for jobs provided by the revolution. We decided to take the next step and carry out a police action to close down the brothels. Police entered them all before dawn one day, arresting the pimps and others who lived off the business. The women were interviewed and then left to watch over the places. We tried to determine their educational level, their background, and their willingness to work.

Many asked right away to be taught a skill so they could work. Generally these were the ones with a better outlook, those who really wanted to get out of the situation they were in. All former prostitutes were given jobs—right away for those with some work experience, and after finishing trade school for others.

Educación y trabajo: vías para erradicación de la prostitución

La Revolución, en su gigantesca obra de transformación social, viene prestando especial atención a las mujeres caídas en la prostitución, imponiéndose la tarea de redimirlas por el único medio hacedero: la educación y el trabajo remunerado.

EN CAMAGÜEY

En el Centro de Producción Artesanal "Mariana Grajales", construído recientemente, han sido ingresadas to-

"In the first years of the revolution, we made ending organized prostitution a high priority. Tens of thousands of women had been forced into prostitution by the economic conditions before the revolution. We thought it would be a long, difficult job to get rid of this evil. We were surprised when it disappeared in less than two years."—Vilma Espín

Cuban daily *Hoy*, March 6, 1962, reports on center established in Camagüey to provide former prostitutes with training for new jobs. Headline says: "Education and work: paths to eradicating prostitution."

Women who had lived their whole lives as prostitutes and obviously needed more help were placed in special schools where they received training for a new life. Those who were mentally handicapped were taken to special centers. Some had serious psychological problems and other illnesses. A medical examination—in some cases by doctors who specialized in psychological disorders—was the first step in determining which women could go to school right away.

We established a large center for former prostitutes in Camagüey, with child care facilities next door. That way children wouldn't be separated from their mothers, who spent time with them in the afternoon. The women received job training, especially in the garment factories that were opening at that time.

We were surprised at how fast it all happened, and happy we could solve such a serious problem in so little time. The women began to marry, a number of them with their own teachers, with police.

The federation worked intensely in creating the schools, in supporting them, in finding work for the women. It was very successful.

Incorporating women in production

Looking back on those years, I recall how we worked to incorporate women fully into jobs. The early years weren't easy, because there were many unemployed fathers with families, people who'd been unemployed since before the revolution. A few years after the revolution, however, no one was jobless any longer. By 1964 we were asking women to take on a whole variety of jobs in services, in factories, in agriculture. More hands were needed.

At the time, a father or husband sometimes said he didn't want his daughters or his wife working. Before the revolution, he would say, he had been unable to provide an adequate income for his family. But now, with the revolution, he had a job and could provide for their needs. The children were going to school. The wife was more secure. So what was this talk about women going to work!

Women, on the other hand, did understand. They felt they not only had a right to work, but a right to get out of the house. They had a right to participate in labor useful for the whole society, not just for the home. Women felt it was a duty to contribute to the revolution through their own labor, as workers. In 1964 and 1965 we had to carry out a major political effort around this question, and women began to confront the arguments of their fathers and husbands.

This opened an era of intense political work for both the federation and the party. The issue began to come up in discussions in workplaces everywhere. We began noticing remnants of the past, subtle discrimination, regarding the appointment of women to leadership responsibilities. And the federation and the party began responding to those manifestations.

Women took an active part in all the programs where the revolution needed them. Every campaign was predicated on women participating. To help women get into centers of production, to get them better trained for jobs, we organized courses in bee-keeping, raising poultry, growing fruit and vegetables, and raising rabbits.

Many women went to work even before the necessary conditions were in place. We didn't yet have child care centers; we were just beginning to build the first ones. Women still had to shoulder the household work of shopping, cooking, washing clothes. We had to fight to create a new consciousness among all family members, parents and children, to get them to share housekeeping chores—and to get parents to pay more attention to their children.

That battle—which arose forcefully as women joined the workforce in a massive way—continues to this day.

Over time the mass of youth—those born after the revolution, as well as those who were children when it began—got into the universities and technical schools. This included women, who, because of their training, have gotten into jobs with more and more responsibility. This speaks highly for the revolution's programs to encourage the participation of women. And it speaks highly for the development of the revolution as a whole.

Women's participation in the workforce has increased enormously since those early years. We began by bringing in many women from houses of prostitution. They began working in agriculture, in garment factories, in a variety of other jobs. In the process, they gained a greater consciousness of their place in society. Housewives and young women who entered the workforce had a similar experience.[36]

An enormous number of young women are enrolled in universities today, and graduate in fields that require intense, time-consuming work, such as researchers or doctors. Some are working in areas far from the cities where they live, and frequently have to travel to other provinces. Some have studied for professions such as geology or agronomy, which require traveling in rural areas.

Today women have jobs as technical workers in all sectors. This includes Moa, Cienfuegos, the big industrial develop-

---

36. In 2008, 59 percent of working-age women were part of the labor force and they made up some 38 percent of all workers. In 1953, 13.5 percent of women were employed, comprising 13.9 percent of the workforce.

ment programs, as well as serving as doctors in schools and in rural areas.[37]

The battle for equality

Enormous changes have come about among women who remain housewives, too. They're not the women they once were, limited to the confines of their homes. The woman of the past went out only for recreational activities or to take the children to school. In rural areas, women were confined to the home and the little patch of land around it. Today's housewife is a woman involved in voluntary labor in agriculture,[38] in construction, in factory work. She's involved in activity through the federation, the CDRs, the Union of Young Communists (in the case of younger women), or the party.

Today there are housewives who are party members. They were recommended for membership because of the political and social work they've carried out. In revolutionary Cuba, when you use the term "housewife," you have to think what it often includes.

As I mentioned earlier, in the first years of the revolution we didn't use the word "equality." We didn't talk about the emancipation, the liberation of women. We didn't use the terminology of the feminist struggle. Instead we spoke of the need for full participation by women in society.

The federation's first congress after our founding was in 1962. There followed years of intense work, when we considered it

37. Moa Bay is the center of Cuba's nickel industry. Cienfuegos, the site of a major oil refinery and shipyard, was also, at the time of this interview, the site of a joint Cuba-Soviet Union project to build a nuclear power plant.

38. Beginning in 1966, the FMC organized women volunteers to join agricultural brigades during harvests. By the early 1970s, more than 100,000 women were part of these brigades each year.

For us, equality is not merely a principle of social justice, but a fundamental human right.... It would be dangerous to start agreeing with the most backward capitalist ideologues on women's participation in the workforce simply due to conjunctural considerations or because we haven't given priority to solving the most pressing family needs.

To propose that women return to the home would be a significant step backward from all standpoints. First of all, this is absurd. It not only abandons the principle of equality and reinforces women's traditional role; it also erases almost a century and a half of social struggle, since the pioneers of Marxism pointed to the indivisible relation between the liberation of society through socialist revolution and women's liberation as part of the revolutionary movement. . . .

That's why we've been careful all these years not to propose apparent solutions to women's double burden such as extending the length of maternity leave, giving mothers subsidies to care for their children, shortening women's work hours, etc. Such steps, instead of reducing inequality, tend to perpetuate it by taking women out of the workforce and slowing their advancement.*

VILMA ESPÍN
FEBRUARY 1989

* "Speech at Meeting of Women Leaders from Socialist Countries," Havana, February 1989. In Vilma Espín, *La mujer en Cuba: familia y sociedad* [Women in Cuba: family and society] (Havana, Ministry of the Revolutionary Armed Forces, 1990), pp. 240–41.

premature to call another congress. By 1974, however, we could no longer postpone assessing what women had achieved.

The theses prepared for our second congress examined in depth women's participation in society—women workers, peasant women, young women, housewives. They dealt with the place of the family in our society. We drafted them to examine what women had achieved up to that time—what they had contributed to the revolution, as well as the possibilities the revolution had given them.

In the congress summary, Fidel said these theses should be studied not only by women but by all members of society, through the mass organizations, the party, and the communist youth.

Fidel also addressed the question of equality for the first time. In the congress discussions we hadn't discussed it in the clear way Fidel did, when he said there was a *battle for equality*. We had discussed only what was missing to achieve equality: in objective material terms, and subjectively, politically.

The concept of the struggle for equality helped us take on all kinds of backward, nonrevolutionary notions that remained in our society—the double standard for men and women on questions of sexual relations, machismo, the legacy of self-centeredness that comes from capitalism, the bourgeois double standard in the home regarding household work and child care.

We examined the responsibilities every family member should have: those of the father and mother to educate their children, to serve as examples. We emphasized the importance, socially and politically, of the entire family participating in the household tasks of laundry, cooking, and cleaning.

We looked at the promotion of women to positions of greater responsibility, and why women didn't yet have the leadership positions they had earned through their work over the years.

"Voluntary labor was a school for the Federation of Cuban Women. It was a way to politically strengthen women—in fact, all our people. . . . At the same time, it's an important part of educating revolutionaries themselves, of educating new generations who perhaps have never been asked to carry out missions demanding a high level of sacrifice."—Vilma Espín

Minibrigade volunteers building apartment complex in Havana, 1990. "Housewives aren't the women they once were," Espín said, "limited to the confines of their home or, in rural areas, to the little patch of land around it. They're involved in voluntary labor in agriculture, in construction, in factory work."

If we compare our present situation with what existed before the revolution, the advances are enormous. . . . But now, in the present stage of the revolution, women have a historical battle to wage.

What is that battle? The struggle for women's equality. The struggle for the full integration of Cuban women into society!

We believe this objective is precisely the focal point of this congress, because, in practice, women's full equality still does not exist. This is not, of course, only a task for women. It is a task for society as a whole! . . .

The party and mass organizations must ensure conditions are present for women to be incorporated into the workforce. First, it's a question of elemental justice. Second, it's an imperative necessity for the revolution.[*]

FIDEL CASTRO
NOVEMBER 29, 1974

The results of the second congress of the Federation of Cuban Women formed the basis for the document *On the Full Exercise of Women's Equality* that was presented to the first congress of our party in 1975.[39] It was also of great use in discussing the Family Code.[40]

39. See pp. 207–8.
40. The Family Code, adopted in February 1975, replaced prerevolutionary laws on marriage, divorce, and alimony. Much of the discus-

[*] Speech at second congress of Federation of Cuban Women, in *Women and the Cuban Revolution*, pp. 76–87. Also in *Mujeres y Revolución*, pp. 152–58.

So 1974 and 1975 were years of intense political work. We fought to increase understanding among the population of the principles of the party, the principles of the revolution, regarding women's right to equality. Women's right to full, unlimited participation in the political, economic, social, and cultural life of Cuba, where we were building and continue to build socialism.

During the discussion on the Family Code, many men took a stronger position on achieving equality for women than they had on the original documents. This gave us another important measure of progress. These men were no longer the youth they had been at the time of the revolutionary victory. Their proposals for the Family Code deeply enriched the discussion.

As preparations for the first party congress began,[41] Fidel said that the *Theses on the Full Exercise of Women's Equality* should be discussed by the entire country—despite the fact that discussion of the Family Code and the FMC document for our 1974 congress had just ended. The most important thing about our laws, about our documents, Fidel said, is that the revolutionary principles behind them be discussed and

---

sion leading up to its adoption focused on articles stipulating that women should have equal rights and responsibilities in marriage and that men should share in housework and raising children. For major excerpts, see *Women and the Cuban Revolution*, pp. 182–200.

41. The first congress of the Communist Party of Cuba was held in December 1975. The Communist Party came out of a consolidation, led by the July 26 Movement leadership, of parties that supported the revolution. In 1961 the July 26 Movement, Popular Socialist Party, and Revolutionary Directorate ceased functioning as separate organizations and the Integrated Revolutionary Organizations (ORI) was created. In 1963 the United Party of the Socialist Revolution (PURS) was formed, and, in October 1965, the Communist Party of Cuba was founded.

The younger generations cannot understand, much less internalize, the degree of discrimination women were subject to before the revolution—simply because they were women. The immense majority of women, who were poor, suffered not only from class exploitation, and, if they were black women, from racial discrimination as well. They were also oppressed as a gender, putting them all at a humiliating social disadvantage.

The situation required a radical transformation, and that's what was done.

I consider it necessary to emphasize that we cannot retreat a millimeter in what we have accomplished over the last fifty years, above all in terms of something as decisive as genuine equal opportunity for men and women on the job.

This too has been a field of action for the federation, which must meet its responsibility to alert the party to any deviation from this established policy. In saying this, I am simply reiterating the point Fidel made thirty years ago, at the third congress of the FMC, when he said:

"It is the duty of the federation to be attentive to all questions that concern women, to defend women's interests within the party and within the state."

To which I would add: "Let no one have the slightest doubt about this!" [*]

VICE PRESIDENT JOSÉ RAMÓN MACHADO
AUGUST 23, 2010

[*] Speech at fiftieth anniversary of founding of Federation of Cuban Women. In *Mujeres*, issue no. 3 (July–September), 2010

The elections held today by this Assembly filled vacancies in the Council of State, including for two vice presidents. One of them is—for the first time—a woman who, in this case, is also comptroller of the republic.

These elections reflect not only the revolutionary and professional qualities of those selected. They also express our explicit intent to increase the ethnic and female composition of leadership positions.

Personally I view as shameful the lack of progress we've made in this area in fifty years of revolution.

It's true that 65 percent of the technical workforce is female, that the citizenry of Cuba comprises a beautiful racial rainbow, and that there are no formal privileges of any kind.

It's true that Cuban society emerged from a radical social revolution in which the population achieved a full and total legal equality and a level of revolutionary education that has shattered the subjective aspect of discrimination.

But discrimination still exists in another form, what Fidel has called objective discrimination, which is rooted in poverty and lack of access to education.

For my part I will exert all my influence to push back these harmful prejudices until they are eradicated once and for all, until women and blacks are promoted to leadership positions at all levels, in accordance with their merits and training.[*]

PRESIDENT RAÚL CASTRO
DECEMBER 20, 2009

understood by each member of society.

Promotion of women to leadership responsibilities has been a constant concern of Fidel's. When the federation was formed, he had a much clearer idea of what we had to do—clearer than those of us who started the FMC—about the degree of inequality that existed in our society and what we needed to do.

Through all those years, at each of the federation's meetings and party congresses, he stressed the need for a greater advancement of women into leadership positions in all areas of our society, in the state, the party, and elsewhere.

Defense of the homeland

In all our struggles, in all our wars, there were women whose glorious names are inscribed in history. As early as the Ten Year War (1868–78) and the Independence War (1895)[42], there were women combatants, some of whom rose to the rank of colonel or captain. These women didn't simply collaborate, carry out underground work, or help their husbands but stood out in their own right. Many died in combat.

There are names with beautiful histories attached to them, like Rosa la Bayamesa, Adela Azcuy, Mercedes Varona. At the beginning of the war of 1868, Carlos Manuel de Céspedes talked of the glorious women who preferred death to yielding to the demands of the Spaniards. Luz Vázquez, an extraordinary woman, was one. The Castillo sisters, marvelous women,

42. See chronology, and "Cuban independence wars" in glossary.

* Speech to closing session of National Assembly of Peoples Power. In the elections held that day, four of the seven new members of the Council of State were women, one of whom was black.

were two others.[43] Many were very young.

Ana Betancourt was ahead of her time. That's precisely the phrase Martí used to describe her actions during the Guáimaro Constituent Assembly of 1869,[44] where she spoke of the need to consider women's emancipation, participation in society, and liberation. In vibrant, beautiful terms, Betancourt called for freeing women from their shackles, so they could participate in everything. Her words, fortunately, were taken down, and we in the federation have often used them. We have put them forward in Cuba and abroad as an example of Cuban women's participation since the earliest years of our struggles.

After March 10, 1952,[45] we began to see women in student demonstrations in the streets. In the last stage of our struggle, in our revolutionary war, the July 26 Movement was strengthened by the many youth and women who joined. In the cities, women took young people hunted by the police into their homes. In the mountains, they welcomed Rebel Army combatants, fed them, and cared for the wounded.

Women found many different ways to participate. We weren't just combatants in the underground, although many risked their lives doing underground work. We also fought in the Sierra Maestra, in the mountains, in the different fronts of the war. Others went as teachers, as nurses, organizers of the camps, or workers in shops making uniforms, knapsacks,

43. See glossary, Rosa María Castellanos, Adela Azcuy, Mercedes Varona, Carlos Manuel de Céspedes, Luz Vázquez, Adriana and Lucía Castillo Vázquez.

44. In Guáimaro, in a section of Camagüey province liberated by independence fighters, Cuba's first constitution was debated and voted on in April 1869.

45. The date of Batista's military coup.

Citizens:

The Cuban woman, in the quiet dark corner of the home, has waited with patience and resignation for this sublime moment in which a just revolution breaks her yoke and unties her wings.

Everything in Cuba was enslaved: by birth, color, and sex. You want to destroy slavery by birth, fighting to the death if necessary. [In the Republic in Arms] slavery based on color no longer exists.

When the moment comes for women to be liberated, the Cuban man, who has overturned slavery by color, will commit his generous soul to the conquest of rights for the one who, in the war today, is his caring, self-sacrificing sister, and who tomorrow will be, as she was yesterday, his exemplary companion.*

ANA BETANCOURT
APRIL 14, 1869

"In vibrant, beautiful terms, Ana Betancourt called a century ago for freeing women from their shackles so they could participate in everything. Her words, fortunately, were taken down and we in the Federation have often used them."

—Vilma Espín

*According to one account, after Betancourt spoke at 1869 Guáimaro Constituent Assembly during first independence war, Carlos Manuel de Céspedes, who delegates elected president of the Republic of Cuba, congratulated her. "Cuban historians, when writing about this day, will record how you, ahead of your time, called for the emancipation of women," Céspedes said.

and other essentials.

Some women served as messengers—one of the most dangerous assignments. Others worked in kitchens, brought in supplies, helped transport people from the mountains to the city or from the city to the mountains. They took care of the wounded, helped set up hospitals, helped establish the schools in the Second Front and in the Sierra Maestra. That's why we felt it was also necessary they be given the opportunity to take up arms and fight as soldiers and officers.

In the final months of the war, Fidel demonstrated his understanding of the political measures the war required. With the tremendous confidence he's always had in women, he organized the Mariana Grajales Women's Platoon in response to the demand of women who had already spent time in the mountains but hadn't had the opportunity to fight arms in hand.[46]

To go to the mountains and fight was, naturally, the yearning of every revolutionary, of all the youth, men and women, who participated in the struggle.

But it wasn't easy to get a chance to do it. As underground fighters, continually persecuted by the superior forces of the tyranny, we always thought about joining the Rebel Army in the mountains and being able to confront the enemy, arms in hand.

So when Fidel formed the Mariana Grajales Platoon, it was a great day for our compañeras who got the opportunity, there in the Sierra Maestra, to take up a rifle and train for combat.

And fight they did, with great success, from the first battle they took part in.

During those difficult moments of constant battle, they

46. See p. 71, footnote 10.

Even though we were doing many essential things, we felt frustrated that we could not fight arms in hand. We were in the places where fighting was taking place.

"If women have to take part in all the duties of the revolution," we said, "why can't we fight for the revolution in the same way as our men fight?"

We asked our commander in chief to allow us to fight arms in hand. He agreed.

On September 3, 1958, Fidel assembled his general staff at the time. There was a discussion that lasted more than seven hours. Fidel had a very big argument there. There were still not enough weapons for everyone, and the men were saying, "How can we give rifles to women when there are so many men who are unarmed?"

Fidel answered: "Because they're better soldiers than you are. They're more disciplined."

"In any event," he said, "I'm going to put together the squad, and I'm going to teach them how to shoot."[*]

TETÉ PUEBLA
2003

showed the capacity of women to fight the enemy despite the harsh conditions in the mountains. It was an extraordinary moment in the history of women's participation in the revolution.

Shortly after the 1959 victory, when the revolutionary government began to organize militias in the workplaces, we got requests right away from women who wanted to participate. The majority were housewives. So the federation created a

[*] In *Teté Puebla and the Mariana Grajales Women's Platoon in Cuba's Revolutionary War* (Pathfinder, 2003), pp. 50–52.

militia unit. As soon as a woman entered a workplace, she was integrated into the militia there. Later, as our concept of the militias changed, in keeping with the structure of workers militias, women joined through their worksites.

During that period, when the revolution was the target of constant threats and aggression from the enemy, women played an active role in defense. When the attack came at Playa Girón, women across the country mobilized. One of our first emergency medical brigades went to the front and was joined by women from the area. Two compañeras died there, Cira García, our regional general secretary in Playa Larga, and Juliana Montano.

Women responded the same way during the October Crisis.[47] When a call was issued on Radio Havana in October 1962, explaining what was happening, women reported for duty. I remember receiving reports and wire service dispatches from other countries at the time. In Mexico, in the United States itself, women were holing up in their homes. They had bought candles, condensed milk. There was tremendous anxiety, terror of a nuclear war.

In our country, on the other hand, people were calm. There was no panic. Women in militia uniforms went to their antiaircraft gun stations. Their children had been evacuated to places where they'd be taken care of, at times with their grandparents. We knew we might disappear from the face of the earth, that none of us might be left alive, but we faced the prospect quietly and coolly.

I always stress this. Because later, as threats continued over the years, women have wanted to be ready at the critical time. They've wanted to know what their responsibility is in case of war, what has to be prepared beforehand, how to make sure

47. See glossary, October 1962 "Missile" Crisis.

the elderly and the children are cared for, where to go, where to take shelter. Through civil defense exercises, our public health brigade members have trained jointly with the armed forces and the Ministry of Health.

In 1980, when the Reagan administration's aggressive policy following the revolutionary victories in Grenada and Nicaragua showed we had to be even better prepared for war, Fidel proposed organizing the Territorial Troop Militias.[48] Women signed up right away. Some volunteers who had small children felt they were being discriminated against and firmly insisted they be allowed to join. Out of that experience, a new policy was initiated—to train women officers for the Territorial Troop Militias. Women who wanted to join the regular armed forces could now be taken into active duty.

After extensive discussion in the federation and the Ministry of the Revolutionary Armed Forces, we concluded that women should be allowed to take on many full-time positions in the armed forces. Until then women had served in the armed forces only in certain technical capacities. They could serve as doctors, nurses—and in aviation and the tank corps as engineers or technicians—but they were not part of the regular command structure. The First Women's Antiaircraft Artillery Regiment was created in March 1984. It opened new possibilities and created hopes and aspirations among the mass of women, especially young women. They joined that first regiment and then the second one, in the Guantánamo region. We've seen great enthusiasm and a desire not only to voluntarily serve in that regiment, but to stay in the armed forces.[49]

48. See glossary, Territorial Troop Militias.

49. Units of both Women's Antiaircraft Artillery Regiments in 1988 took part in the final stage of the internationalist mission in Angola that defeated the forces of apartheid South Africa.

When we talk about "war of the entire people," this isn't just an idea. It's a reality to organize the people and the armed forces. It's a reality that can be seen in each defense activity we carry out.

The first Bastion exercise[50] revealed a unanimous desire among our people to know exactly what they could do. Women above all made this point forcefully, through the federation and the party. That is, if they weren't part of a regular formation in the Territorial Troop Militias, what would they be asked to do in case of war? Could they get a rifle, a grenade?

I remember that Raúl once said, "Even a pot of hot water can be used to fight the enemy."

New methods began to be outlined, new conceptions, in which every member of our population had a responsibility, a weapon, and a place in combat if the enemy invaded. Under the concept of war of the entire people, everyone now knows—women in particular—what they have to do if the enemy dares to try to invade us.

Women's increased political consciousness, as demonstrated by their participation in defense of the homeland, has led many to take part in internationalist missions, as well. The morale of our people is extraordinarily high. We are prepared to defend ourselves even in the most difficult situations. The fact that this is known—that it's something we've publicized—has been and remains a deterrent for the imperialist enemy.

50. The Bastion military exercises were based on the concept of a "war of all the people" in case of US invasion. The exercises involving the civilian population as well as the armed forces were first conducted in September 1980. They continued in 1983, 1986, 2004, and in 2009, when nearly four million took part.

"When the First Women's Antiaircraft Artillery Regiment was created in March 1984, it opened new possibilities and created hopes and aspirations, especially among young women. They joined that first regiment and then the second one, in the Guantánamo region. We've seen great enthusiasm not only to voluntarily serve in that regiment, but to stay in the armed forces."—Vilma Espín

Members of Women's Antiaircraft Artillery Regiment of Guantánamo at encampment in Havana, prior to deployment to Angola, in 1988. They defended newly built airfields in the south of Angola against attack by forces of South African apartheid regime. Espín is in white blouse.

Chronology

1868 — Carlos Manuel de Céspedes launches first war for Cuba's independence against Spanish colonial rule.

1869 — Independence fighters organize assembly of Republic in Arms in April in Guáimaro, in a section of Camagüey province they had liberated. Delegates adopt Cuba's first constitution, which declares, "All the inhabitants of the Republic are absolutely free," including slaves. Ana Betancourt participates and speaks of need to fight for women's participation in social and political life.

1870 — On December 25 Céspedes, elected president at Guáimaro assembly, annuls curbs on emancipation adopted by Republic's new legislature and reaffirms full civil and political rights for freed slaves.

1878 — First independence war ends. Majority of independence forces sign Zanjón Pact with Madrid, maintaining Spanish rule and freeing only slaves and indentured workers who were members of anticolonial army. Insurgents led by Antonio Maceo reject pact, pledging to continue struggle until independence is won and slavery abolished.

1879 — Some independence forces launch what becomes known as the "Little War," which lasts into 1880.

1886 — Spanish crown abolishes slavery in Cuba.

1895 — Led by José Martí, the Cuban Revolutionary Party reinitiates war for independence.

1898 — US government sends troops to intervene in anticolonial war, snatching victory from Cuban independence forces.

Defeated Spain signs Treaty of Paris, ceding Puerto Rico, the Philippines, and Guam to Washington, and placing Cuba under US military occupation.

1901 — US government imposes so-called Platt Amendment on Cuban constitution at Constituent Assembly in June. Amendment affirms Washington's "right to intervene" in Cuba and to establish naval bases on the island.

1902 — Cuba gains formal independence, but US imperialist interests dominate its government and increasingly take control of its agriculture and other production and commerce.

1903 — US-dictated "treaty" imposes US naval base at Guantánamo.

1931–39 — Spanish revolution. Civil war (1936–39) ends in defeat of republican forces and establishment of Francisco Franco's fascist regime, a blow to working class worldwide.

August 1933 — Revolutionary general strike leads to overthrow of Machado dictatorship in Cuba and establishment of "Hundred Days Government," which implements measures contrary to US capitalist interests in Cuba.

January 1934 — US-backed coup by army chief of staff Fulgencio Batista overthrows "Hundred Days Government." For next six years Batista dominates Cuban government through presidents beholden to him.

1940 — Batista elected president, forms "national front" government that includes Popular Socialist Party (Communist Party) in cabinet.

1944 — Authentic Party leader Ramón Grau San Martín elected president.

May 1947 — Founding of Cuban People's (Orthodox) Party led by Eduardo Chibás. Party attracts new generation repelled by government's corruption and subservience to Washington. Fidel Castro leads radical youth wing.

July 1947 — Fidel Castro joins armed expedition—backed and financed by Grau government—to overthrow US-backed dictator Rafael Trujillo in Dominican Republic. The operation, known as Cayo Confites expedition after Cuban island where preparations took place, is called off by Grau in September under US government pressure.

June 1948 — Authentic Party's Carlos Prío Socarrás elected president.

March 1949 — After year-long battle by students and teachers, newly established University of Oriente in Santiago de Cuba wins official recognition and funding.

October 1949 — Imperialist-backed forces of Chiang Kai-shek's Nationalist Party (Kuomintang) are defeated and flee mainland China. People's Republic of China is proclaimed.

August 5, 1951 — Eduardo Chibás fatally shoots himself at close of his weekly radio program, after speech denouncing government corruption. Funeral becomes huge antigovernment demonstration.

1952

March 10 — Military coup by Batista ousts Prío two and a half months before June 1 presidential election. Coup is met by student protests in Havana and other cities. Batista establishes brutal dictatorship defending US imperialist interests. Fidel Castro begins organizing revolutionary movement, recruited primarily from Orthodox Party youth, to overthrow tyranny.

April 9 — Revolutionary upsurge in Bolivia, with tin miners in vanguard, topples military regime. Largest tin mines are nationalized, trade unions legalized, land reform initiated, and Bolivia's indigenous majority enfranchised.

1953

January 27 — "March of the Torches," student demonstration in Havana marking centennial of José Martí's birth, denounces Batista regime. Revolutionary movement led by Fidel Castro makes first public appearance with contingent of 500.

April 5 — National Revolutionary Movement (MNR) leaders arrested for planned anti-Batista revolt in military aimed at seizing base in Havana.

July 26 — Some 160 revolutionaries led by Fidel Castro launch insurrectionary assault on Moncada army garrison in Santiago de Cuba and Carlos Manuel de Céspedes barracks in Bayamo. Attacks fail. Fifty-six captured revolutionaries are murdered in following days.

July 27 — Armistice ends three-year-long Korean War. Korea's workers and peasants and Chinese People's Liberation Army block Washington from dominating entire Korean peninsula and invading China to roll back revolution.

August 22 — Washington and London organize coup in Iran toppling government of Mohammad Mossadegh, which had nationalized British oil holdings. Install monarchy of Shah Mohammed Reza Pahlavi.

September–October — Trial of captured Moncada combatants. Fidel Castro and 31 others are sentenced to up to 15 years in prison.

1954

February 20 — Haydée Santamaría and Melba Hernández, the two Moncada combatants who are women, are released from prison after serving seven-month sentences.

May 7 — French forces surrender to Vietnamese liberation fighters at Dien Bien Phu, signaling defeat of French colonial rule in Indochina. Geneva Accords codify partition of Vietnam, with Washington dominating southern half of country.

June — Seeking to crush worker and peasant struggles in Guatemala and turn back initial steps toward land reform, CIA-backed mercenary forces invade the country and oust government of Jacobo Arbenz.

October — Defenders of July 26 combatants clandestinely print and begin circulating *History Will Absolve Me*, Fidel Castro's courtroom speech written down by him in prison and smuggled out. Supporters distribute tens of thousands of document that becomes program of revolutionary movement.

1955

May 15 — Growing amnesty campaign forces Batista to release more than 200 political prisoners, including Moncada combatants. Haydée Santamaría and Melba Hernández are among leaders of campaign.

June 12 — July 26 Revolutionary Movement is founded through fusion of Moncadistas and other currents. These include members of Revolutionary National Movement, such as Armando Hart and Faustino Pérez, and Santiago-based Revolutionary National Action led by Frank País. Among latter is Vilma Espín.

July 7 — Fidel Castro arrives in Mexico. Begins preparations for expedition to return to Cuba to launch revolutionary war against Batista.

August 15 — Fidel Castro sends letter to leaders of Orthodox Party, urging party to join insurrectionary movement.

December 5 — Boycott of racially segregated buses begins in Montgomery, Alabama, opening battle in rising mass struggle by Blacks to bring down racist Jim Crow segregation across US South.

December — Nationwide strike in Cuba by 200,000 sugar workers protests government moves to cut wages. A number of towns in central Cuba are briefly taken over by workers and supporters.

1956

February 26 — José Antonio Echeverría and other student leaders in Havana form Revolutionary Directorate to carry out armed actions against dictatorship.

April 3 — Conspiracy by anti-Batista army officers known as "Los Puros" (the pure ones) is discovered. Twelve active-duty officers are arrested and jailed, including José Ramón Fernández.

June — Vilma Espín returns to Cuba after graduate studies in United States. Meets with July 26 leadership in Mexico en route and rejoins underground struggle in Santiago de Cuba.

August 30 — Fidel Castro and José Antonio Echeverría sign Mexico Letter, to coordinate action by July 26 Movement and Revolutionary Directorate.

November 25 — Eighty-two members of July 26 Movement, under Fidel Castro's command, set sail from Mexico aboard *Granma* yacht to initiate revolutionary war in Sierra Maestra mountains of eastern Cuba.

November 30 — July 26 Movement in Santiago, led by Frank País, organizes armed action in support of scheduled *Granma* landing. In its wake, Batista's police begin wave of arrests and murders, especially in Santiago and throughout Oriente province.

December 2 — Delayed by storms, *Granma* lands in eastern Cuba. The revolutionary war begins.

December 5 — Rebel Army combatants surprised by Batista's troops in first battle of revolutionary war, suffering heavy casualties.

1957

January 6 — July 26 Movement organizes demonstration in Santiago of several thousand women to protest police murder of 15-year old William Soler, a member of movement's action squad.

February 17 — National Directorate of July 26 Movement meets in Sierra Maestra, a month after the Rebel Army's first victory. Frank País and Vilma Espín come from Santiago to take part.

New York Times correspondent Herbert Matthews interviews Fidel Castro. Publication of interview and photo exposes Batista's lie that Castro has been killed.

March 13 — Revolutionary Directorate organizes attack on presidential palace in Havana. Echeverría and most combatants are killed during action or hunted down and murdered afterward.

March 15 — First Rebel Army reinforcements—51 cadres from underground struggle in Oriente province—reach Sierra Maestra. Operation is organized by Frank País, Celia Sánchez, and Vilma Espín.

May 10 — In Santiago courtroom, 22 captured *Granma* expeditionaries are convicted and sentenced to prison. In same trial, Frank País and some 70 others charged in connection with November 30 action are acquitted.

May 28 — Rebel Army wins battle against well-fortified army garrison at El Uvero.

July 20 — Vilma Espín assigned to coordinate underground action in Oriente province as Frank País assumes responsibilities as July 26 Movement's national action coordinator.

July 21 — Ernesto Che Guevara is first combatant promoted

by Fidel Castro to rank of commander, in charge of Rebel
Army's second column, no. 4.

July 30 — Frank País and Raúl Pujol murdered; general strike
shuts down Santiago.

July 31 — 60,000 join funeral march for Frank País; demonstration by women in Santiago confronts US ambassador, demands end to US aid to Batista.

September 5 — July 26 Movement combatants join with anti-
Batista forces inside naval base in Cienfuegos to seize city;
revolt is brutally crushed following day.

1958

January 10 — Armando Hart and two others are arrested on
way down from Sierra Maestra. July 26 Movement's quick
action publicizing arrests saves their lives. Hart remains
in prison until revolutionary victory.

January 23 — Popular rebellion in Caracas overthrows Venezu-
elan dictator Marcos Pérez Jiménez.

March — Rebel Army establishes Frank País Second Eastern Front,
led by Raúl Castro in northeastern Oriente province, and
Third Front, led by Juan Almeida northeast of Santiago.

April 9 — July 26 Movement calls general strike throughout
Cuba. Strike fails and movement meets with fierce repression by Batista dictatorship. Exploiting setback to rebels,
regime prepares "encircle and annihilate" offensive in Sierras by 10,000-strong force.

May — Demonstrations in Argentina, Paraguay, Bolivia, Peru,
Venezuela, and other countries protest Latin America tour
by US vice president Richard Nixon and denounce US
domination of region.

May 3 — Meeting of July 26 Movement in Sierra Maestra assesses outcome of April 9 strike. Center of July 26 Movement national leadership is shifted to Sierra Maestra, under

Fidel Castro's direct command.

June 28 — Rebel Army forces in Second Front under Raúl Castro capture 29 US marines from nearby Guantánamo base and hold them—along with 20 US and Canadian civilians—as shield against Batista bombing raids. Fidel Castro orders their release when informed in early July.

June — Vilma Espín is transferred to Second Front, assigned to political instruction of combatants and coordination of logistical support from areas nearby.

July 20 — Rebel Army victory at battle of El Jigüe breaks back of Batista army's "encircle and annihilate offensive." Preparation of counteroffensive begins.

August — Asela de los Santos is transferred to Second Front, assigned to organize Education Department, which opens 400 schools by end of year.

August 21–31 — Camilo Cienfuegos and shortly afterwards Che Guevara lead Rebel Army columns toward western and central Cuba, respectively.

September 4 — Fidel Castro organizes Mariana Grajales Women's Platoon formed in Rebel Army's Column 1. Women's platoon engages in first combat September 27.

September 21 — At Congress of Peasants in Arms near headquarters of Second Front, 200 delegates ratify support for Rebel Army and land reform.

October — Guevara's Column 8 reaches Las Villas province, and Guevara takes command of rebel forces in Escambray mountains.

October 10 — Rebel Army issues Law no. 3 codifying right of peasants to land they work, a revolutionary measure already being carried out in rebel-held areas in Oriente province.

November–December — Strategic victories liberate growing number of cities in both Oriente and Las Villas, strengthening Rebel Army's counteroffensive against Batista's troops.

December 31 — Guevara's forces liberate Santa Clara, capital of Las Villas province, as combined forces of Rebel Army fronts in Oriente, commanded by Fidel Castro, close in on Santiago.

1959

January 1 — Batista flees Cuba. Regime's forces in Santiago surrender to Rebel Army. Fidel Castro issues call for island-wide insurrection and revolutionary general strike.

January 2 — Massive uprising by Cuban workers. Rebel Army columns led by Cienfuegos and Guevara enter Havana and take garrisons. "Freedom Caravan" under command of Fidel Castro leaves Santiago for march to Havana.

January 8 — Freedom Caravan enters Havana.

February 13 — Counterrevolutionaries set fire to cane fields in central Cuba.

February 16 — Fidel Castro becomes prime minister, replacing bourgeois opposition figure José Miró Cardona.

February 27 — Revolutionary government reduces electricity rates.

March 6 — Revolutionary government reduces rents by 30 to 50 percent.

March 22 — Government announces measures to outlaw racial discrimination in public facilities and employment. In response to initiative by workers, Fidel Castro calls for creation of popular militias.

May 17 — First agrarian reform law limits private landholdings to 1,000 acres. Estates of foreign and Cuban owners that exceed limit are confiscated by government decree and mobilizations of peasants and workers. More than 100,000 peasants receive titles to land they work.

October 11–21 — US-based planes begin firebombing Cuban cane fields, sugar mills. B-26 plane bombs Havana, killing two, wounding 50.

October 26 — Formation of Revolutionary National Militias, consolidating local workers and peasants units established earlier in year.

November — Cuban delegation of more than 80 women, headed by Vilma Espín, participates in international women's conference in Chile. Work building delegation helps lay basis for what will become Cuban women's organization.

November 1 — Two thousand workers and students in Panama cross into Canal Zone to plant Panamanian flag. Tear-gassing and assaults by club-wielding US forces spark further actions demanding Panama's sovereignty over canal.

1960

March 4 — *La Coubre*, French ship carrying grenades and munitions purchased from Belgium, explodes in Havana harbor, killing 101 people.

March 17 — President Dwight Eisenhower orders CIA to begin preparation of US-based Cuban mercenary forces to invade Cuba.

July 6 — Eisenhower orders 95 percent reduction in sugar Washington had agreed to purchase from Cuba, under US-Cuba quota accords in place for many years. Soviet Union agrees to buy Cuban sugar.

August 6 — Responding to mounting US economic aggression, revolutionary government decrees nationalization of major US companies in Cuba, backed by massive popular mobilizations and workers' occupations of enterprises.

August 23 — Federation of Cuban Women founded. Fidel Castro addresses meeting held at Confederation of Cuban Workers auditorium in Havana.

September 2 — Rally of one million in Havana approves by acclamation First Declaration of Havana, condemning US imperialism and pointing to revolutionary road for working people in Latin America.

September 28 — Neighborhood-based Committees for Defense of the Revolution (CDRs) founded, involving tens of thousands of working people, in response to growing attacks.

October 13 — Cuban and foreign-owned banks nationalized, as are more than 380 large Cuban-owned enterprises.

October 14 — Housing nationalized. Cubans guaranteed titles to apartments or houses where they live.

October 24 — Remaining US companies nationalized.

1961

January 1 — Year-long literacy campaign begins. Some 250,000 volunteers teach more than 700,000 adults 14 and over, the majority women, to read and write.

January 3 — Washington breaks diplomatic ties with Cuba.

March 31 — President John F. Kennedy abrogates US contracts for sugar purchases from Cuba.

April 10 — Revolutionary government opens first three child care centers in Havana.

April 17–19 — US-organized mercenary invasion at Bay of Pigs defeated by Cuban people at Playa Girón.

May 17 — National Association of Small Farmers (ANAP) founded.

July 31 — First class of 800 peasant women graduate from Ana Betancourt School.

December 11 — 8,000 graduate from Ana Betancourt School. Through three courses between July and December, 12,000 graduate overall.

December 22 — At a massive celebration in Havana, Cuba is able to declare itself a "territory free of illiteracy."

1962

January 22–31 — Meeting of US and Latin American foreign ministers in Uruguay expels Cuba from Organization of American States and supports military moves against revolution.

February 3 — President Kennedy orders total embargo on US trade with Cuba.

February 4 — Assembly of one million in Havana's Plaza of the Revolution adopts Second Declaration of Havana, proclaiming Cuba's support to revolutionary struggles throughout Latin America.

February 26 — First polio vaccination campaign; 70,000 volunteers vaccinate 2.2 million children.

July 5 — Algeria wins independence from France.

October 1 — First congress of Federation of Cuban Women focuses on helping women enter workforce. Organization has 375,000 members.

October 22–28 — Kennedy administration provokes "Missile" Crisis after learning Cuban government, in face of Washington's invasion plans, has permitted installation of Soviet nuclear missiles as part of mutual defense pact. Kennedy demands removal and orders naval blockade of Cuba, placing US forces on nuclear alert. Premier Nikita Khrushchev, without consulting Cuban government, announces removal of missiles. Mass mobilizations of Cuban workers and farmers stay Washington's invasion plans.

1963

May 24 — Algeria welcomes 55 Cuban volunteer doctors, dentists, and nurses, first internationalist medical mission of Cuban Revolution.

October 6 — Revolutionary government enacts second agrarian reform, nationalizing private landholdings larger than 167 acres. Some 10,000 capitalist farmers, owning 20 percent of Cuba's agricultural land, are expropriated.

December 6 — 9,200 graduate from third course of Ana Betancourt School.

1974

January — Maternity law adopted, providing six weeks paid leave before birth and twelve after. A woman can also take nine additional month's leave without pay and return to former job.

November 25–29 — Second Congress of FMC confirms course to advance fight for full equality of women.

1975

February 14 — Family Code adopted by Cuban government, affirming women's rights in workplace and home and replacing prerevolutionary laws on marriage, divorce, adoption, and alimony.

November — Cuban government responds to Angola's request for help in defeating invasion by forces from white-supremacist South Africa; 16-year internationalist mission begins.

December 17–22 — First congress of Communist Party adopts document "On the Full Exercise of Women's Equality."

1979

March 13 — Led by Maurice Bishop, New Jewel Movement in Grenada overthrows US-backed dictatorship, opening revolution in that Caribbean country. Cuban internationalists serve as volunteer construction workers, medical personnel, and teachers.

July 19 — Popular insurrection in Nicaragua, led by Sandinista National Liberation Front, overthrows decades-long Somoza dictatorship. Over next ten years, thousands of Cuban internationalists volunteer as teachers, doctors, and technical advisors.

1980

March 5–8 — Third Congress of FMC. Now has membership of more than 2.3 million, some 80 percent of women in Cuba over age 14.

1981

January — In response to increased US military threats, Territorial Troop Militias begin to be formed. Hundreds of thousands of Cubans join, nearly half of them women.

1984

March — First Women's Antiaircraft Artillery Regiment established as part of integration of women more broadly into Revolutionary Armed Forces.

1985

March 5–8 — Fourth congress of FMC assesses progress in women's integration into workforce and fight for equality on job.

1986

February and December — Third congress of Cuban Communist Party marks beginning of rectification process. More than 100 child care centers built in Havana by end of 1988, largely by minibrigades using volunteer labor.

1988

Women's Antiaircraft Artillery Batteries participate in Cuba's internationalist mission in Angola, taking part in military campaign that culminated in defeat of invading forces of apartheid South Africa.

Glossary of Individuals, Organizations, and Events

AAA – See Triple A.

Action for Liberty (Acción Libertadora) – Founded 1952 under leadership of Justo Carrillo. Advocated armed action to encourage army officers to carry out coup against Batista. After arrests and exile of many members, disappeared by early 1955. Many members joined July 26 Movement.

Acosta, Clodomira (1936–1958) – Rebel Army messenger. Arrested, tortured, and murdered by Batista's police in Havana, September 1958; body thrown in sea.

Agrarian Reform Law – Enacted by the revolutionary government May 17, 1959. Limited individual landholdings to 1,000 acres, resulting in confiscation of vast estates, many owned by wealthy US families. Some 100,000 landless peasants received title to land they tilled. Second agrarian reform in 1963 limited holdings to 167 acres, affecting 10,000 capitalist farmers.

Almeida, Juan (1927–2009) – Member of Communist Party Central Committee and Political Bureau from its founding in 1965 until his death. A bricklayer in Havana at time of Batista coup, he participated in 1953 Moncada attack. Released May 1955 following amnesty campaign. Participated in *Granma* expedition 1956. In February 1958 promoted to commander, later headed Third Eastern Front. After 1959 responsibilities included head of air force, vice minister of Revolutionary Armed Forces, vice president of Council of State. One of three Sierra combatants to hold rank of Commander of the Revolution. Hero of the Republic of Cuba. President of Association of Combatants of Cuban Revolution at time of death.

Almendros, Herminio (1898–1974) – Professor of education. Supported republicans in Spanish Civil War; left Spain after victory of fascists. Joined University of Oriente faculty 1952. After 1959 worked in Ministry of Education, including in Sierra Maestra.

Alomá, Tony (1932–1956) – Member of July 26 Movement underground in Santiago de Cuba. Killed in combat during November 30, 1956, armed action.

Amat, Carlos (1930–) – Member of July 26 Movement underground in Santiago de Cuba. Worked at telephone exchange. After 1959 minister of justice and ambassador at Cuba's Permanent Mission to UN in Geneva.

Ameijeiras, Efigenio (1931–) – Division general in Revolutionary Armed Forces. Joined revolutionary struggle against Batista regime March 1952. *Granma* expeditionary in 1956, finished war as commander of Rebel Army Column 6 and second in command of Second Eastern Front. Head of Revolutionary National Police and its battalion that fought at Playa Girón April 1961. Commanded Cuban internationalist mission in Algeria 1963. Led Cuba's volunteer mission in Angola 1984.

ARO – Oriente Revolutionary Action. Founded in 1954 by Frank País. Later, as it grew beyond Oriente, renamed Revolutionary National Action (ANR). Fused with Moncada veterans and others to form July 26 Movement in 1955.

Atala Medina, Ibis and Nayibe – Members of Santiago underground.

Authentic Organization – Military organization set up by leaders of Authentic Party to oppose Batista following 1952 coup.

Azcuy, Adela (1861–1914) – Joined Cuban independence army 1896, serving as a nurse. Became a captain.

Barrera, Pedro – Colonel in Batista's army, first commander sent to fight Rebel Army in Sierra Maestra January 1957.

Batista, Fulgencio (1901–1973) – Military strongman in Cuba, 1934–58. Elected president 1940–44. Led coup March 10, 1952, establishing US-backed military-police tyranny. Fled Cuba January 1, 1959, in face of advancing Rebel Army and popular insurrection.

Batista, Rubén (1933–1953) – First student martyr in struggle against Batista dictatorship. University student in Havana who participated in protest actions against 1952 coup. Shot by police on January 15, 1953, at demonstration against desecration of monument to Julio Antonio Mella just outside university. Died a month later.

Bay of Pigs – See Playa Girón.

Benítez, Conrado (1942–1961) – Volunteer literacy teacher in Escambray mountains. Killed by counterrevolutionary bandits January 5, 1961, together with peasant Eliodoro Rodríguez Linares, who was Benítez's student.

Betancourt, Ana (1832–1901) – Participant in Cuba's first war of independence against Spain, 1868–78. Took part in 1869 Guáimaro assembly that adopted Cuba's first constitution. Arrested by colonial regime and deported.

Boti, Regino (1878–1958) – Supporter of Cuban independence from Spain; a leading Cuban poet of first half of twentieth century.

Camacho, Julio (1924–) – Member of Orthodox Party, Action for Liberty, and Revolutionary National Movement. Founder of July 26 Movement in 1955 in Guantánamo and leader of November 30, 1956, armed action there. Helped lead September 5, 1957, uprising in Cienfuegos, then joined Rebel Army in Sierra Maestra. Member of Communist Party Central Committee since founding in 1965.

Cañas Abril, Pedro (1902–1992) – Professor at University of Oriente in Santiago. After revolution headed Institute of Geography of Academy of Sciences from 1966 to 1981.

Carbonell, Fe – Member of Santiago underground.

Castellanos, Rosa María (Rosa la Bayamesa) (c.1830–1907) – Freed from slavery and joined liberation army at outset of 1868–78 independence war. Ran hospital for combatants then and during 1895–98 independence war.

Castillo Vázquez, Adriana and Lucía – Daughters of Luz Vázquez and Francisco Castillo Moreno, revolutionaries during Cuba's first independence war. When Bayamo was about to fall to Spanish troops in 1869, helped burn city and fled to countryside where both died of illness.

Castro, Fidel (1926–) – Central leader of revolutionary movement in Cuba since beginning of struggle against Batista dictatorship in 1952. Organized July 26, 1953, attack on Moncada garrison in Santiago de Cuba and Carlos Manuel de Céspedes garrison in Bayamo. Captured and sentenced to fifteen years in prison. Released 1955 after amnesty campaign. Led fusion of revolutionary organizations to found July 26 Revolutionary Movement. Organized *Granma* expedition from Mexico to launch revolutionary war in Cuba 1956. Commander in chief Rebel Army 1956–59 and commander in chief Revolutionary Armed Forces 1959–2008. Cuba's prime minister, February 1959 to 1976. First secretary Communist Party of Cuba 1965–2011; president of Council of State and Council of Ministers 1976–2008.

Castro, Ramón (1924–) – Older brother of Fidel and Raúl Castro. Helped organize supplies for Rebel Army during revolutionary war and served primarily in agriculture-related responsibilities since 1959 victory.

Castro, Raúl (1931–) – President of Council of State and Council of Ministers and first secretary of Communist Party of Cuba. An organizer of student protests at University of Havana against Batista dictatorship, he participated in 1953 Moncada attack and was captured and sentenced to thirteen years in prison. Released May 1955 following amnesty campaign. Founding member of July 26 Movement and participant in 1956 *Granma* expedition. Rebel Army commander of Second Eastern Front 1958. Minister of Revolutionary Armed Forces 1959–2008. Vice premier 1959–76. First vice president of Council of State and Council of Ministers 1976–2008 and second secretary of Communist Party from 1965.

Causse Pérez, José Nivaldo (1928–1994) – Brigadier general in Revolutionary Armed Forces. Participant in clandestine struggle in Santiago de Cuba; assigned to Rebel Army after November 30, 1956, uprising. An organizer of first school to train Rebel Army teachers; operated Second Front radio station.

Céspedes, Carlos Manuel de (1819–1874) – Lawyer, plantation owner, and revolutionary democrat in Oriente province. On October 10, 1868, freed his slaves, proclaimed Republic of Cuba, and launched first war against Spanish rule, attacking garrison in nearby town of Yara in what became known as Call of Yara. Supreme commander of Cuban independence army and later first president of Republic in Arms until October 1873. Killed in battle February 27, 1874.

Chabás, Juan (1900–1954) – Joined Communist Party of Spain during Civil War. In exile taught in Cuba, including at University of Oriente.

Chaviano – See del Río Chaviano, Alberto.

Chibás, Eduardo (1907–1951) – A leader of Student Directorate in fight against Machado dictatorship in 1920s and 30s. In 1947 founding leader of opposition Orthodox Party (Cuban People's Party), which had broad popular support. Elected senator 1950. On August 5, 1951, in protest against government corruption, shot himself at close of radio address; died 11 days later.

Cienfuegos, Camilo (1932–1959) – *Granma* expeditionary 1956. Captain in Rebel Army Column 4 led by Che Guevara, promoted to commander 1958. From August to October 1958 led Antonio Maceo Column 2 westward from Sierra Maestra. Operated in northern Las Villas until end of war. Became Rebel Army chief of staff, January 1959. Killed when plane lost at sea while returning to Havana, October 28, 1959.

Civic Front of Martí Women (Frente Civico de Mujeres Martianas) – Founded in 1952 to unite women in struggle against Batista coup. Worked closely with July 26 Movement. Disbanded in January 1959, its supporters worked in revolution's education, health, and other campaigns and many were founding members of Federation of Cuban Women.

Colomé, Abelardo (Furry) (1939–) – Army corps general and, since 1989, Minister of Interior. Joined July 26 Movement 1955. Participant in November 30, 1956, armed action in Santiago de Cuba. Part of first reinforcements sent to Rebel Army in Sierra Maestra March 1957. Promoted to commander December 1958. Internationalist mission in Argentina and Bolivia 1962–64 to prepare guerrilla front in Argentina led by Jorge Ricardo Masetti. Head of Cuban mission in Angola 1975–76. Member of Communist Party Central Committee since founding in 1965. Member of Political Bureau and Council of State. Hero of Republic of Cuba.

Committees for Defense of the Revolution (CDRs) – Organized September 28, 1960, on a block-by-block basis to exercise vigilance against counterrevolutionary activity and organize participation in public health efforts, civil defense, and other campaigns of revolution.

Congress of Peasants in Arms – Meeting of 200 peasant delegates, representing 84 local committees, near headquarters of Second Front, September 21, 1958. Formed regional peasant committee to implement land reform and strengthen alliance with agricultural workers.

Cowley, Fermín (1907–1957) – Lieutenant colonel in Batista's army. In December 1956, as military chief of Holguín regiment, directed kidnapping and murder of 23 opponents of dictatorship. In May 1957 ordered killing of 15 captured survivors of *Corynthia* expedition organized by Authentic Organization. Brought to justice November 23, 1957, by order of July 26 Movement.

Cuadras, Gloria (1911–1987) – Veteran of anti-Machado fight in early 1930s. A leader of national amnesty campaign for imprisoned Moncadistas. In 1955 a founder of July 26 Movement and head of propaganda in Oriente. Active in underground during revolutionary war. After 1965 served on Oriente provincial committee of Communist Party of Cuba.

Cuban independence wars – From 1868 to 1898 Cubans waged three wars for independence from Spain: Ten Years War (1868–78), "Little War" (1879–80), and war of 1895–98 leading to end of Spanish rule. US military occupied Cuba after Spain's defeat and imposed so-called Platt Amendment on constitution, authorizing Washington to "exercise the right to intervene" in Cuba and to establish naval bases on the island.

Cuban People's Party – See Orthodox Party.

de la Torre, Carlos (1858–1950) – Educator, rector of University of Havana in 1920s, exiled 1930–34 for opposition to Machado dictatorship.

del Río Chaviano, Alberto (b. 1911) – Under Batista, commanding officer of First Regiment based at Moncada garrison in Santiago de Cuba. After July 26, 1953, assault on Moncada, he directed massacre of 56 captured revolutionaries. Promoted to brigadier general. Fled Cuba January 1959.

Díaz, Emiliano (Nano) (1936–1957) – Member of Revolutionary

National Action (ANR), led by Frank País in Santiago, which joined in founding July 26 Movement in 1955; participant in November 30, 1956, armed action; joined Rebel Army as part of March 1957 reinforcements; killed at El Uvero, with rank of lieutenant May 28, 1957.

Doce, Lidia (1916–1958) – Rebel Army messenger. Arrested, tortured, and murdered by Batista's police in Havana, September 1958; body thrown in sea.

Domínguez, Guillermo (1932–1957) – Member July 26 Movement urban underground in Puerto Padre; joined Rebel Army March 1957 as part of first group of reinforcements; became lieutenant; captured and killed near Pino del Agua May 17, 1957.

Domitro, América (1935–1971) – Active in underground in Santiago de Cuba, Havana, Camagüey. Companion of Frank País. Assigned to Rebel Army's Second Front November 1958. After January 1, 1959, worked in ministries of defense and foreign relations.

Domitro, Taras – Member of July 26 Movement urban underground in Santiago de Cuba, participant in November 30, 1956 armed action. Brother of América Domitro.

Duque de Estrada, Arturo (1928–1963) – Member of Oriente Revolutionary Action from 1954, then July 26 Movement in Santiago de Cuba. Secretary to Frank País. Received telegram from Mexico November 27, 1956, that *Granma* expedition had set sail for Cuba.

Echeverría, Delia (1908–1998) – Member of Young Cuba revolutionary organization 1930s and fiancée of Antonio Guiteras. Exiled for anti-Batista activities; returned January 1959. Worked in Casa de las Américas. At founding of Federation of Cuban Women in 1960 served as first vice-president.

El Uvero, battle of – Rebel Army, strengthened by reinforcements from Santiago underground, mounted frontal assault on and took El Uvero garrison May 28, 1957.

Escalona, Juan (1931–) – As University of Oriente student, campaigned to win state recognition. Member of Popular Socialist Party and, from September 1958, Rebel Army, serving in Second Front. Brigadier general in Revolutionary Armed Forces (retired); member of Communist Party Central Committee 1980–2011; minister of justice 1983–90, 1993–2010; president of National Assembly 1990–93.

Espín, Nilsa (d. 1965) – Active in student movement at University of Oriente and July 26 Movement underground; sister of Vilma Espín.

Ferrer, Nilda (d. 1990) – Member of July 26 Movement in Santiago de Cuba. Together with María Antonia Figueroa carried out first demonstration supporting imprisoned Moncadistas as they arrived for trial September 1953.

Figueroa, Max (1913–1996) – Professor at University of Oriente, supporter of struggle against Batista. In exile in Honduras 1953–59. After 1959 held responsibilities in Ministry of Education, including director of Central Institute of Teaching Sciences.

Galbe, José Luis (1904–1985) – Republican exile from Spanish Civil War; came to Cuba 1940. Joined University of Oriente law faculty. After 1959 in Cuban foreign service, serving as attaché in Greece, Cyprus, Italy.

García, Cira (1920–1961) – Militia member and leader of local unit of Federation of Cuban Women at Playa Larga on Bay of Pigs. Killed in bombing raid during US-organized invasion.

García, Guillermo (1928–) – Peasant from Sierra Maestra who joined July 26 Movement before *Granma* landing. Helped organize regroupment of Rebel Army forces December 1956. From early 1957 combatant in Column 1 led by Fidel Castro. Commander in Third Eastern Front led by Juan Almeida, late

1958. Member Communist Party Central Committee since 1965, Political Bureau 1965–86. Member of Council of State. One of three Sierra combatants to hold title Commander of Revolution.

García Bárcena, Rafael (1907–1961) – Veteran of anti-Machado struggle of 1920s and 30s. Professor at University of Havana and Orthodox Party member. After Batista's 1952 coup founded Revolutionary National Movement (MNR), promoting military coup by anti-Batista officers. Arrested, tortured, imprisoned April 1953; Armando Hart was defense attorney. Named Cuba's ambassador to Brazil in 1959.

Grajales, Mariana (1808–1893) – When Cuban independence wars against Spain began in 1868, encouraged all eight sons to enlist. Her husband and five sons were killed in combat. Son Lieutenant General Antonio Maceo, known as Bronze Titan, renowned as military leader, strategist, example of revolutionary intransigence; killed in battle 1896.

Griñán Peralta, Leonardo (1892–1962) – History professor at University of Oriente. Author of books about Antonio Maceo and Cuba's wars against Spain.

Guevara, Ernesto Che (1928–1967) – Argentine-born leader of Cuban Revolution. Recruited in Mexico in 1955 to *Granma* expedition as troop doctor. First Rebel Army combatant promoted to commander 1957. After 1959 responsibilities included head of National Bank, minister of industry. Led Cuban internationalist volunteer detachments in Congo 1965 and Bolivia 1966–67. Wounded and captured by Bolivian army during CIA-organized counterguerrilla operation, October 8, 1967; murdered following day.

Guillén, Nicolás (1902–1989) – Poet and National Committee member of Popular Socialist Party before revolution. Persecuted by dictatorship, lived in exile during revolutionary war, returning to Cuba 1959. Became president of National Union

of Writers and Artists of Cuba (UNEAC) in 1961. Member
Communist Party Central Committee at time of death.

Guitart, Renato (1930–1953) – Member of leadership committee of movement led by Fidel Castro prior to Moncada attack.
One of five combatants killed during attack.

Guiteras, Antonio (1906–1935) – Leader of student struggles
against dictatorship of Gerardo Machado in 1920s and early
1930s, and of anti-imperialist forces during 1933 revolution
that overthrew that regime. Interior minister in "Hundred
Days Government" brought to power in September 1933 and
overthrown in January 1934 "Sergeants' Revolt" led by Batista.
Murdered in January 1935 while leading revolutionary struggle against military regime.

Gutiérrez Baró, Elsa (1928–) – Founding member of Orthodox
Party 1947, underground combatant in July 26 Movement. Vice-
president of FMC at founding 1960, first director of Ana Betancourt School 1960–62, first editor of FMC magazine *Mujeres*,
1961. Physician and psychologist; founder of Clinic for Teenage
Youth, 1975.

Hart, Armando (1930–) – Leader of Revolutionary National
Movement after Batista coup. In 1955 a July 26 Movement
founding member and its national coordinator from early
1957 to January 1958. Captured and imprisoned until January 1, 1959. Minister of education 1959–65; Communist Party
organization secretary 1965–70; minister of culture 1976–97.
Member Communist Party Central Committee since 1965, and
Political Bureau 1965–86. Since 1997 director of Martí Program
Office of Council of State.

Hart, Enrique (1929–1958) – Member Revolutionary National
Movement. In charge of July 26 Movement action and sabotage in Havana during revolutionary war. Organized militias of July 26 Movement in Matanzas. During the April 9,
1958, strike attempt, helped seize radio station and addressed

population. Killed April 21, 1958, while making bomb. Brother of Armando Hart.

Hatuey (d. 1511) – Taino Indian chief who led uprising in Cuba against Spanish colonialists; captured and burned at stake 1511. According to tradition, when offered last rites so his soul could go to heaven, Hatuey asked if that's where souls of Spaniards went. When assured it was, he declined rites, saying he preferred his soul go elsewhere.

Heredia, José María (1803–1839) – Opponent of Spanish rule. Cuba's national poet in early nineteenth century.

Hernández, Melba (1921–) – One of two Moncada combatants who were women. Captured, sentenced to seven months in prison. Released February 1954 and helped lead national amnesty campaign for Moncada combatants. At founding of July 26 Movement in 1955, member of its National Directorate. Returned to Cuba from Mexico after *Granma* landing, carried out underground activity, later joined Rebel Army. Member Central Committee of Communist Party. In 2001 received honorary title Heroine of Republic of Cuba.

History Will Absolve Me – Fidel Castro's reconstruction of courtroom defense speech at 1953 trial for leading attack on Moncada garrison. Later circulated clandestinely throughout Cuba, serving as program of July 26 Movement.

Ibarra, Laureano – Notorious Batista police official. Fled to US after victory of revolution in 1959.

Ibarra Planas, Zoila (d. 1986) – Second in command of Education Department in Second Eastern Front. In 1959 head of Education Department of Rebel Army.

Imperatori Grave de Peralta, Alicia (1913–) – Founding administrator of Ana Betancourt School for peasant women, Havana 1960–61. Supporter of July 26 Movement during revolutionary war, selling bonds to raise funds. Joined Revolutionary National Militia when formed in 1959. Participated in

1959–60 preparatory work that launched Federation of Cuban Women. Member of FMC National Committee since founding, shouldering responsibilities in its National Secretariat. Executive secretary to president of FMC. Awarded honorary title Heroine of Labor in 2011.

Independence wars – See Cuban independence wars.

Integrated Revolutionary Organizations (ORI) – Formed 1961 at initiative of July 26 Movement, fusing with Popular Socialist Party and Revolutionary Directorate. Helped lay basis for founding of Communist Party of Cuba in 1965.

Jiménez Lage, Reynerto (1930–1987) – Member of July 26 Movement and participant in November 30, 1956, uprising in Santiago de Cuba. Joined Rebel Army March 1957 with first group of reinforcements; served in Columns 1, 6, 16. After 1959 colonel in Revolutionary Armed Forces.

July 26 Revolutionary Movement – Founded June 1955 by Fidel Castro and other participants in Moncada attack, fusing with other revolutionary forces, including Revolutionary National Action (ANR) led by Frank País. In May 1958 national leadership was centralized in Sierra Maestra, with Fidel Castro serving as general secretary as well as Rebel Army commander in chief. Led fusion with Popular Socialist Party and Revolutionary Directorate in 1961 as step toward founding Communist Party of Cuba in 1965.

La Bayamesa, Rosa – See Castellanos, Rosa María.

López Rendueles, Julio (1893–1986) – Spanish republican exile. Joined faculty at University of Oriente as chemistry professor 1950. During revolutionary war helped July 26 Movement make munitions.

Machado, Gerardo (1871–1939) – Headed US-backed dictatorship in Cuba 1927–33. Elected president in 1924, forcibly extending term in 1927, unleashing protests that were brutally suppressed. August 1933 revolutionary upsurge sent him into exile.

Machado Ventura, José Ramón (1930–) – First vice president of Council of Ministers and Council of State since 2008 and second secretary of Communist Party since 2011. Joined Rebel Army in latter half 1957, serving as physician and attaining rank of commander. Served in Second Eastern Front. Minister of public health 1960–68, first secretary of Communist Party's Havana provincial committee 1971–76. Member of party Central Committee since 1965, Political Bureau since 1975, and Central Committee Secretariat since 1976.

Mambises – Fighters in Cuba's three wars of independence from Spain between 1868 and 1898. Many were freed slaves and other bonded laborers. The term "mambi" is of African origin.

Marinello, Juan (1898–1977) – Chairman of Popular Socialist Party 1939–61. Rector of University of Havana following revolution. President of National Assembly and member of Communist Party Central Committee at time of death.

Marrero, Levi (1911–1995) – Historian, professor of geography at University of Havana. Author of *Geografía de Cuba*. Left Cuba 1961.

Martí, José (1853–1895) – Cuba's national hero. Noted poet and writer. Arrested and exiled for independence activity at age 16. Founded Cuban Revolutionary Party in 1892. Led fight to oppose Spanish colonial rule and US designs on Cuba. Organized and planned 1895 independence war; killed in battle.

Masetti, Jorge Ricardo (1929–1964) – Argentine journalist who came to Sierra Maestra January 1958 and was won to Rebel cause. Founded Cuba's Prensa Latina news service after 1959. Died while leading guerrilla front in northern Argentina.

Masferrer, Rolando (1914–1975) – In 1950s organized paramilitary force known as "Tigers," used as death squads during revolutionary war. Member of Cuban Communist Party in 1930s; fought in Spanish Civil War. Became wealthy pro-Batista senator, campaigned in Oriente in 1958 electoral farce. Fled Cuba December 31, 1958. Killed by car bomb in Miami in gangland assassination.

Matthews, Herbert (1900–1977) – *New York Times* correspondent who in February 1957 was first journalist to interview and photograph Fidel Castro in Sierra Maestra, disproving Batista regime's lies that rebels had been wiped out. Covered Spanish Civil War for *Times* in 1930s.

Mella, Julio Antonio (1903–1929) – Founding president of Federation of University Students (FEU) in 1923. A founding leader of Communist Party of Cuba in 1925. Arrested by Machado's police in 1926, escaped to Mexico, continuing to organize against dictatorship. Assassinated in Mexico City by Machado's agents, January 1929.

Meruelo, Otto – Pro-Batista television commentator, arrested 1959 for complicity with dictatorship's crimes. Sentenced to 30 years, served 20, left Cuba.

MNR (Revolutionary National Movement) – Founded by Rafael García Bárcena in May 1952. Sought to encourage coup by forces within military, with popular backing. Attempted April 1953 putsch in Havana failed. Most cadres, including Armando Hart and Faustino Pérez, joined July 26 Movement.

Moncada attack – On July 26, 1953, some 160 revolutionaries under command of Fidel Castro launched insurrectionary attack on Moncada army garrison in Santiago de Cuba and simultaneous attack on garrison in Bayamo, opening armed struggle against Batista dictatorship. Five died in combat at Moncada. After attack's failure, Batista's forces massacred 56 captured revolutionaries. Fidel Castro and others were later captured, and he and 31 others were sentenced to up to 15 years in prison. Broad national amnesty campaign won their release May 15, 1955.

Montané, Jesús (1923–1999) – A leader of 1953 Moncada attack, released in May 1955 amnesty. Participant in *Granma* expedition. Captured December 1956 and in prison for rest of war. After 1959 headed Central Committee's International Department; organized Central Committee; minister of communication. Member Communist Party Central Committee from 1965 until his death.

Montseny, Demetrio (1925–) – Brigadier general (retired) in Revolutionary Armed Forces. Railroad worker from Guantánamo, active in July 26 Movement in Santiago de Cuba. Joined Rebel Army 1958; became head of Column 20. After 1959 represented Ministry of Industry in Oriente, served as military attaché, director of foreign relations of armed forces ministry, and president of Santiago unit of Association of Combatants of the Cuban Revolution.

National Association of Small Farmers (ANAP) – Founded May 1961. Organization of farmers organized today in Credit and Service Cooperatives (CCSs) working privately held land and Agricultural Production Cooperatives (CPAs) of farmers collectively working land.

Navarrete, Agustín (Tin) – Member of July 26 Movement underground in Havana and Santiago de Cuba. Named Rebel Army commander in 1959. Later vice minister of steel industry.

Núñez Jiménez, Antonio (1923–1998) – Joined Guevara's column in 1958 on eve of battle of Santa Clara with rank of captain. Well-known geologist and geographer. Responsibilities after 1959 included executive director of National Institute of Agrarian Reform, president of Academy of Sciences, vice minister of culture, ambassador to Peru.

October 1962 "Missile" Crisis – In face of escalating preparations by Washington for invasion, Cuban government signed mutual defense agreement in early 1962 with Soviet Union. In

October 1962 US president John Kennedy demanded removal
of Soviet nuclear missiles installed in Cuba, ordered naval
blockade, stepped up preparations to invade, and placed US
armed forces on nuclear alert. Cuban workers and farmers
mobilized in millions to defend revolution. On October 28 Soviet premier Nikita Khrushchev, without consulting Cuban
government, announced decision to remove missiles.

Oriente Revolutionary Action – See ARO.

Orthodox Party (Cuban People's Party) – Known as the *ortodoxos*, formed in 1947 on platform of opposition to US imperialist domination and government corruption. Principal leader
Eduardo Chibás. Party's youth wing provided initial cadres
for revolutionary movement Fidel Castro organized after Batista's 1952 coup. Leadership moved rightward after Chibás's
death in 1951; party fragmented after coup.

País, Frank (1934–1957) – Based in Santiago, a central leader of
July 26 Movement from founding in 1955. Earlier a student at
Teachers Institute and University of Oriente in Santiago; vice
president Federation of University Students (FEU) in Oriente.
Action coordinator for Oriente in Revolutionary National
Movement (MNR); central leader of Oriente Revolutionary
Action (ARO) and Revolutionary National Action (ANR). Led
ANR combatants into July 26 Movement in 1955; its central
leader in Oriente province, became national action coordina-
tor and head of its urban militias. Murdered by dictatorship's
forces July 30, 1957.

País, Josué (1937–1957) – Active in Martí Student Bloc in Havana. Joined July 26 Movement; participated in Santiago de
Cuba uprising November 30, 1956. Captain in July 26 Movement urban militia in Santiago; murdered by government
troops June 30, 1957. Brother of Frank País.

Parada Marañón, Lucía – Active in underground movement
in Santiago de Cuba. After 1959, worked for more than 20

years as one of Raúl Castro's secretaries.

Parellada, Otto (1928–1956) – Member of Action for Liberty, worked closely with Frank País. Imprisoned 1954 for attempt to bomb Batista motorcade; released in amnesty May 1955. Founding member of the July 26 Movement; killed in Santiago de Cuba uprising November 30, 1956.

Pedraza, José Eleuterio (1903–1989) – As head of Cuban army, tried to depose Batista in 1941 during latter's first regime. Forced out of army, returned as inspector general during revolutionary war. Fled Cuba January 1, 1959; worked closely with Trujillo dictatorship in Dominican Republic.

People's Power – Cuba's popularly elected government bodies at municipal, provincial, and national level, established by 1976 constitution. National Assembly of People's Power, elected every five years, is highest legislative body and elects Council of State and its president, who is head of state and of government.

Pérez, Faustino (1920–1992) – Member of Orthodox Party. Following 1952 coup joined Revolutionary National Movement and in 1954 along with Armando Hart became an MNR leader. Jailed October 1954, freed by amnesty May 1955. A founder of July 26 Movement in June 1955, part of its first National Directorate. *Granma* expeditionary. Headed July 26 Movement underground in Havana until April 1958. Became Rebel Army commander in Sierra. Member of Communist Party Central Committee from 1965 until his death.

Playa Girón – On April 17, 1961, 1,500 US-based Cuban mercenaries organized, financed, and deployed by Washington invaded Cuba at Bay of Pigs on southern coast. In less than seventy-two hours, they were defeated by Cuba's revolutionary militias, armed forces, and police. On April 19 remaining invaders were captured at Playa Girón (Girón Beach), the name used in Cuba for invasion and battle.

Popular Socialist Party (PSP) – Name taken by Communist Party of Cuba in 1944. Opposed Batista dictatorship but rejected political course of Moncada combatants and of July 26 Movement and Rebel Army in launching revolutionary war in 1956–57. PSP cadres collaborated with July 26 Movement in final months of struggle. After 1959 victory, July 26 Movement initiated fusion with PSP and Revolutionary Directorate in 1961, leading to founding of Communist Party of Cuba in 1965.

Portuondo, José Antonio (1911–1996) – Writer, veteran of revolutionary upsurge against Machado dictatorship in 1930s; member of Popular Socialist Party; professor at University of Oriente 1953–58. Ambassador to Mexico 1960–62; founding member and vice president of National Union of Writers and Artists of Cuba (UNEAC); rector of University of Oriente 1962–65; ambassador to Vatican 1976–82.

Prío Socarrás, Carlos (1903–1977) – Leader of Authentic Party. President of Cuba from 1948 until Batista's March 1952 coup. A leading figure in exile bourgeois opposition during revolutionary war. In early 1961 left Cuba for US.

PSP – See Popular Socialist Party.

Puebla, Delsa "Teté" (1940–) – Brigadier general in Revolutionary Armed Forces. One of first women to join Rebel Army July 1957, rising to rank of lieutenant. Founding member and second in command of Mariana Grajales Women's Platoon. Founding member of Federation of Cuban Women and Communist Party. Member of party's Central Committee 1980–86 and of its provincial committee in Havana since 1980. Since 1985 director of office of Assistance to Combatants and Family Members of Internationalists and Martyrs of the Revolution.

Pujol, Raúl (1918–1957) – Member of Civic Resistance in Santiago de Cuba. Murdered together with Frank País July 30, 1957.

Ramos Latour, René (Daniel) (1932–1958) – July 26 Movement national action coordinator after Frank País's death, heading its urban militias. Joined Rebel Army as commander May 1958. Killed in battle July 30, 1958, in closing days of Batista army's failed offensive in Sierra Maestra.

Randich Jústiz, Luis Mariano (d. 1957) – Classmate of Frank País at Teachers Institute in Santiago de Cuba; joined provincial police. Confirmed País's identity to cops who then killed País July 30, 1957. Brought to justice by July 26 Movement.

Realengo 18 – Site of long battle over land in eastern Cuba, settled in 19th century by veterans of independence wars. From 1920s, under battle cry "land or blood," peasant families, backed by agricultural workers, fought sugar barons' land grab. With support of courts, Guardia Rural, and Batista following 1934 coup, landlords prevailed until Rebel Army's liberation of area in 1958.

Revolution of 1933 – Revolutionary upsurge and general strike that toppled Machado dictatorship in August 1933. Replaced by proimperialist regime led by Carlos Manuel de Céspedes, son of initiator of Cuba's 1868 independence war; toppled same year in coup led by noncommissioned officers, students, and civilians, known as "Sergeants' Revolt." "Hundred Days" coalition government formed; included anti-imperialist leaders such as Antonio Guiteras; decreed eight-hour day; annulled US "right to intervene" in Cuba (Platt Amendment). Fulgencio Batista, army chief of staff at time, led second coup January 14, 1934, with support of US embassy.

Revolutionary Directorate – Founded 1955 by José Antonio Echeverría and other Federation of University Students leaders. In 1956 cosigned Mexico Letter with July 26 Movement to cooperate in actions against dictatorship. Organized March 13, 1957, attack on Presidential Palace; some 40 members and leaders, including Echeverría, killed that day and in cop massacre weeks later. In October 1958 its guerrilla column in Escambray mountains joined front commanded by Che Guevara. Fused with July 26 Movement and Popular Socialist Party in 1961.

Risquet Valdés, Jorge (1930–) – Popular Socialist Party member, joined Rebel Army 1958. Secretary of Integrated Revolutionary Organizations (ORI) in Oriente Province after March 1962; later minister of labor. In Congo-Brazzaville 1965 as head of Column 2 to support internationalist mission led by Che Guevara in eastern Congo. Member Communist Party Central Committee since 1965. Head of Cuban civilian internationalist mission in Angola 1975–80. Deputy in National Assembly.

Rivero, Rafael (d. 1965) – Active in July 26 Movement underground, later captain in Revolutionary Armed Forces. Husband of Nilsa Espín.

Rodríguez, Léster (1927–1998) – Participant in Moncada attack. At founding of July 26 Movement in 1955 its coordinator in Oriente province. Helped organize Santiago uprising November 30, 1956. Arrested, acquitted May 1957, went into exile. July 26 Movement delegate in United States through October 1957. In 1958 returned to Cuba and joined Rebel Army, becoming captain. After 1959 held various responsibilities, including in steel industry.

Salas Cañizares, José María – One of most notorious of Batista's killers, commanded police squad that assassinated Frank País in July 1957. Lieutenant colonel and Military Intelligence Service (SIM) commander in Santiago de Cuba. Fled Cuba January 1, 1959.

Salas Cañizares, Rafael (1913–1956) – Havana chief of police following Batista's march 1952 coup. Notorious torturer and murderer. Died from wounds sustained during October 1956 raid on Haitian embassy, where cops murdered ten anti-Batista activists who had sought refuge there.

Sánchez, Celia (1920–1980) – First woman to become Rebel

Army combatant, serving on general command from October 1957. Ten years earlier was founding member of Orthodox Party and a leader of its youth. Leader in Oriente province of amnesty campaign for Moncada prisoners. In 1955 a founding member of July 26 Movement and its central organizer in Manzanillo. Together with Frank País, organized urban supply and recruitment network for Rebel Army. At her death a member of Communist Party Central Committee and secretary of Council of State and Council of Ministers.

Sánchez Arango, Aureliano (1907–1976) – Student activist in struggle against 1925–33 Machado dictatorship. Minister of education in Carlos Prío government 1948–52, notorious for corruption. Formed Triple A, which proclaimed aim of organizing armed struggle against Batista dictatorship but didn't do so. Following victory of revolution, engaged in counterrevolutionary activity and fled to US.

Santamaría, Abel (1927–1953) – Second in command of 1953 attack on Moncada garrison; captured, tortured, and murdered by Batista forces. A store clerk and student, after March 1952 coup he led group of young Orthodox Party members pressing party leadership to fight dictatorship. In May 1952 joined forces with Fidel Castro and helped lead propaganda, agitation, organization, and military training of 1,200 recruits preparing for Moncada action.

Santamaría, Haydée (1922–1980) – Participant in 1953 Moncada attack, in which her brother Abel was captured, tortured, and murdered. She was arrested, tried, and imprisoned for seven months. A founder of July 26 Movement and member of its National Directorate. Helped organize November 30, 1956, uprising in Santiago de Cuba. Sent to US in 1958 to organize support among exiles. Founder and director of Casa de las Américas cultural organization in Havana from 1959 until her death. Member Communist Party Central Committee 1965–80.

Second Front – Frank País Second Eastern Front, initiated March 1958, became liberated zone in northeastern Oriente province under command of Raúl Castro. Encompassed 4,700 square miles with population of 500,000.

Smith, Earl (1903–1991) – Wall Street broker, US ambassador to Cuba 1957–59.

Somoza – Family of dictators who ruled Nicaragua, 1933–79; overthrown by 1979 revolution led by Sandinista National Liberation Front (FSLN).

Spanish Civil War – Overthrow of monarchy in Spain in 1931 opened way for rising working-class movement to fight for and conquer political power. Capitalist rulers, backed by other imperialist powers, turned to General Francisco Franco's fascist forces in 1936 to defeat elected republican government. Civil war spurred revolutionary working-class and peasant struggles for land, national rights, and workers power. Last republican stronghold fell to fascists January 1939.

Tabernilla Dolz, Francisco (1888–1972) – General who backed Batista's 1952 coup, subsequently army chief of staff with rank of major general. Fled Cuba January 1, 1959.

Territorial Troop Militias – Volunteer militias organized across Cuba in 1981 in face of US military threats in response to revolutionary victories in Grenada and Nicaragua. Composed of some 1.5 million workers, farmers, students, and housewives, who train before and after work and help finance their military expenses. Important component of Cuban revolutionary defense strategy of "war of the entire people."

Tey, José (Pepito) (1932–1956) – Student leader in Santiago de Cuba and close collaborator of Frank País in Action for Liberty (1952–53), Revolutionary National Movement (1953–54), Oriente Revolutionary Action (1954), Revolutionary National Action (1955), and July 26 Movement (1955–56). Killed during November 30, 1956, uprising in Santiago de Cuba.

Triple A – Armed organization founded by Aureliano Sánchez Arango after 1952 coup, including veterans of anti-Machado struggle of 1930s. Funded by Authentic Party leaders; aimed to convince members of military to topple Batista. Virtually disappeared by start of revolutionary war in December 1956.

United Revolutionary Women (Unidad Femenina Revolucionaria) – Organized in early 1959, largely in rural areas. Closely associated with Popular Socialist Party. Dissolved into Federation of Cuban Women, founded August 1960.

Varona, Mercedes (d. 1870) – Active collaborator of Cuban independence fighters, captured by Spanish authorities. First woman killed in war when Spanish column escorting her and other prisoners was attacked by independence forces, to whom she sought to give support.

Vázquez, Leyla – Member of Santiago underground.

Vázquez, Luz (1831–1870) – With Bayamo about to fall to Spanish troops in 1869, she and her family helped burn down city and fled to countryside. There she and several of her children died.

Ventura Novo, Esteban (d. 2001) – Havana police chief, one of Batista's most notorious assassins. Fled to US January 1, 1959.

With Cross and Country (Con la Cruz y con la Patria) – Organization of Catholics who supported revolution, founded 1960. Germán Lence, its leading spokesperson, was suspended from priesthood by Cuba's bishops after their August 1960 statement denouncing "Communist regime."

Women's International Democratic Federation – International women's organization, founded in Paris, December 1945, and led by Communist Parties in Soviet Union and world over.

Index

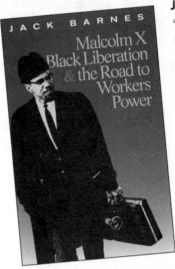

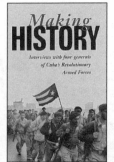

A revolution within . . .

Marianas in Combat: Teté Puebla and the
Mariana Grajales Women's Platoon in Cuba's Revolutionary War 1956–58

For more than 50 years, the struggle to transform women's social status has been central to Cuba's socialist revolution. Brigadier General Teté Puebla joined the fight to overthrow the US-backed Batista dictatorship in 1956, at age fifteen. This is her story—from the urban underground, to officer in the Rebel Army's all-women's unit until today. $14. Also in Spanish and Farsi.

Making History
Interviews with Four Generals of Cuba's Revolutionary Armed Forces
Enrique Carreras, Harry Villegas, José Ramón Fernández, Nestor López Cuba

Through the stories of four outstanding Cuban generals, we understand how the people of Cuba, as they build a new society, have held Washington at bay for more than 5 decades. $17. Also in Spanish and Farsi.

With Our Memory on the Future

Produced in 2005 for the 45th anniversary of the Federation of Cuban Women, this film examines the progress women have made since workers and farmers took power in 1959. Through interviews in workplaces and schoolyards, attitudes towards women's equality, divorce, child rearing, and sexual relations are frankly discussed. $15. DVD, 53 minutes. In Spanish, English subtitles.

Renewal or Death: Cuba's Rectification Process
Fidel Castro
In *New International* no. 6

Two speeches by Fidel Castro registering a turning point in the Cuban Revolution in the late 1980s known as rectification. It marked a turn away from copying many political and economic policies from the Soviet Union, and a revitalization of working-class methods, popular mobilization, and voluntary work. Introduction by Mary-Alice Waters. $16

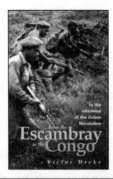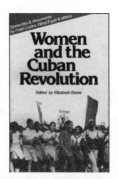

. . . Cuba's socialist revolution

First and Second Declarations of Havana

Nowhere are questions of revolutionary strategy confronting workers and farmers in the Americas addressed with greater clarity than in these two documents, adopted by million-strong assemblies of the Cuban people in 1960 and 1962. These uncompromising indictments of imperialist plunder and "the exploitation of man by man" continue to stand as manifestos of revolutionary struggle by working people the world over. $10. Also in Spanish, French, Arabic.

From the Escambray to the Congo:
In the Whirlwind of the Cuban Revolution
Víctor Dreke

The author describes how easy it became after the Cuban Revolution to take down a rope segregating blacks from whites in the town square, yet how enormous was the battle to transform social relations underlying all the "ropes" inherited from capitalism and Yankee domination. Dreke, recounts the creative joy with which working people have defended their revolutionary course—from Cuba's Escambray mountains to Africa and beyond. $17. Also in Spanish.

Women and the Cuban Revolution
Speeches and Documents by Fidel Castro, Vilma Espín, and others

The victory of the Cuban Revolution, said Fidel Castro in 1966, "has meant a double liberation" for women, "who were discriminated against not only as workers but also as women." Includes the 1975 Family Code, documents of Cuba's Communist Party, and speeches by party leaders. $16

www.pathfinderpress.com

Fidel Castro on Cuba's revolutionary victory

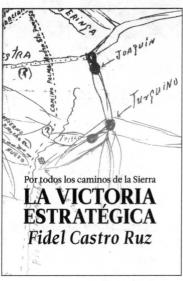

Along every road in the Sierra
STRATEGIC VICTORY

Fidel Castro's firsthand account of 74 days of battle in the summer of 1958, when 300 revolutionary fighters—with the support of workers and peasants across Cuba—defeated the Batista dictatorship's 10,000-strong "encircle and annihilate offensive." Includes maps, photos, historical documents, illustrated glossary of weapons. 855 pp. In Spanish. $35

Por todos los caminos de la Sierra
LA VICTORIA ESTRATÉGICA
Fidel Castro Ruz

From the Sierra Maestra to Santiago de Cuba
STRATEGIC COUNTEROFFENSIVE

Castro's day-by-day account of the final months of the revolutionary war in late 1958. How worker and peasant combatants, having defeated an army more than 30 times their size, launched a 147-day counteroffensive to extend the revolutionary struggle throughout Cuba, taking power January 1, 1959. Includes communiqués, letters, maps, and photos. 593 pp. In Spanish. $25

$50 for two-volume set.

Published by Cuba's Council of State.

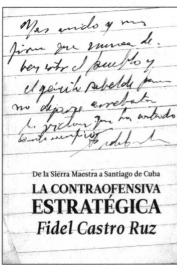

De la Sierra Maestra a Santiago de Cuba
LA CONTRAOFENSIVA ESTRATÉGICA
Fidel Castro Ruz

The expanding union of the workers, and class politics

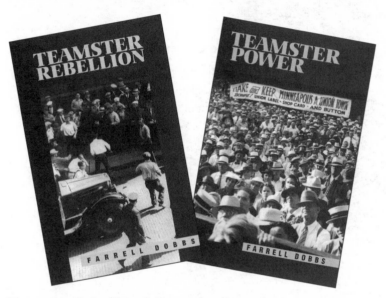

Teamster Rebellion & Teamster Power
Farrell Dobbs

The 1930s strikes and organizing drives that built the industrial union movement in Minneapolis and extended union power from the Dakotas to Texas to Ohio. The first two books in a four-volume series by a central leader of these battles and of the communist movement in the US. Vital sources for those engaged in sharpening class battles in the 21st century. $19 each. Also in Spanish.

From the dictatorship
of capital ...

The Communist Manifesto
Karl Marx, Frederick Engels

Founding document of the modern revolutionary workers movement, published in 1848. Why communism is not a set of preconceived principles but the line of march of the working class toward power—a line of march "springing from an existing class struggle, a historical movement going on under our very eyes." $5. Also in Spanish, French, and Arabic.

State and Revolution
V.I. Lenin

"The relation of the socialist proletarian revolution to the state is acquiring not only practical political importance," wrote V.I. Lenin just months before the October 1917 Russian Revolution. It also addresses the "most urgent problem of the day: explaining to the masses what they will have to do to free themselves from capitalist tyranny." In *Essential Works of Lenin*. $12.95

Their Trotsky and Ours
Jack Barnes

To lead the working class in a successful revolution, a mass proletarian party is needed whose cadres, well beforehand, have absorbed a world communist program, are proletarian in life and work, derive deep satisfaction from doing politics, and have forged a leadership with an acute sense of what to do next. This book is about building such a party. $16. Also in Spanish and French.

www.pathfinderpress.com

...to the dictatorship of the proletariat

Lenin's Final Fight
Speeches and Writings, 1922–23

V.I. Lenin

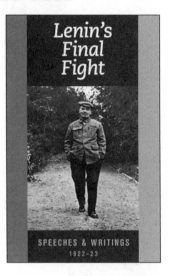

In 1922 and 1923, V.I. Lenin, central leader of the world's first socialist revolution, waged what was to be his last political battle. At stake was whether that revolution, and the international movement it led, would remain on the proletarian course that had brought workers and peasants to power in October 1917. Indispensable to understanding the world class struggle in the 20th and 21st centuries. $20. Also in Spanish.

NEW INTERNATIONAL NO. 11
U.S. Imperialism Has Lost the Cold War

Jack Barnes

Contrary to the capitalist rulers' expectations in the wake of the collapse of regimes claiming to be communist across Eastern Europe and the USSR, the workers and farmers there have not been crushed. They remain an intractable obstacle to imperialism's advance, one the exploiters will have to confront in class battles and wars. $16. Also in Spanish, French, Swedish, and Icelandic.

The History of the Russian Revolution

Leon Trotsky

The social, economic, and political dynamics of the first socialist revolution as told by one of its central leaders. How, under Lenin's leadership, the Bolshevik Party led the overturn of the monarchist regime of the landlords and capitalists and brought to power a government of the workers and peasants. Unabridged, 3 vols. in one. $38. Also in Russian.

The Cuban Revolution and

Cuba and the Coming American Revolution
Jack Barnes

This is a book about the struggles of working people in the imperialist heartland, the youth attracted to them, and the example set by the Cuban people that revolution is not only necessary—it can be made. It is about the class struggle in the US, where the revolutionary potential of workers and farmers is today as utterly discounted by the ruling powers as was that of the Cuban toilers. And just as wrongly. Foreword by Mary-Alice Waters. $10. Also in Spanish and French.

Dynamics of the Cuban Revolution
A MARXIST APPRECIATION
Joseph Hansen

How did the Cuban Revolution unfold? Why does it represent an "unbearable challenge" to US imperialism? What political obstacles has it overcome? Written as the revolution advanced from its earliest days. $25

Cuba's Internationalist Foreign Policy
Fidel Castro

Cuba's foreign policy, says Castro, starts "with the subordination of Cuban positions to the international needs of the struggle for socialism and national liberation." Speeches from 1975–80 on solidarity with Angola, Vietnam, the Nicaragua and Grenada revolutions, and more. Includes "Cuba in Angola: Operation Carlota" by Gabriel García Márquez. $22

Episodes of the Cuban Revolutionary War, 1956–58
Ernesto Che Guevara

A firsthand account of political events and military campaigns that culminated in the January 1959 popular insurrection that overthrew the US-backed dictatorship in Cuba. With clarity and humor, Guevara describes his own political education. He explains how the struggle transformed the men and women of the Rebel Army and July 26 Movement, opening the door to the first socialist revolution in the Americas. $30

World Politics

Aldabonazo
INSIDE THE CUBAN REVOLUTIONARY UNDERGROUND 1952–58
Armando Hart

This firsthand account by a historic leader of the Cuban Revolution complements the interviews here with Vilma Espín and Asela de los Santos. Hart tells the story of men and women who led the urban underground and provided decisive support to the Rebel Army in the struggle that brought down the US-backed Batista tyranny in the 1950s. The actions of this revolutionary generation changed the history of the 20th century—and the century to come. $25. Also in Spanish.

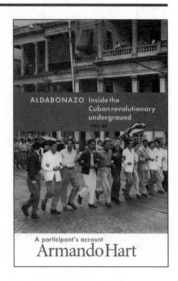

To Speak the Truth
WHY WASHINGTON'S 'COLD WAR' AGAINST CUBA DOESN'T END
Fidel Castro and Che Guevara

In historic speeches before the United Nations and UN bodies, Guevara and Castro address the peoples of the world, explaining why the US government so fears the example set by the socialist revolution in Cuba and why Washington's efforts to destroy it will fail. $18

IN NEW INTERNATIONAL NO. 10
Defending Cuba, Defending Cuba's Socialist Revolution
Mary-Alice Waters

In face of the greatest economic difficulties in the history of the revolution in the 1990s, Cuba's workers and farmers defended their political power, their independence and sovereignty, and the historic course they set out on at the opening of the 1960s. $16. Also in Spanish, French, Swedish, and Icelandic.

www.pathfinderpress.com

WOMEN'S LIBERATION & SOCIALISM

Cosmetics, Fashions, and the Exploitation of Women

JOSEPH HANSEN, EVELYN REED,
AND MARY-ALICE WATERS

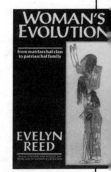

How big business plays on women's second-class status and social insecurities to market cosmetics and rake in profits. The introduction by Mary-Alice Waters explains how the entry of millions of women into the workforce during and after World War II irreversibly changed US society and laid the basis for a renewed rise of struggles for women's emancipation. $15

Woman's Evolution

From Matriarchal Clan to Patriarchal Family

EVELYN REED

Assesses women's leading and still largely unknown contributions to the development of human civilization and refutes the myth that women have always been subordinate to men. "Certain to become a classic text in women's history"—*Publishers Weekly.* $32

Abortion Is a Woman's Right!

PAT GROGAN, EVELYN REED

Why abortion rights are central not only to the fight for the full emancipation of women, but to forging a united and fighting labor movement. $6. Also in Spanish.

Communist Continuity and the Fight for Women's Liberation

DOCUMENTS OF THE SOCIALIST WORKERS PARTY 1971–86

How did the oppression of women begin? Who benefits? What social forces have the power to end women's second-class status? 3 volumes, edited with preface by Mary-Alice Waters. $30

Available from www.pathfinderpress.com

New International
A MAGAZINE OF MARXIST POLITICS AND THEORY

NEW INTERNATIONAL NO. 12

CAPITALISM'S LONG HOT WINTER HAS BEGUN

Jack Barnes

Today's sharpening interimperialist conflicts are fueled both by the opening of what will be decades of economic convulsions and class battles, and by a far-reaching shift in Washington's military policy and organization. Class-struggle-minded working people must face this historic turning point for imperialism, and draw satisfaction from being "in their face" as we chart a revolutionary course to confront it.

$16. Also in Spanish, French, and Swedish.

NEW INTERNATIONAL NO. 13

OUR POLITICS START WITH THE WORLD

Jack Barnes

The huge economic and cultural inequalities between imperialist and semicolonial countries, and among classes within them, are reproduced and accentuated by the workings of capitalism. For vanguard workers to build parties able to lead a successful revolutionary struggle for power in our own countries, our activity must be guided by a strategy to close this gap.

$14. Also in Spanish, French, and Swedish.

NEW INTERNATIONAL NO. 14

THE CLINTONS' ANTILABOR LEGACY: ROOTS OF THE 2008 FINANCIAL CRISIS

$14. Also in Spanish, French, and Swedish.

Also from
PATHFINDER

The Working Class and the Transformation of Learning
The Fraud of Education Reform under Capitalism
JACK BARNES

"Until society is reorganized so that education is a human activity from the time we are very young until the time we die, there will be no education worthy of working, creating humanity." $3. Also in Spanish, French, Swedish, Icelandic, Farsi, and Greek.

Is Socialist Revolution in the U.S. Possible?
A Necessary Debate
MARY-ALICE WATERS

In two talks—part of a wide-ranging debate at the Venezuela International Book Fairs in 2007 and 2008—Waters explains why a socialist revolution in the US is possible. Why revolutionary struggles by working people are inevitable, forced upon us by the crisis-driven assaults of the propertied classes. As solidarity grows among a fighting vanguard of working people, the outlines of coming class battles can be seen. $7. Also in Spanish, French, and Swedish.

Women and the Family
LEON TROTSKY

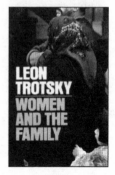

How the October 1917 Russian Revolution, the first victorious socialist revolution, transformed the fight for women's emancipation. Trotsky explains the Bolshevik government's steps to wipe out illiteracy, establish equality in economic and political life, set up child-care centers and public kitchens, guarantee the right to abortion and divorce, and more. $13

www.pathfinderpress.com

The Cuban Five
Who they are, Why they were framed,
Why they should be free
MARTÍN KOPPEL, MARY-ALICE WATERS,
AND OTHERS

Held in US prisons since 1998, five Cuban revolutionists were framed up for being part of a "Cuban spy network" in Florida. Gerardo Hernández, Ramón Labañino, Antonio Guerrero, Fernando González, and René González were keeping tabs for the Cuban government on rightist groups with a long record of armed attacks on Cuba from US soil. Articles from the *Militant* on the truth about the frame-up and the international fight against it. $5. Also in Spanish.

Malcolm X Talks to Young People

Four talks and an interview given to young people in Ghana, the United Kingdom, and the United States in the last months of Malcolm's life. This new edition contains the entire December 1964 presentation by Malcolm X at Oxford University in the United Kingdom, in print for the first time anywhere. The collection concludes with two memorial tributes by a young socialist leader to this great revolutionary. $15. Also in Spanish and French.

The Jewish Question
A Marxist Interpretation
ABRAM LEON

Traces the historical rationalizations of anti-Semitism to the fact that, in the centuries preceding the domination of industrial capitalism, Jews emerged as a "people-class" of merchants, moneylenders, and traders. Why the propertied rulers incite renewed Jew-hatred in the epoch of capitalism's decline. $22

Puerto Rico: Independence Is a Necessity
RAFAEL CANCEL MIRANDA

One of the five Puerto Rican Nationalists imprisoned by Washington for more than 25 years until 1979 speaks out on the brutal reality of US colonial domination, the campaign to free Puerto Rican political prisoners, the example of Cuba's socialist revolution, and the ongoing struggle for independence. $6. Also in Spanish.

PATHFINDER AROUND THE WORLD

Visit our website for a complete list of titles and to place orders

www.pathfinderpress.com

PATHFINDER DISTRIBUTORS

UNITED STATES

(and Caribbean, Latin America, and East Asia)

Pathfinder Books, 306 W. 37th St., 10th Floor,
New York, NY 10018

CANADA

Pathfinder Books, 7107 St. Denis, Suite 204,
Montreal, QC H2S 2S5

UNITED KINGDOM

(and Europe, Africa, Middle East, and South Asia)

Pathfinder Books, First Floor, 120 Bethnal Green Road
(entrance in Brick Lane), London E2 6DG

AUSTRALIA

(and Southeast Asia and the Pacific)

Pathfinder, Level 1, 3/281-287 Beamish St., Campsie, NSW 2194
Postal address: P.O. Box 164, Campsie, NSW 2194

NEW ZEALAND

Pathfinder, 4/125 Grafton Road, Grafton, Auckland
Postal address: P.O. Box 3025, Auckland 1140

Join the Pathfinder Readers Club
to get 15% discounts on all Pathfinder titles
and bigger discounts on special offers.
Sign up at www.pathfinderpress.com
or through the distributors above.